Bibliographic Organization

BIBLIOGRAPHIC ORGANIZATION

PAPERS

*Presented before the Fifteenth Annual Conference
of the Graduate Library School
July 24–29, 1950*

Edited by

JESSE H. SHERA

AND

MARGARET E. EGAN

THE UNIVERSITY OF CHICAGO PRESS

CHICAGO · ILLINOIS

THE UNIVERSITY OF CHICAGO STUDIES IN LIBRARY SCIENCE

THE UNIVERSITY OF CHICAGO PRESS, CHICAGO 37
Cambridge University Press, London, N.W. 1, England
W. J. Gage & Co., Limited, Toronto 2B, Canada

PREFACE

THE acceleration of publication in all areas of intellectual activity has made it increasingly difficult for the librarian to meet the bibliographic needs of scholar, technician, and the general public. The existing chaos in the world of graphic materials emphasizes the need for better means of quick and accurate access to them through a coordinated attack upon the problems of bibliographic organization. It has been the purpose, therefore, of this the Fifteenth Annual Conference of the Graduate Library School to clarify current thought concerning bibliographic organization, to recapitulate the attention it has recently received from many agencies—public and private, national and international—and to present the problems which must be solved before the need for an effective organization of the world of recorded materials can be met.

Attempts to define precisely the meaning of the term bibliographic organization have been singularly unsuccessful. Such definitions have been either so broad as to contribute little to the clarification of our thinking, or so specific as to circumscribe too drastically the areas in which it operates. Basically, the task of bibliographic organization is the matching of two patterns: (a) the pattern of all those human activities in which the use of graphic records plays a part, and (b) the entire pattern of intermediary services which transmit recorded materials from the producer to the ultimate consumer. To such a concept of bibliographic organization, however, two important qualifications must be made. Though bibliographic organization is to be regarded as one of the instrumental devices of our modern system of graphic communication, it must, by definition, exclude all direct communication between individual and individual, or communication among groups so small in numbers that any intermediary service or agency is unnecessary. Furthermore, from bibliographic organization, as it is to be understood in the pages that follow, must be eliminated the great bulk of all mass communication media; communication which is completely under the control of the transmitting agent, e.g. radio broadcasting, the daily newspaper, the motion picture, for such are of concern in bibliographic organization only when they, or a sample of them, are transmitted through time as historical documents. Bibliographic organization, then, is concerned with *indirect* communication in that it encompasses those parts of the process of communication which require intermediary agencies or services.

Because bibliographic organization presupposes the existence of such an intermediate agent between the producer and the consumer of the recorded word, one may say, as the editors of the present volume have previously written: "There are two ways in which bibliographic [organization] may be considered—internally and externally. It may be examined from the standpoint of the librarian and scholar who devise and use it. . . . The other way is to view it against its background of intellectual activities in general. The sociologist might view it as one part of the more general problem of communication, since in its entirety it involves (1) communication *within* a group of specialists, (2) communication *between* various groups of specialists, and (3) communication between specialist and lay public. The sociologist's approach would seem to be potentially fruitful in that it would tend to promote a generalized body of knowledge and set up operating principles closely related to the structure of scholarship and its techniques of transmission."[1] This is the viewpoint that has dominated the thinking of the directors of this Conference, and has shaped the planning of the papers herein presented.

In the past the production of bibliographies has been fragmentary, inequitably distributed, and completely lacking in coordination. Furthermore, the production of bibliographies has been completely separated from all those processes which make the materials physically available. This trend cannot be continued if our efforts to bring recorded materials under the control of those who need them are to meet with success. Bibliographic organization is the very life blood of a system which is essentially unitary, which resists dismemberment, and the component elements of which cannot be compartmentalized into isolated, self-sufficient, and autonomous segments. No part of the entirety of literature is separable from the remainder; the exercise of the human mind in any specific subject area may require the use of the records of several subject fields; and a breakdown in the flow of literature at any one point, or within any one branch of bibliographic organization, eventually impedes the flow throughout the entire system. The directors of this Conference have,

---

1. Margaret E. Egan and Jesse H. Shera, "Prolegomena to Bibliographic Control," *Journal of Cataloging and Classification*, V (winter, 1949), 17.

therefore, constantly endeavored to emphasize the wholistic approach to bibliographic organization, and to resist those centrifugal forces which threaten the atomization of the process.

It is not the aim of this Conference to solve the many harassing problems by which bibliographic organization is beset, or even to propose steps which might conceivably result in their immediate solution. Effective bibliographic organization is not so easily attained. Only by full discussion based upon further investigation of the patterns indicated above, and by repeated emphasis upon the need for a coordinated attack, can the foundations be adequately laid for the solution of bibliographic problems. No solution can be regarded as satisfactory unless the resultant system of bibliographic organization directs the inquirer to the material which he needs, indicates its location, and provides the means for placing it before him. This Conference, therefore, treats of the problems of (1) what materials are characteristically most used in each field, (2) what services are available for the location of such materials, (3) what agencies are responsible for the preservation and organization of the materials, and (4) what techniques may be employed to expedite the entire process. No solution can be considered final inasmuch as the patterns of use within each field are subject to constant change. Therefore the Conference has attempted to emphasize these changes in the patterns of communication characteristic of each area, and the need for continuous study and adaptation to such changes. Nor can any solution be practicable unless it takes into account the technological potentialities which are, or appear to be, immediately available, and the economic feasibility of such devices for the manipulation of bibliographic materials. Hence the Conference has directed attention toward the development of tools for the servicing of bibliographic data and the problems of management which these instruments create.

The general plan of the Conference follows a five-fold organization by orienting the discussion about:

1. The problem in its entirety and the history of some attempts to organize and coordinate bibliographic activity.

2. The classification of knowledge as an approach to the matching of the intellectual concept or thought-unit with the bibliographic unit. Here it might well be pointed out that three attempts at such a matching process were presented at the Conference in the papers of Taube, Shera, and Ranganathan, and that these evoked the live-

liest interest and discussion on the part of the audience, thus demonstrating that the need was more widely felt among librarians than has, perhaps, been previously recognized.

3. The differing needs in different subject fields. Limitations of time and space necessitated division into the broadest possible subject areas, but every attempt was made to emphasize the necessity for minute and specific study of the multitudinous and diverse groups who use literature. It was not possible, for example, to examine the requirements of such specific groups as lawyers, accountants, dietitians, producers of synthetic fibres, etc., yet that such groups are conscious of their bibliographic needs is clearly indicated by the spontaneous development of their own bibliographic services.

4. Physical accessibility as provided by different types of library agencies, by library techniques for locating and reproducing bibliographic materials, and by mechanical devices to expedite such services. The economic efficiency of each was surveyed in terms of the conservation of space, time, and human energy in relation to the quantity and quality of output.

5. A summary of present trends as they may be expected to be reflected in modifications of existing agencies and practices, in future investigations of bibliographic problems, and in the development of bibliographic services.

Throughout the Conference discussion has almost inevitably been centered upon the requirements of the scholar and the research worker. But attention has been called, particularly in the papers of Taeuber, Cory and Egan, to the important fact that scholarly or scientific exploration is useless unless its results can be channeled to those who must apply the resultant findings in technological and social activities, and unless the general public can be kept sufficiently well informed to win its understanding and acceptance of the rapid changes in modern living. These last two needs also imply effective bibliographic organization, but at different levels.

In order to facilitate the discussion of concrete problems by small interested groups, opportunity was given for the audience to request or to organize special seminars on such problems. Three such *ad hoc* discussions, which obviously are not represented by published papers in the present volume, were:

1. "The Production of the *Public Affairs Information Service Bulletin*," presented by Miss Marian C. Manley, Librarian, Business Branch of the Newark Public Library, and member of the Board of

Directors of P.A.I.S. CHAIRMAN: Allen J. Sprow, Assistant Editor, *Psychological Abstracts*.

2. "Bibliographic Problems of Special Libraries." CHAIRMAN: Miss Elizabeth Joy Cole, Librarian, Calco Chemical Division, American Cyanamid Company, and former president of the Special Libraries Association.

3. "The UNESCO/LC Bibliographical Survey," presented by Verner W. Clapp, Chief Assistant Librarian of Congress. CHAIRMAN: Jesse H. Shera, Graduate Library School.

The directors of the Conference wish again to express their gratitude to the participants who wrote and presented papers; to the chairmen who so ably led the discussion periods; to the members of the audience, from thirty states and five foreign countries, whose interested and lively discussions contributed so much to the success of the meetings; to Dean Bernard R. Berelson and the faculty of the Graduate Library School for their constant interest and support; and to Nina Mills and Cassandra Norton, for their numerous and varied services.

JESSE H. SHERA
MARGARET E. EGAN
Directors of the Conference

GRADUATE LIBRARY SCHOOL
UNIVERSITY OF CHICAGO
September 22, 1950

TABLE OF CONTENTS

INTRODUCTION

THE FUNCTIONAL APPROACH

THE SUBJECT APPROACH

CONTENTS

THE MANAGEMENT APPROACH

IMPLICATIONS AND CONCLUSIONS

SYNTHESIS AND SUMMARY

INDEX

INTRODUCTION

THE ROLE OF BIBLIOGRAPHIC ORGANIZATION IN CONTEMPORARY CIVILIZATION

VERNER W. CLAPP

T HE title of this paper may well seem to demand from me an estimate, in some terms, of the value of bibliographic services in relation to other human activities. I may as well confess immediately that I shall not dwell long on such considerations. It might be interesting to investigate the amount of effort which goes into bibliographic activity and its cost in comparison with that of other occupations. It may be important to conjecture just what would happen, financially or otherwise, to research, to scholarship, to national security or public health or private happiness, or to industry and trade and education, if the supporting bibliographic services were withdrawn. These may be interesting and perhaps important kinds of information, but I have not had the means, the time, nor indeed the urge to investigate them. We have the word of various folk that the use of DDT, the invention of the airplane, the study of heredity and the application of research in vitamins were all delayed for decades because of the deficiencies in the bibliographic services which should have brought these matters to the attention of those to whom they might have been of use. We have Dr. Larkey's statement that staggering amounts of money are being wasted in medical research in the United States because of inadequacies in medical bibliography.[1] We can all, out of our experience, point to instances in which scientifically important, or socially useful, or commercially or industrially valuable achievements were made possible with bibliographical assistance. These facts still do not tell us what is the value of bibliography.

It is obvious that bibliography is one of the arts of communication. It is obvious, too, that among these arts bibliography is at a secondary level of utterance, for the reason that it treats of and is dependent upon prior records of communication. By providing information regarding these prior records bibliography makes them useful and the information contained in them available. The importance of the role of bibliography, then, is a function of the importance of the information or ideas contained in these prior records, qualified by an expression of the ability of the users of these records to gain access to the information or ideas without the use of bibliography. By any estimation of the number of records, the importance of their contents, and the degree of their inaccessibility without bibliographic assistance, the value of the role of bibliography would, I think, be rated very high.

BIBLIOGRAPHIC ORGANIZATION—DEFINITION

At this commencement of a series devoted to bibliographic organization, it is perhaps worth while to attempt to define what it is we are talking about. I propose the following definition, which may, however, well require revision during the ensuing discussions.

Bibliographic organization may be defined as the pattern of effective arrangements which results from the systematic listing of the records of human communication. Such listings are themselves called bibliographies, and the art of making them is bibliography.

It is necessary to call attention to several words in this definition. One of these is the word "effective." It is not enough that there should be a complex of arrangements resulting from bibliographic listing; in order to deserve the title "organization" the arrangements should also prove effective; and effectiveness implies a purpose and its satisfaction.

Another group of words to which attention should be called is the phrase "records of human communication." This phrase is used designedly so as not to restrict the field of bibliography to graphic records, and even less to written and printed records. It seems probable that, in spite of the restricting etymology of the word, we shall be compelled to extend the concepts, methods, and even the terms of bibliography to records of human communication of all kinds. Can we, for example, give the name bibliography to a list of works which merely represent speech in writing or printing while we refuse it to a list of records which are capable of reproducing speech itself? Can we admit the title for the little black dots which symbolize musical sounds and refuse it to the records of the sounds themselves? Or admit it for albums of pictures and refuse it for isolated photographs and motion picture films? We admit it now for certain tactual records, such as Braille; why not then for the whole range of records which may be employed for the transmission of ideas, whether they be in graphic, auditory, tactual, olfactory or gustatory form?

While saying this I am quite conscious of the fact that at the present time the principal record of ideas is in written or printed forms, and it is these which create most, though by no means all, of our bibliographic problems. However, it may be expected that if we can solve the problems for these forms, the way will be prepared for the others.

In passing, it may be pointed out that the concept of "bibliographic organization" is not very far separated in content, though somewhat in point of view, from what has been called "bibliographic control." The first term is descriptive of the condition, while the second refers rather to the effect of bibliographic work. "Bibliographic control" has been defined as "the mastery over written and published records which is provided by and for the purposes of Bibliography," and as being synonymous with the phrase "effective access through bibliographies."[2]

DEVELOPMENT OF THE ROLE OF BIBLIOGRAPHIC ORGANIZATION

There was a time—we like to say uncritically—when it was possible for a diligent scholar to possess himself of substantially all recorded learning. While this statement was never literally true, yet there is no doubt that there were periods in human history in which it was possible for the polymath or the polyhistor to be informed of the contents of much of that part of the extant record of human activity which most nearly concerned him.

In such an age there was but little need of bibliography or of bibliographical organization. Bibliographies, like city directories, come into existence only when the number of facts which require to be readily known become too numerous to be learned by individual experience or to be held in individual memory. And indeed, the comparison with the city directory which is suggested here may serve to cast a light upon the role and social usefulness of bibliography.

We have all watched city directories grow—in direct ratio to the increase in the number of families, of houses or apartments, or of telephone subscribers. A directory which listed the entire population of the United States in 1949 would be simply twice as large as the one for 1899. The task of bibliography is something else again.

In the first place, the rate of increase of publications seems to have run continuously ahead of the rate of increase in population. For example, for the whole period of nearly 250 years prior to 1876, Scudder was able to find only 4,390 scientific serials,[3] while for the

33-year period 1900–1933 the *World List* recorded 24,029.[4] It is a
little hard to get at the exact facts regarding the proportionate increase of publications and population, and the following tables in-
corporate only readily available, uncriticized and approximate data.
These data seem to indicate that with respect to printed publications
within the continental United States the increase during the past
fifty years was about ten per cent more rapid than the increase in
population. This finding, however, takes no account of the increased
size of publications during the period, nor does it take any account
of the printed publications of universities, state governments, ecclesi-
astical, commercial, industrial, labor and other organizations, for
which there are no reliable figures. If, however, an estimate of the
number of processed publications is introduced, it would appear that
publications increased almost six times as rapidly during the past
fifty years as did population. The records of copyright deposit tend
to confirm this. Here it appears that in the categories listed in the
table (not all of which are publications, however) there has been an
increase in deposits during the past 50 years two and three-quarter
times as rapid as the increase in population.

Such increases in the absolute number of publications would not of
themselves be greatly troublesome, any more than are the increases
in the absolute number of families in the compilation of a city directory. It is from other characteristics of publications than their absolute number that the trouble arises. The first of these characteristics
is their variety. The increase in number of families involves no increase in variety which must be reflected in their listing. With publications, however, the opposite is the case, for the purpose of publication is to give expression to variation, and the increase in number of scientific serials between the periods recorded by Scudder
and the *World List* is largely an indication of the specialization and
differentiation which occurred in the interim within the sciences and
the arts. And not only do the distinctions of subject matter and
other characteristics require bibliographic attention to keep them
distinct, but, *per contra*, the similarities which run through the distinctions likewise require bibliographic treatment to bring them
together.

Still another of the characteristics of publications which gives
trouble in their listing is their universality. The citizen of Chicago
does not require that his directory list the persons with whom he
might possibly like to communicate in London or Auckland. Users

TABLE 1

INCREASE IN PUBLICATIONS IN THE CONTINENTAL UNITED
STATES COMPARED WITH INCREASE IN POPULATION

Publication	1799	1899	1949
Books................................	....	5,321[6]	10,892[7]
Periodicals.........................	....	20,918[8]	19,075[9]
Newspapers.....................	1,900[5]	....	12,115[9]
Publications of federal government	....	5,760[10]	26,370[11]
Subtotal..................	1,900	31,999	68,452
Ratios........................	1	17	36
	....	1	2
"Processed" publications[12]........	....	[13]	147,946[14]
Total....................	1,900	31,999	216,398
Ratios.......................	1	17	114
	....	1	7

TABLE 2

INCREASE IN PUBLICATIONS IN THE CONTINENTAL UNITED STATES
COMPARED WITH INCREASE IN POPULATION

Copyright Deposits	1799	1899	1949
Books proper........................	....	5,834	13,493
Other books........................	....	4,196—	35,797
Periodicals (numbers)........	....	9,777	54,163
Musical compositions.........	....	19,776	48,210
Maps............................	....	1,478	2,314
Total............................	....	41,061[15]	153,977[16]
Ratios..............................	....	1	3

TABLE 3

INCREASE IN PUBLICATIONS IN THE CONTINENTAL UNITED STATES
COMPARED WITH INCREASE IN POPULATION

Population	1799	1899	1949
Population................	5,170,556[17]	74,689,889[17]	147,946,000[18]
Ratios..................	1	14 / 1	28 / 2

of bibliographies, however, frequently expect services of just this kind and the bibliographer in such cases must have reviewed not only the publications of a locality, but of the whole world.

There are still other distinctions. The city directory, just as does a list of books in print, lists only the living inhabitants. But for many purposes, no publication is dead; it may reappear, in bibliography after bibliography, perhaps to the end of time. Finally, as against the single, though perhaps repetitive, listing which the city-dweller may receive, contrast the potential number of different kinds of listings, from a few to several thousands, which every new publication launched into the world may receive. For example, if the publication is an American book, it may be listed in its publisher's preliminary announcements, and, after publication, in his catalogs; then in *Publishers' Weekly* and in the *Catalog of Copyright Entries*, in innumerable lists of "Books Received," in the *Cumulative Book Index* in several cumulations, in lists of "best books of the year," in the *ALA Book List* and the *United States Quarterly Book List*, in the catalogs of the hundreds or even thousands of libraries which may acquire copies of it, in subject bibliographies devoted to the various subjects under which it may be considered, in bibliographies of its author, its illustrator and book designer, in lists of recommended reading, in lists of sources upon which other works become dependent, in antiquarian book-sellers' catalogs, in *American Book Prices Current*. All for one book. There is indeed a great difference between the city directory and the bibliography, though both are based upon the simple process of listing facts which would otherwise be easily unregarded and unknown; and the difference can, in the final analysis, be attributed to the needs of the users of the product. The needs of the users of the city directory are relatively simple, similar, delimited and stable; the needs of users of bibliographies are relatively complex, dissimilar, varied and changing.

THE MAKERS OF BIBLIOGRAPHIES

It is perhaps worth giving a moment's attention to the question: Who are the producers of bibliographies? To the objection that this is a silly question, and deserves no more consideration than would the question of who produces books in general, it may be pointed out again that books in general are produced intentionally to effect variety, whereas with bibliographies the intention is to effect a synthesis out of a preceding variety by emphasizing similarities. We might, therefore, expect to find in the condition of production or among the producers of bibliographies some distinctions which may be diagnostically revealing or prognostically useful.

In such an expectation we are likely to be disappointed. Enough of the world's great bibliographies have been produced by individual effort, by commercial publishers, even by publishers specializing in bibliographical publications, by professional associations, by governmental institutions, by agencies having a subject interest or by agencies merely concerned with the collection and use of records—as are archives and libraries—to show that there is very little pattern here which is indicative of any forces tending to centralize responsibility in one group or kind of institutions as opposed to another. Indeed, there is so little pattern in this matter that the kind of bibliography which in one country is produced by a commercial concern may in the next be produced by a governmental agency, and in another by an association of private individuals.

The bibliographic work of libraries may, however, claim our special attention for a moment. Libraries have come into bibliographic work accidentally, and as it were through the back door. Their first job was to collect, store and arrange books, and to produce them on demand; listing them came only when the collection outgrew the capacity of a single room, or when the list was needed for purposes of inventory, or to gratify the owner. Librarians were a little embarrassed to find that in making lists and catalogs of their collections they had used bibliographical techniques and had created bibliographies. For a long time, indeed, they successfully confused the issue by using wretched techniques and by making their catalogs as bibliographically unserviceable as possible. We still have much of this tendency with us. Librarians depend for the most part upon others for the production of bibliographies, and, on the whole, prefer to do so. Indeed, much of the qualification for reference work consists in familiarity with important bibliographies and a proclivity for suspecting the existence of others. But the matter has not rested there. Bibliographies made by non-librarians have been useful, very useful; but they have never yet been adequate as exclusive tools for the organization or service of particular library collections. On the one hand they are not sufficiently adaptable to these particular collections; on the other they are too numerous, too costly, too duplicative, too lacking in promptness to match the librarian's activity in acquisition, too lacking in the selectivity which may be required by local conditions. Thus they have never provided assistance for organization and service except to portions of particular collections. As a result, librarians have been forced increasingly into bibliographic activity, and have in the process developed important bibliographic techniques and forms. The techniques are related particularly to the exploitation of more or less extensive, permanent, and heterogeneous collections of books—techniques such as book classification, descriptive and subject cataloging; the forms are related particularly to the location of copies—forms such as the libraries' own catalogs and shelf-lists of various kinds, union catalogs and union lists.

It is worth emphasizing that the librarian's work, if not his interest, has always been focussed upon the inventorial problem—the problem of the location of the book. Where, in his bibliographical work, he has gone beyond giving locational information, it has been almost with reluctance, and with the inventorial problem in mind. For example, probably no library in this country uses the national bibliography as its catalog, because the national bibliography (*Cumulative Book Index*, for example) does not provide shelf-location marks. On the other hand, probably no library lists in its catalog the individual articles which are recorded in *Reader's Guide to Periodical Literature* or in *Chemical Abstracts*. The latter would be no more of a duplication than would be the former; the difference is that the location problem in the case of the *Reader's Guide* is not important: the location of the serials which it analyzes is well known in any collection. To take another example, libraries which keep their federal documents according to the Superintendent of Documents' classification can use his *Monthly Catalogue* as the finding medium; while those which interfile these documents in their total collections must expend bibliographical effort on them and enter them separately in their catalogs. It is the locational factor which is controlling. Other considerations, such as a desire for a single index to the entire collection, or for subject or other analysis, have always of necessity been subordinate.

What then is the position of librarians in relation to the problems of bibliographic organization? I think it is something like the following:

In the first place, the cost of even such bibliographic work as librarians now perform in the organization of their collections has grown so large that they are looking for ways to reduce it, even at the risk of reverting to earlier, cheaper, and less satisfactory methods.

Meanwhile, their readers continue to press for more and more information, for which librarians would fain refer them to bibliographies prepared and published either by cooperation among librarians or wholly outside the library group. Such bibliographies fall short, however, of being satisfactory for the purpose of making collections serviceable. Their very number and heterogeneity make them inefficient for many library purposes; their lack of adaptation to particular collections increases this inefficiency; their duplicativeness and high cost make it frequently impossible to justify their acquisition; their lack of promptness in publication and the great gaps in their coverage result in inability—temporary in some cases, permanent in others—to use them for adequate service for materials which may be actually on hand.

It is natural, under these circumstances, that librarians should be inclined to suppose that greater orderliness in the production of bibliographic services would meet more satisfactorily the needs of the general public as well as their own requirements as custodians of collections. It is natural, too, that they should feel that some of the techniques developed in libraries might be applied profitably in effecting this greater orderliness. These techniques—for systematizing the universe of knowledge represented by all books, or the smaller worlds represented by the literatures of particular disciplines; for controlling large collections of materials which are diverse in form, age, language, and subject; and for reconciling the varied uses of information of many different kinds—have been more fully and more generally developed at their hands than by any other group. Yet so many workers in so many different fields have known and accepted these techniques within libraries that it seems reasonable to suppose that their use in bibliographic services would find equal acceptance.

As a librarian, I regard these suppositions as having much merit, and for this reason: the usefulness of bibliographies ultimately rests upon successful access to copies of the works listed. Location is crucial, and librarians in the long run control location. Bibliographies, for the most part, ignore or assume location and access; from this arise many of their defects. If they should give some regard to location, a great element of orderliness would automatically be introduced. If the *Cumulative Book Index* were to print shelf-marks in a form utilizable by libraries, how long would libraries continue to construct their own catalogs for *CBI* books? Or, to cite another example, what library will now be willing to spend much time in cataloging the publications of the United Nations and of its Specialized

Agencies if the *United Nations Documents Index*—a bibliography which has location as one of its basic considerations—fulfills its promise?

THE MATERIALS TO BE ORGANIZED—LEVELS AND VARIETIES OF ORGANIZATION

What are the materials which should be submitted to bibliographic control? There is an easy and a difficult answer to this question. An easy answer can be made because both librarians and the users of libraries would agree upon it; the answer becomes difficult when either librarians or the users of libraries are required to define it. The easy answer is, everything should be submitted to bibliographic control which eventually is contained in libraries or similar repositories. In this answer, it will be observed, the importance of location and access becomes once more apparent. As to what should eventually be held in libraries there is already a large margin of agreement between librarians and the users of libraries—a margin certainly ample enough to work out the principles of bibliographic organization. We agree on most books, periodicals, newspapers, government documents, etc. There are doubtful areas in each of these categories, but not nearly as doubtful as with regard to "processed" publications, broadsides, posters and leaflets, photographs, sound recordings, and the like. And, meanwhile, no one is likely to be doing important bibliographic work with the records of small businesses, with radio scripts or with bus tickets so soon as to embarrass libraries with regard to collecting and preserving them.

The level and variety of bibliographic organization raises more questions than that of extensiveness, and there are no easy answers to these questions. Librarians have accustomed their clients to a bibliographic organization which is comparatively superficial in level of analysis and lacking in variety of point of view. Many librarians stoutly maintain that even this level and this much variety is more than is really justified by the need or by their obligation to provide access; that the subject specialist—around whose need the service should be constructed—wants little or nothing more from them than the simplest guides to location. I profoundly doubt this. In any case, no one knows better than a librarian who has tried to do bibliographic work in his own collection, how superficial the organization of his own collection is.

The truth is that, for any task involving the use of informational sources, the inquirer needs analysis sufficiently deep to reveal the relevant information. Sometimes the level of analysis may be appropriately shallow, as—for example—to isolate the category "city directories," or "war posters." Much more frequently it needs to be somewhat deeper so as to isolate, for example, a work on the history of book production in the United States, an article on the Australian lungfish, or a novel on the times of Richard III. Most requests for subject information go still deeper than this, however, and what the inquirer wants is an individual fact like the number of periodicals published in the United States in 1899, the presence or absence of a specific compound in the liver of the lungfish, or the text of the will of Richard III. For the isolation of such facts our present methods of analysis are for the most part very badly organized. They assume a narrowing down of the inquiry, with adequate analysis at each level; but neither the levels nor the varieties of interest at each level are well defined. At the uppermost level of analysis stand the guides to collections; at the lowest, the concordances which list every word. Just above the latter, in refinement of analysis, stand the analytic indexes to concepts, proper names, formulas, etc., which are found in the backs of books and which so often fail our readers because of inadequate, inaccurate or non-standard analysis. Each of these tools of analysis, it will be noted, comes within the scope of our definition of a bibliography. It will also be noted that the levels of analysis of the concordance and the analytical index are the ultimate toward which all others are approximations. In highly skilled work and in complex subjects, such as biology, medicine, chemistry or law, they are professional necessities. Whenever the communications of which we preserve the records have sufficient social usefulness, this is the kind of analysis which should finally be available. But the micro-analysis which is needed to respond to inquiries at the most refined level must not be permitted to interfere with the macro-analysis which is needed at other levels. If the two are to be combined, a further development of techniques for the purpose is required. Our card catalogs now are a jumble of references at wholly different levels of analysis—from references to the encyclopedic work which treats of everything to the references to the off-print which may discuss one word in a dead language. The same thing is true of other bibliographic tools—the periodical index and the abstracting journal.

As for variety in bibliographic organization, it is a commonplace that the activity which is to produce this organization—namely, the making of bibliographies—has the widest possible latitude as to form, purpose, content and method. We are accustomed to seeing bibliographies as books, as periodicals, as files of cards, whether manuscript, typewritten or printed. We may soon be accustomed to them in the form of punched cards, perforated tape, or magnetized drums. We recognize many variations in the purpose of bibliographies—to sell books, or to encourage their reading; to document the sources whence information has been drawn; to provide information regarding records, in particular categories, which exist, which have existed, or which may or should exist. We recognize many differences in bibliographic method, quite apart from the level to which analysis is carried.

The latitude which is permitted to the listing process (apart from content) is consequently great. Perhaps the single inflexible requirement upon it is that it should bring together, by listing, materials which have one or more characteristics in common. But these characteristics, in their turn, offer infinite variety. In one case the common characteristic may be the fact of existence in a particular library or even in a particular room in that library. In another, the common characteristic may be the fact of non-existence, as with lost books or bibliographic ghosts. Between these extremes lies the whole gamut of possible common characteristics. They may be characteristics of common purpose, as in lists of doctoral dissertations; of physical form, as in lists of manuscripts; of literary form, as in lists of novels; of bibliographic form, as in lists of periodicals; of form of distribution, whether published or unpublished; of origin, as deriving from the same author, publisher, illustrator, book-designer, period of time, language, alphabet, or geographic area; of distribution, as being located in a particular country, region or library, or as having suffered a particular fate such as condemnation by the Congregation of the Index. Finally, of course, there is that most important category of common characteristics, subject-content or subject-relevance; and in this category alone there is possible endless variety.

Because of the enormous variety of records which lend themselves to bibliographic treatment it can be only in the rarest instances that the common characteristics which are adopted as criteria of selection can be few. To take a typical instance, a list of medieval scientific manuscripts in British libraries would utilize—to draw conclusions from its title—criteria of form, subject-content, date of origin, and location. Nor would it be wholly unexpected if it were found that there were additional criteria not evident in the title, such as geographic origin (e.g., the Western World as opposed to the Far East), or language or alphabet (e.g., European languages to the exclusion of Arabic and ancient Egyptian).

When the varieties in content are complicated by the varieties in purpose, form, method and level of analysis of the bibliography itself, it can be appreciated that the range of possibilities in bibliographic work is very great. The truth is that bibliographies, like other records of human communication which they reflect, are particular and fragmentary manifestations of human interest and human intellectual activity. As such, their variety is infinite; and we face the situation that the activity which was to have brought order and synthesis into the records of other activities, and which was to have extracted a unity out of their variety, has itself fragmented in endless variations. But we may take comfort in the fact that these variations are not, for practical purposes, as many as they seem; that there are a workable number of types of bibliographies which have responded to certain typical situations and needs. It seems to me that, in constructing a pattern of bibliographic organization, it will be necessary to examine these types, to ascertain the contributions made by each, and to select from among them those which may most suitably be adapted to the additional uses which are required. In doing this it should be noted that there are levels of dependence in bibliographic work. Librarians, for example, use publishers' and dealers' catalogs, lists of periodicals and of recommended books in the building of their collections. The catalogs of these collections at a later stage themselves constitute bibliographies from which other bibliographies are in turn compiled. Similar lines of dependence and interdependence can be drawn between the bibliographies compiled through the use of the *Reader's Guide* and the *Bibliography of Agriculture* for example, and the lists which these services themselves used in order to establish their coverage. Thus while there is probably only the rarest instance of a bibliography which does not stand on the shoulders of previous bibliographies, there nevertheless are types which, because of their superior opportunities for reporting promptly and accurately, and with sufficient comprehensiveness or conversely with sufficient selectivity, on the existence of records such as publications, are better suited than others for performing a wide and fundamental service in bibliographic organization. Few librarians would hesitate to make a choice, if compelled to do so, between the *ALA Book List*, *CBI*, and the *Catalog of Copyright Entries—Class A, Books*, though each of these services reports currently on American book production. One is too selective and another is too unselective (aside from other characteristics) to be the best to serve general bibliographic uses.

Nor do the so-called national bibliographies represent the only type of bibliography which performs a general and fundamental service. *Chemical Abstracts*, the *Reader's Guide*, *PAIS*, the *Monthly Catalogue of the Superintendent of Documents*, the National Union Catalog—these all represent types of bibliographic services which, with differing purposes, excellences and defects, contribute in varying degrees to bibliographic organization.

Is it not perhaps possible to identify, among the various types, some which by virtue of their present general usefulness might be developed to serve an even wider and deeper usefulness? Can we not perhaps find in certain of these types the fixed points around which to construct a pattern of services, interdependent in a rational manner, which would achieve the comprehensibility, the simplicity, the synthesis, the unity from variety which bibliography promised but which it has failed to give? As an example of a development of this kind, minute though it may be in the framework of the entire problem, I mention again the *United Nations Documents Index*. This bibliography, at one stroke, has taken the place of a dozen or more bibliographies, actual and potential. It attempts, within a certain definition, to be comprehensive, yet by the use of an absurdly simple device, it serves the purpose of a selective list. Because it is based on considerations of shelf-order, it is potentially capable of serving locational requirements for every library which receives the documents described.

WHAT DO WE EXPECT OF BIBLIOGRAPHY?

What then do we expect of bibliography? The answer to this question will manifestly vary with the point of view. The bookseller expects of his catalog that it will sell books; an author of a monograph expects of his bibliography merely that it record and permit verification of his sources. As custodians of book collections we most frequently think in somewhat different terms, which, however, represent generally the needs of the users of books.

In the simplest and most general terms, we expect that bibliography should lead the inquirer, through channels as well-defined as are the entrances to harbors, to the particular record or records of communication which contain the information or other matter which he seeks. Specifically, we desire—even if we have been led not to expect—that bibliography should have assembled all the material relevant to the subject of the search; that it should provide comprehensive coverage to the extent that comprehensive coverage is needed, yet permit selectiveness where that is required. Because the subjects of inquiry are frequently subjects of international interest, bibliography should be able to leap over barriers of nationality, language and alphabet. Because the same subjects are often considered in different aspects by more than one discipline, bibliography ought to be able to reconcile these differences of point of view, often manifested merely in differences of terminology. Bibliography should, when these services are needed, evaluate, characterize or criticize the sources of information which it lists in order to narrow down the search or to produce a synthesis or provide a conspectus. Still another expectation which I have heard expressed and which has some ring of plausibility is that bibliography should in some manner signalize new contributions to learning so as to call them to the attention of workers in other fields where these contributions might be employed, adapted or developed. Whether this is possible or not I do not know. It may, however, not unreasonably be expected of bibliography that it should be able to locate for the inquirer the original or a copy of the work to which it has referred him. Finally, bibliography may be expected to be so organized as to present to the inquirer the minimum of delay and difficulty, either in the choice of bibliographical services to be used in the search for particular kinds of information at particular levels of analysis, in the prosecution of his search, or in redundant searching in needlessly multiplied and overlapping services.

AVENUES FOR FURTHER EXPLORATION OF PROBLEMS

It is obvious that these expectations are not readily to be realized for all—if indeed ever for any—of the subjects of inquiry. Yet it is probable that much can be done to reduce existing deficiencies and to effect improvements. I am going to mention a few lines along which it seems to me that discussion, investigation and experiment can profitably be pursued. Some of these avenues will be given attention in later papers in this series.

1. *Types.*—We need a taxonomic study of bibliographies; one

that would categorize the principal types so as to identify those which have the possibilities of widest usefulness, around which a pattern might be constructed, and which are most likely to reward the effort and cost of development. A mere *Index Bibliographicus*[19] or *World Bibliography*[20] does not provide this taxonomic information. Nor is it enough merely to know what the differentiating characteristics are; they should be studied in relation to the entire job of bibliography. Why do bibliographic services differ so markedly? What are the purposes and what the effects of the differentiating characteristics? What is their relation to location? When is multiplicity a virtue and when is consolidation desirable or possible? Must *CBI*, the *Monthly Catalogue* of the Superintendent of Documents, the *Monthly Check List of State Publications*, and *Doctoral Dissertations Accepted by American Universities* (to name four fragments of the national bibliography of the United States) be eternally kept separate, or can or should they be consolidated?

2. *Gaps.*—What are the gaps in bibliographic organization which should or can be closed? We expect that bibliography should have assembled all material relevant to any search; and it has been indicated above, in another connection, that bibliographic control should extend to all materials which eventually repose in libraries. This gives us some guide to coverage, though it provides little clue to level or variety of analysis. Presumably we shall require coverage of every monograph down to the last mimeographed report which will eventually repose in a library (though it may be noted that it may find its way there solely because it was listed in a bibliography). Presumably, we shall want *Ayer's Directory* to list every last house-organ of which a file may somewhere seem worthy of preservation as a record of communication. But shall we also require that every periodical be indexed somewhere, or that every newspaper be indexed with the refinement applied to the *New York Times?* Most of us would shudder at the thought; yet there is already an enormous amount of indexing of this very kind going on which would make collections more useful and information more accessible if the results of this indexing could be efficiently incorporated with what we now have. What makes us shudder is the thought of further multiplicity and complexity of bibliographic services, further overabundance of references to material of little or no value, and further costliness. If these disadvantages could be avoided we would welcome additional accessibility. Meanwhile, we all know that important materials are

being omitted from bibliographies at every level of analysis. The three principal reasons for these omissions are (*a*) oversight—lack of information on the part of the bibliographers regarding what is published; (*b*) economic factors—high cost of bibliographic publishing on the one hand, lack of sufficient demand on the other; and (*c*) insufficient development of bibliographic activity. These three factors apply in varying proportions to the bibliographic production of every country in the world.

The problem of gaps is therefore multiple, and will require efforts at solution on many fronts. We shall need to make value decisions and—more difficult—find the bases for these decisions before we can decide ultimately what materials to keep, what materials to list collectively, what to list individually but briefly, and what to analyze deeply. We must invent devices for making general use of the results of bibliographic work which is now hidden away in particular institutions, offices or files. Our primary responsibility is for our own national bibliography; our predecessors were capable of influencing and developing it, and so may we be. For the bibliographic developments of other countries—which are important to us also—we can work through other groups with international interests and with international organizations; in particular through UNESCO, which is active in this field and which welcomes our participation.

3. *Duplication.*—The *ALA Bulletin* is listed in I do not know how many lists of periodical publications, and its contents are indexed in at least three indexing journals. Forty-six per cent of the contributions abstracted in *Physics Abstracts* during the first six months of 1948 were also abstracted in *Chemical Abstracts*.[21] Bradford's findings on duplication and gaps are well known.[22] Is this duplication necessary or desirable? Whatever answers we as librarians give to this question, we are not always the court of last resort. Duplication has obvious reasons and justification in serving the convenience of particular groups of inquirers; and these groups are not infrequently important and even powerful bodies whose over-all contributions to bibliography make a certain amount of duplication a small price to pay. However, it is possible that rationalization (by which I do not necessarily mean an arbitrary elimination of duplication) may be promoted even in such cases. For the most important and powerful groups bibliographic publication is a costly business; and librarians in any case can, through their purchasing or non-purchasing power and other resources, often affect many bibliographic undertakings.

But, to affect them profitably, we must be prepared with a plan of rationalization.

4. *Informativeness.*—In every field of inquiry there are conflicting requirements for comprehensiveness of listing and for either selectivity or the information which makes selection possible. The relation between this conflict and the problem of duplication is obvious. It is not an easy conflict to resolve in a single bibliographic service, though attempts have been made to do so. Unless we invent new techniques for reconciliation, it is likely that what we shall get in the way of informativeness will depend upon the same factors that affect the closing of gaps in coverage, and among these the economic factors are probably the most important. Meanwhile, however, we can search for methods which will here and there reduce costs, which will enable us to adapt the product of bibliographic activity to various uses, as, for example, in combining comprehensive and selective lists. We can at all stages of bibliographic work insist upon standards of accuracy and of other excellences of workmanship, and of scholarship where that is needed.

5. *Physical location.*—Bibliography without accessibility to the material is frustration. Physical location without bibliography imposes intolerable limitations on use. The two are essential halves of a whole. The sooner we realize this and draw conclusions from it, the better off bibliography will be.

6. *Cooperation.*—This is explicit in every activity involving bibliography, but cooperation is conditioned by numerous factors; the existence and adequacy of common standards as well as the extent of adherence to them, the necessity for variation from such standards because of local circumstances; cost; requirements of promptness or speed; the physical limitations of bibliographic vehicles; language; terminology; etc. But if, as has been frequently stated, there is enough bibliographic energy now being expended to do the whole bibliographic job if properly coordinated, the bases for increased cooperation are well worth deliberate investigation.

7. *Classification, coding, subject headings.*—It is largely because of their successful development of these techniques that librarians appear to have some authority in matters of bibliography. There is no doubt that these tools of library organization have an enormous potential force toward the rationalization of all bibliographic work. The problem to be explored is how that potentiality may be realized.

8. *Mechanical devices.*—As I have pointed out in another connection, all bibliography depends upon mechanical devices over and above those which were required to produce the records of communication which bibliography describes. At their simplest, these devices were slips of paper on which the bibliographer copied down titles prior to arranging them in an order. At the most complicated, the device may be a rapid selector or an electronic computer. The card catalog, a most successful device, stands between these. In spite of its success it has marked deficiencies for many present bibliographic needs. We need cheaper, more compact, more easily reproducible, more easily available, more flexible devices. We should work toward such devices with present bibliographic needs in mind. Even if we are not wholly successful at first, our attempts will throw light on the entire bibliographic process, will sharpen our perception of needs, and will tend to clarify many of the related problems.

Whose job is all this? While it is probably true that more bibliographic work of general use is being performed by non-librarians than by librarians, yet it is probably true again that librarians do more bibliographic work than any other one professional group. It is probably true also that more than any other group they see the bibliographic problem as a whole, if not clearly. They are inescapably concerned with physical accessibility of the materials listed by bibliography. Yet librarians have not grasped the problem as a whole. They wrestle only with particular aspects of it, while the rest of the world is to a very large extent ignorant of the library's general concern. We librarians are frequently not consulted regarding the establishment of a new bibliographic service, save as prospective purchasers. At the present time two great bibliographic services are negotiating with each other regarding abbreviations for journal titles, without any regard to the work done in this field by librarians or to the librarians' concern for the outcome.

We have a lot at stake; I think we can contribute much. Bibliographic planning should be a principal concern of our organized profession. We shall find no lack of other professional groups with whom to cooperate, and there are many signs that they would welcome cooperation and even a certain amount of leadership. Internationally, as I have already said, UNESCO needs our collaboration.

CONCLUSION

This paper began with the statement that to deserve the title "organization" the arrangements which bibliography provides must prove effective. I have not attempted to define narrowly the role which bibliography does, or should, or must play in contemporary civilization, nor have I stated in other than general terms the purposes which it should entertain or the extent to which it should satisfy these purposes. These are all inextricable parts of the pattern of a civilization which is based upon recorded communications. This conference is necessarily concerned with the problems rather than with the accomplishments of bibliography. Yet the two are counterparts. As has recently been said in the UNESCO survey, "the problems of bibliographical activity arise from its very concern with those most individual and most unregimentable manifestations, the products of man's intellect. From this source come its woes; from this source come also its importance and indeed its splendor. The problems of bibliography may seem at any one moment to predominate over its achievements; but its accomplishments are majestic. Without bibliography the records of civilization would be an uncharted chaos of miscellaneous contributions to knowledge, unorganized and inapplicable to human needs. It is, very simply, the importance and effectiveness which bibliography already possesses which make the further and continuous improvement of bibliographical services a matter worthy of the sincerest efforts of international collaboration."[23]

REFERENCES

1. Sanford V. Larkey, Presidential address at the meeting of the Medical Library Association, Boston, June, 1950. To be published in the Association's *Bulletin*, October, 1950.

2. The UNESCO/Library of Congress Bibliographical Survey, *Bibliographical Services, Their Present State and Possibilities of Improvement* (Washington, 1950), p. 1.

3. Samuel H. Scudder, *Catalogue of Scientific Serials of All Countries Including the Transactions of Learned Societies in the Natural, Physical, and Mathematical Sciences, 1633–1876* (Cambridge: Harvard University Library, 1879).

4. *A World List of Scientific Periodicals Published in the Years 1900–1933* (2d ed.; Oxford: Oxford University Press, 1934).

5. Charles Evans (in his *American Bibliography*, Vol. XII [Chicago: Privately printed, 1934]), lists 785 entries for 1799, covering the letters *A–M* only. For 1798 he records 903 works for the same letters, and 1,808 for all.

6. *Publishers' Weekly* (New York), LVII (1900), 192.

7. *Ibid.*, CLVII (1950), 239.

8. *N. W. Ayer and Son's American Newspaper Annual* (Philadelphia) (1900), p. 8.

9. *Ibid.* (1950), pp. 12–13.

10. Estimated number of main entries in U.S. Superintendent of Documents, *Monthly Catalogue* (Washington), January–December, 1899.

11. Total number of numbered entries from *idem*, January–December, 1949.

12. By "processed" publications are meant those which are produced by duplicating equipment used in offices, or otherwise than with equipment usual to book and periodical publication.

13. No estimate made, although there were undoubtedly a smaller number of publications issued by the hectograph and perhaps other processes.

14. Estimated at one publication per annum per thousand of population.

15. U.S. Library of Congress, *Annual Report of the Librarian of Congress* (Washington), *1901* (1901), p. 66.

16. *Ibid., 1949* (1950), p. 154.

17. By interpolation from the *World Almanac* (New York), LXV (1950), 435.

18. *Ibid.*, p. 434.

19. Institut International de Coopération Intellectuelle, *Index bibliographicus: Catalogue internationale des bibliographies courantes. Deuxième édition ... Publiée par Marcel Godet & Justus Vorstius* (Berlin & Leipzig: W. de Gruyter & Co., 1931).

20. Theodore Besterman, *A World Bibliography of Bibliographies* (2d ed.; London: The Author, 1947–49).

21. American Institute of Physics (New York), "Study of Physics Abstracting," *Physics Coverage of CHEMICAL ABSTRACTS Compared with That of PHYSICS ABSTRACTS* (AIP/45: M-16, October 27, 1949).

22. S. C. Bradford, *Documentation* (London: Crosby Lockwood & Son, Ltd., 1948), pp. 108 ff.

23. T. Grivet, *Present State of Science Abstracting Services and Possible Improvements* (UNESCO/NS/SAC/1; Paris, April 15, 1949), p. 62.

HISTORY OF SOME ATTEMPTS TO ORGANIZE
BIBLIOGRAPHY INTERNATIONALLY

KATHRINE O. MURRA

IN A subject as beset with semantic difficulties as is bibliography, it is important at the outset of a discussion, even of the historical aspects of the subject, to identify boundaries. To do that, one runs a necessary risk of belaboring the obvious. Two elements which might easily be assumed to be a necessary part of a discussion of attempts to organize bibliography internationally should be examined. It might be assumed that an international organization or organizations, or, at least, international financing, must necessarily be a part of any attempt. This is not true. Organizations which are in no sense of the word international have done impressive work in organizing bibliography internationally, particularly by subject. Individuals have also been so largely responsible for some of the attempts that no organization can be credited—or charged with them, as the case may be.

A second too-easy supposition is that the primary result of attempts to organize bibliography internationally is international bibliography—defining international bibliography as a list containing written or published records whose place of production or location is not a primary criterion for their inclusion in the list. International bibliography has not been the result of, nor the intended result of, all attempts to organize bibliography internationally, and has existed considerably longer than attempts to organize it.

If our topic is neither necessarily concerned with international organizations nor with international bibliography what, then, is its primary characteristic? To be correctly included in this discussion, the attempt must have been one of consciously seeking to organize man's record in whatever form for greater usefulness and accessibility for those who might want it for whatever purpose, regardless of national boundaries. Attempts characterized by this element will be found to include: (1) instances of international organizations stimulating improvement of bibliography within nations; (2) the production of international bibliography by a group within one na-

24

tion; (3) development of mechanisms for obtaining coverage of the literature of a subject or of literature generally, whether by a private, national or international body. Thus indentificaton is made on the basis of characteristics of aims rather than the means. These distinctions will, I hope, be further clarified as I proceed.

Attempts to organize bibliography internationally *per se*, or by large groups of subjects such as the natural sciences, or for a specific subject field such as zoology, have been so numerous that there is presently no list, within my knowledge, sufficiently complete to rely upon. Attempts have been made to make such a list. For example, as a background study for use of the Assembly of Librarians of the Americas in 1947, Gietz and Daniels extracted eighty-four resolutions pertaining to bibliography and book matters passed by some twenty-five Inter-American conferences of various types held between 1888–1943. A number of these pertained directly or indirectly to some aspect of the international organization of bibliography.[1] Yet, as is well known, others preceded the Americas in international intellectual cooperation.

A number of approaches to our topic might have been profitably adopted. Mention of a few will serve to indicate some of the many facets of the subject. It would have been possible to name the *major* international organizations which have concerned themselves with bibliographic matters and to give a thumbnail sketch of each. It would also have been possible, and doubtless useful, to survey the various bibliographically rich countries to see what has been the contribution of each to international organization of bibliography. Most interesting studies could be made of the contributions of learned societies, professional groups, library associations and cultural institutions to the improvement of bibliography on an international basis. I would like to know the full story of the Royal Society of London's contribution to the international organization of bibliography. The story of these attempts might also be told in terms of the men and women who have done the most to organize it internationally—in terms of biographies employing the most objective and scholarly methods. There are many more approaches to the tremendously rich and inadequately cultivated literature of this subject.

I have chosen to develop in some detail the story of seven attempts. In my opinion, practically every problem, hazard, success and failure of such an operation is mirrored in these undertakings.

Our ability to grasp present day bibliographic problems can be strengthened by a thorough understanding of these precedent experiences. There is need for a more complete analytical history of these attempts which will further develop the data here presented and augment it with case studies of auxiliary, subsidiary and independent attempts. Such a history in the hands of those at the managerial and the operational levels might substantially advance international organization of bibliography.

The seven attempts which will be described in more or less detail are: two attempts of the Royal Society of London, the *Catalogue of Scientific Papers*, the story of which extends roughly from 1851 to 1925, and the *International Catalogue of Scientific Literature*, from 1894 to 1935; the Brussels Institute from 1890 to the present; the Concilium Bibliographicum from about 1892 to 1940; the International Institute of Intellectual Cooperation from 1924 to 1946; the International Federation of Library Associations from 1927 to the present; and the entirely post-World-War-II work of UNESCO, the United Nations Educational, Scientific, and Cultural Organization. There will necessarily be mention of some other ventures, but only for purposes of illustration.

It should be said, parenthetically, that too many librarians in the United States are inclined to regard bibliography as one of the original provinces of librarianship—to be sure, a kind of Siberian province as yet not fully explored and developed, but, nevertheless, peculiarly theirs. This feeling is not borne out by history. Bibliography, concern for the organization of bibliography, and international undertakings in that direction have been dominated by what, for lack of a better phrase, we call the subject specialists. They were not specialists in the modern sense a century ago. They were scholars working in much broader fields of knowledge than today's specialists but having, at least in miniature, much the same informational needs as today's specialists. In general, librarians are new-comers to the field. Because they have done a relatively good job of organizing the materials committed to their custody, the subject specialists, after a century-long struggle with the swelling tide of their own record, are turning more and more to librarians to remedy their bibliographic ills.

In 1848, it was "America's foremost physical scientist,"[2] the first secretary of the Smithsonian Institution, who initiated one of the most impressive experiments in international bibliographic

organization on record, and one generally ignored in the history of
international organization. The neglect of the *Catalogue of Scientific
Papers* in such studies as this and the attention to its successor, the
International Catalogue of Scientific Literature, stems, perhaps, from
one of the common assumptions mentioned earlier: namely, that our
topic must necessarily deal with the international character of the
agency which does bibliographic work rather than with characteristics of the goals sought.

To return to the first Secretary of the Smithsonian, perhaps it was,
as Coulson suggests, largely Joseph Henry's pride smarting from the
neglect of his scientific contributions by Europeans which egged him
on to seek a better means of disseminating information about scientific research.[3] For whatever reasons, he said in his annual report for
1851:

"It is estimated that about twenty thousand volumes, including
pamphlets, purporting to be additions to the sum of human knowledge, are published annually; and unless this mass be properly arranged, and the means furnished by which its contents may be
ascertained, literature and science will be overwhelmed by their own
unwieldy bulk. The pile will begin to totter under its own weight, and
all the additions we may heap upon it will tend to add to the extension of the base, without increasing the elevation and dignity of the
edifice.

"One of the most important means of facilitating the use of libraries, particularly with reference to science, is well digested indexes
of subjects, not merely referring to volumes or books, but to memoirs, papers, and parts of scientific transactions and systematic
works."[4]

When the money was not available for implementing his proposed
indexing project, he wrote to the British Association for the Advancement of Science saying that he would assume responsibility for
the indexing of the American literature if they could undertake the
rest. In 1855, the British Association appointed a three man committee to consider the proposal. Messrs. Cayley, Grant, and Stokes,
who were appointed, were all members of the Royal Society[5] so that
it is not altogether surprising that the aid of that body was secured.
The collaboration offered by Professor Henry was not needed because in 1858 the Royal Society assumed responsibility for preparation of a "Manuscript Catalogue of the Titles of Scientific Memoirs

SEVEN EXPERIMENTS IN ORGANIZING BIBLIOGRAPHY INTERNATIONALLY

Data	I	II		III	
	Catalogue of Scientific Papers (*The Catalogue**)	*International Catalogue of Scientific Literature* (*The International Catalogue**)	International Institute of Bibliography	International Institute of Documentation (The Brussels Institute*)	International Federation for Documentation
Purpose†	To index scientific periodicals of the Nineteenth Century	To index the scientific literature of the Twentieth Century	To establish a world bibliographical information center	To ascertain the existence and nature of bibliographical services and coordinate their activity	To coordinate activities of member groups of the Federation
Period of publication, or organizational activity, as the case may be	1800–1900	1901–1914	1895–1931	1931–1937	1937–to date
Dates covered by this history of the enterprise	1851–1925	1894–1935		1890 to date	
Auspices	Royal Society of London	International organization in collaboration with the Royal Society of London	International association of individuals and the Belgian Government‡	International federation of international specialized scientific associations and national bodies of general nature‡	International federation of national sections on documentation plus associate members both individuals and private institutions
Financed by	1. Royal Society of London 2. British Government 3. Sale of sets of the *Catalogue* 4. Gifts from individuals	1. Subscriptions of participating nations 2. Royal Society of London 3. British Government 4. Gifts from individuals	1. Belgian Government 2. Gifts of individuals	1. Gifts of individuals 2. Royal Dutch Oil Company 3. Rockefeller Foundation 4. Affiliates	1. Gifts of individuals 2. Affiliates
Major types of bibliographic service rendered	1. Published an author list of articles in scientific periodicals of the Nineteenth Century 2. Published subject indexes for pure mathematics, physics, and mechanics	1. Published a subject index to the literature of seventeen branches of science covering 1901–1914	1. Published a journal which served as a medium for exchange of information on bibliographic organization 2. Attempted to serve as a clearing house of bibliographic information 3. Issued expanded schedules of decimal classification 4. Aided in compilation of world union catalog 5. Convened international meetings on bibliographic organization	1. Continued publication of a journal serving as a medium for exchange of information on bibliographic organization 2. Issued expanded schedules of decimal classification 3. Convened international meetings on bibliographic organization	1. Continued publication of a journal serving as a medium for exchange of information on bibliographic organization 2. Issued expanded schedules of decimal classification 3. Convened international meetings on bibliographic organization

Data	IV Concilium Bibliographicum (The Concilium*)	V International Committee on Intellectual Cooperation (The International Committee*)	V International Institute of Intellectual Cooperation (The I.I.I.C.*)	VI International Federation of Library Associations (I.F.L.A.*)	VII United Nations Educational Scientific and Cultural Organization (UNESCO*)
Purpose†	To organize the literature of zoology internationally	To study and aid in the better organization of literary, artistic and scientific works	To encourage, coordinate and assist intellectual effort and improve the condition of intellectual workers	To select time and place and prepare programs for international library conferences	To serve the ends and objects of the United Nations To foster and promote all aspects of education, science, and culture
Period of publication, or organizational activity, as the case may be	1895–1940	1921–1946	1925–1946	1927 to date	1946 to date
Dates covered by this history of the enterprise	1892–1926	1921–1946	1924–1946	1926 to date	1946 to date
Auspices	International association of learned societies and zoologists	League of Nations	League of Nations, International Committee on Intellectual Cooperation	As title indicates	United Nations
Financed by	1. Learned societies 2. Government grants 3. Gifts of individuals 4. Sale of publications	League of Nations	French government and others	Member associations	Participating nations
Major types of bibliographic service rendered	1. A bibliographical service on cards with decimal classification symbols on each 2. A bibliographic index in bulletin form with an edition printed on both sides of a page, and one on only one side	Brought together subject specialists for study of bibliographic problems of their fields	1. Gave grants in aid for bibliographic work including bibliographies, directories, journals, etc. 2. Provided a forum for discussion of problems of bibliographic organization in the subject fields	1. Holds international meetings at which information on library and bibliographic problems is exchanged 2. Publishes proceedings of its meetings which are an important informational resource on international library and bibliographic work	1. Gives grants in aid for bibliographic work for use in international organization of bibliography 2. Convenes meetings to study and work out solutions for problems of organization of international bibliography

* Abbreviated form of name most frequently used in this paper.
† The statements given under this heading are general and do not attempt to give purposes in detail with indication of changes over the years.
‡ Changed to international federation of international specialized scientific associations and national bodies of a general character in 1924.

Contained in the Scientific Periodicals in all Languages" from 1800 to 1860.[6] The titles were written in quadruplicate in order to form four distinct catalogs as follows: (1) a serial index, (2) an alphabetical author index, (3) a classified index, (4) an extra set for which a use had not as yet been designated.

By December, 1862, the president of the Society reported there were sixty-two MS volumes completed in the first set—the serial index. These had been placed in the Society's library for reference use and the other sets were to be placed there when completed. President Sabine said that the catalog contained 150,000 titles and that there were at least 10,000 titles representing the holdings of the Royal Society's library to be added. Compilation thus far had cost £980.

In 1864, Major-General Sabine reported to the Society that the MS catalogs were nearly complete and that coverage had been extended to include publications through 1863. Foreign societies and academies had been asked to supply suitable titles not already included. The number of titles had thus been increased to more than 180,000.

The MS catalog was offered to the British Government for publication at public expense with the suggestion that some sets be presented to "Scientific Institutions" throughout the world and the remainder be offered for sale at "the cost of paper and printing only." The government accepted the proposition.[7]

The contemplated printed catalog was to consist of an alphabetical author catalog *and a subject index*. The Society had already spent £1,400 for preparation of the *Catalogue* and estimated that the preparation of the subject index would cost from three to four hundred pounds more.[8]

There is ample indication that the Society, and others, considered a subject catalog the zenith of its work. However, it was not until 1869 that announcement was made that Professor Julius Victor Carus of Leipzig had been hired "to prepare the alphabetical index of subjects."[9] The Franco-Prussian War prevented his going to London to conduct the work. It was therefore delegated to the Library Committee of the Royal Society. This group had been engaged in building the library's holdings as the work on the *Catalogue* revealed important lacunae in its collections.[10] Nevertheless, the "Index Rerum" did not thrive. After the war Carus was ill and the Committee otherwise engaged. No mention of the subject index is made in the presidential address for thirteen years. In 1886 the president deplored the lack of one but announced that the cost was prohibitive.[11]

A decennial volume for the period 1864–1873 was approved by the Council of the Royal Society in 1874. The six volumes which comprised the period 1800–1863 had cost £8,936 12s, of which amount the Society had paid £3,720 15s 6d.[12]

When the government agreed in 1876 to publish this first decennial volume, the Council of the Society voted to make the *Catalogue* one of its permanent undertakings.[13] The first complaint of increasing cost of production of the author catalog appears in the presidential address the following year. Because of the cost, the president reported, application had been made for government aid in the *preparation* of the *Catalogue*.

In spite of this less favorable financial situation, the Council authorized a second decennial volume covering the period 1874–1883.[14]

The full impact of greatly accelerated scientific publication was being felt. The next year the president told the Society that "the task of preparing the MS of the *Catalogue of Scientific Papers*, decade 1874 to 1883, has proved far heavier than was anticipated, and the matter very far exceeds in bulk that of the previous decade."[15] His statement is underwritten by Iwinski, who reported that there were in the world 3,179 periodicals of all kinds including newspapers in 1826; 14,240 in 1866; 20,882 in 1872—a gain of 6,642 in six years; 25,901 in 1880; and 35,296 in 1882—a gain of 9,395 titles in *two* years.[16]

The demand for subject indexing for various fields was increasing. Illustration of this fact can be given by interrupting for a moment the story of the *Catalogue of Scientific Papers*. A few examples from our own country indicate a trend of the times. In 1882 the American Association for the Advancement of Science appointed a Committee on Indexing Chemical Literature. In its first report in 1883 the committee listed three methods of collecting material for the index which appeared to be open to it; (1) to index the chemical literature of the *Catalogue of Scientific Papers;* (2) to have certain journals assigned to individuals for indexing and then collate the results; (3) to utilize chemists who would volunteer to index the journals available to them for the element of their special interest. The last mentioned was selected.[17] Henceforth for twenty years the

Smithsonian circulated a bibliography of these independently prepared subject indexes to the literature of chemistry.[18]

In 1876, when John Shaw Billings circulated a *Specimen Fasciculus* to a proposed dictionary catalog of subjects and authors, *The Index-Catalogue of the Library* of the U.S. Surgeon General's Office, it was to serve both as a catalog of the library and as an index to the "*principal* original papers in medical journals and transactions," having grown out of earlier separate author and subject catalogs.[19] When it was first published, beginning in 1880, there was no intent to continue it nor to use it as a medical *bibliography*. Both of these circumstances eventuated.[20]

To return to the original thread of the story. By 1888 the Royal Society of London seemed to be thinking of international aspects of the *Catalogue*—perhaps, of international financing.[21] The government refused to print the volumes covering 1874–1883. However, they did grant £1,000 as an aid to publication. The Royal Society arranged with Clay and the Syndics of the Cambridge University Press to publish it. By the investment of what was left from the grant "in a policy" under the terms of which £1,000 would be available for the *Catalogue* in October 1899, the future was somewhat assured.[22] Once again, the president voiced the hope that the subject index would materialize.

The government grant failed to forestall the growing stringency of the situation. To better it, Dr. Ludwig Mond, a chemist, and Fellow of the Society, gave £2,000 to aid the Catalogue. This munificent shot in the arm again aroused hope of a subject index.[23] The staff was enlarged and a special committee provided to supervise it. As time went on the chief concern of the committee was to determine whether the subject-index to the *Catalogue* as already published should be classified or alphabetical.

By the 1890's, how to obtain subject-indexing of the world record in the various subject fields had become the major bibliographic concern of many professional and learned societies. At the Congress of Chemists held in Chicago in 1893, H. Carrington Bolton, Chairman of the Committee on Indexing of Chemical Literature, mentioned earlier in this paper, presented a plan for an international index to chemical literature.[24]

Bolton suggested that the chemical society journal in each country publish an index to the current chemical literature of its own country according to internationally agreed upon rules of entry. An international bibliographic committee composed of a representative from each society would draw up these rules. At that time, the German and French societies and to some extent those of other countries tried to include abstracts of materials of other countries in their journals. They neglected to record all of the significant work of their own countries. Since, for obvious reasons, this was recorded by no one else, the energy expended on the abstracting of foreign literature tended to worsen rather than to improve the chemist's control of the material in his field. Dr. Bolton proposed that an International Committee on Chemical Bibliography be established to investigate a scheme, his or any other, for cooperative international indexing. For retrospective coverage, he advocated subject indexing of the Royal Society's *Catalogue*.

A resolution was passed by the Congress to implement his plan.[25] The next annual report of the Committee voiced the hope that "future World's Chemical Congresses may arrange the publication of an exhaustive Index to the Chemical Literature of the World by international cooperation."[26]

The first International Congress of Applied Chemistry, meeting in Brussels under the aegis of the Belgian government in 1894, was presented with a plan for the international organization of chemical literature, in the name of the Belgian Chemists Association, by Monsieur H. Van Laer. It was proposed that an international bureau be established which would carry on liaison between chemical associations, provide for exchange of publications, and prepare a review index of the literature of applied chemistry which the Belgian Association would publish regularly in its journal. Material was to be fed into the central bureau from national committees set up for the purpose.[27]

In the meantime, a promising and wealthy young Harvard graduate in zoology, Herbert Haviland Field, had, during the course of study and travel throughout Europe, discussed with zoologists, librarians, and others the need for international subject indexing of the literature of zoology. From 1892 to 1895 he gradually developed a plan for a bibliographic service for the field. The plan called for a central bureau of zoology and comparative anatomy with headquarters at Zurich and sub-bureaus in Bohemia, Gallicia, Hungary, and Russia, the countries whose languages constituted formidable barriers to international organization of the literature. As founded by the International Congress of Zoology, a central bureau was to issue a fortnightly bulletin divided into topical chapters and biblio-graphical references on cards with classification symbols enabling the user to file related material together. Arrangements were being made for reprinting the material issued on certain topics annually in established journals. For example, the morphological titles would appear in *Zoologischer Jahresbericht*. The bureau was opened in 1896 in Zurich with Field as director. The Swiss confederation of the canton, the city of Zurich, scientific societies in different countries, and, presumably, the director backed it financially.[28]

Meanwhile, in 1890 a bibliographic section of the Society for Social and Political Studies at Brussels was organized by an idealistic lawyer and politician, Henri LaFontaine. The group immediately began a card catalog of material on sociology.

The following year a bibliographic group was set up within the Brussels bar association to study problems of legal bibliography and to publish a periodical summary of material appearing in legal journals.

Paul Otlet, also a Brussels lawyer, published an article in 1892 on problems of bibliography in the social sciences. It attracted the attention of LaFontaine. The two men met and began a now famous, life-long, bibliographic partnership characterized by a devotion to purpose and remarkable tenacity in the face of formidable obstacles.

They began their partnership by merging the sociological and legal indexing projects they had begun, which combined a total of about forty thousand references.

In 1893, with the support of the Belgian government, they set up an International Office of Sociological Bibliography. The deeper LaFontaine and Otlet probed the riddle of making fully accessible the rising tide of literature, the broader the subject of their investigations appeared.[29]

International cooperation functioning through a central agency which would combine the work of a clearing house of bibliographic information, a library complete with a world bibliographic catalog, and a liaison function seemed the obvious solution. When the first international conference on bibliography was convened in Brussels in 1895, LaFontaine and Otlet had a plan covering the above desiderata well in hand—even to a classification scheme. The story of the classification marathon which the intrepid lawyers won is well known. Having secured a copy of Dewey's Decimal Classification six weeks before the conference, they made some adaptations in it and, by way of illustrating its value, applied it to the four hundred thousand cards in their catalog before the conference opened.[30]

The conference was not international in the sense desired because planning and issuance of invitations came too late to permit wide participation. Nevertheless, it established an Institut International de Bibliographie, sanctioned further adaptation of the Dewey system, recommended it for classifying bibliographies throughout the world, authorized preparation of a Répertoire Bibliographique Universel, and finally agreed on the nature of the International Office of Bibliography. A few days later the Belgian government created that office and to it was assigned the preparation of the universal catalog.

The plans, purposes, and methods of operation of the Institute became a bibliographic storm center almost as soon as they were known. Even the pristine dignity of the Royal Society of London could not delete the chill which hung about its report on the Institute in the *Proceedings* for 1895. The receipt of the invitation having arrived too late for participation in the conference, the Senior Secretary visited Brussels later in the year and provided the following information:

"All must admire the energy and enterprise which has thus been displayed in Belgium. At the same time the magnitude of the work and the importance of the interests involved are such that it appears most desirable that the action which the Royal Society has already taken for an International Conference should be persevered in, so that decisions may be arrived at which may ensure, if possible, complete success. The enterprise is one in which we, in consequence of our long connection with such work, are most deeply interested; it is also one which may well become of exceeding value to science generally. But it is impossible to overrate the difficulties connected with it; and to avoid unnecessary complications in the future it is essential that very many questions—especially the division of the subject matter in the various branches of science and the nomenclature to be used—be taken into consideration by competent bodies and settled by general agreement."[31]

In the early days the Institute was made up of individual members from various countries. Through these members, it hoped such national bibliographic improvements as would facilitate compilation of the Répertoire Universel would be stimulated. Current complete national bibliographies were advocated as one of the steps required. Through the information center in Brussels and the Institute's

Bulletin, it was hoped that a bibliographic clearing house could operate which would not only provide bibliographies prepared by specialists on particular subjects, but also provide technical information on the preparation of bibliographies and on the organization of information generally. For the organization of information the Institute believed the Universal Decimal Classification was ideal.

Although LaFontaine, Otlet, and their followers were pulling away from European library and archival tradition and practice,[32] they were unable to disassociate themselves from the ancient dream of scholars that a comprehensive yet flexible scheme for the classification of all knowledge could be devised which at best would serve as a kind of universal language through which the scholarly world might communicate as far as access to material was concerned, and at least would serve as a device which would enable great masses of references so classified to be sorted and arranged by clerical workers. They believed—and I use the verb intentionally, as it appears to have been highly emotional—they believed that the Universal Decimal Classification was that device. The winning of adherents for it soon became a crusade.[33]

It is difficult to evaluate the work of the Institute objectively. There are so few accounts of it which even attempt to be impartial and those which do are, for the most part, only sketches, so that evaluation depends upon the balancing of one prejudiced source against another. Practically up to this hour people have been either for or against the Institute, for or against LaFontaine and Otlet, for or against the concept of documentation which it developed, for or against U.D.C. There is scarcely any middle ground.

Yet, in the face of all this, it will be found that the statement of one of the Institute's most devoted disciples is true. Donker-Duyvis said in 1940 that LaFontaine and Otlet "created a lasting, spiritual background for the present international organization of documentation."[34]

I must parenthetically protect the rear from semantic attack and pause to say that documentation may be defined, as Bradford suggests, as the process of collecting, classifying and making readily accessible the records of all kinds of intellectual activity.[35] However, I think, Miss Ditmas has defined it better for our use by calling it "the aspect of bibliography in which the stress is laid most heavily on the development of aids to the active utilization of recorded knowledge, as opposed to custodianship."[36]

As an experiment in a structure for the international organization of bibliography the Institute is tremendously important. In the period under review, resistance to it demonstrated: (1) a widespread distrust of centralization;[37] (2) an even greater distrust of any group which placed as disproportionate an emphasis on one phase of its program as the Institute did on U.D.C.;[38] and (3) the inflexibility which such emphasis gave to the Institute's ability to respond to accelerated bibliographic needs. In view of the widespread attention to subject indexing among influential scholarly societies reported earlier, I cannot subscribe to Miss Ditmas' contention that adequate support of the Institute was not forthcoming because "there was, then, no widespread realization of the need for comprehensive subject-indexes."[39] There seems to have been ample awareness of the kind that would really count in carrying along such a project.

On the credit side, as an experiment during the period under review—pre-World War I—it brought to light a rather widespread cognizance of the need for international organization of bibliography. It cultivated this interest—often through the very antagonisms it aroused—and provided a more fertile soil for subsequent international work both for itself and others.

In the meantime, in 1894, the Royal Society appointed another Special Committee to investigate the possibilities of producing a subject catalog to the scientific literature of the twentieth century through international cooperation. The group had already addressed a proposal to societies and institutions throughout the world suggesting that (1) such a catalog should begin with the century, (2) a central office or bureau should be maintained by international contributions, and (3) such an office should be supplied with the information necessary for the catalog by means of international cooperation. The desiderata for a catalog given in the communication highlighted some of the defects of the existing *Catalogue*. (1) It said that a catalog should cover monographs and books as well as periodicals. Because Darwin's works did not appear in periodicals they were not included in the *Catalogue of Scientific Papers*.[40] (2) A new catalog should be by subject as well as by author. Mendel's paper on the *Principles of Heredity* was listed under the author's name in the *Catalogue of Scientific Papers*.[41] Mendel was a scientific nobody at the time and his work was as surely buried as though it had not been listed. (3) It would be desirable for the subject listing to be so set up that the index for each subject could be obtained separately. (4) It should appear promptly.

In this country, the Society's communication with a number of replies from institutions and individuals was published in *Science* for 1895. At the suggestion of some eminent librarians, it was reprinted in volume twenty of *Library Journal* so that the English-speaking library world was informed almost immediately of this important bibliographic development. Dr. Herbert Putnam of the Boston Public Library urged librarians to enter into discussion of the proposals either in the pages of the *Journal* or by direct communication with the Royal Society, and some of them did.

After carefully considering these and many more the Society issued invitations for an international bibliographic conference to be convened in London in July, 1896.

The delegates from the United States were John Shaw Billings and Simon Newcomb, the latter from the U.S. *Nautical Almanac*. Billings, in a letter to *Science* in April, 1895, had questioned the value in terms of cost and utility of a complete card index of science available to everyone.[42] He doubted whether investigators who had such a tool at their disposal would be any the better for it because of the bulk of material thus concentrated in one place, and the difficulty of obtaining copies of much that was listed. His bibliographic eminence and experience carried great weight at the conference.[43]

By an interesting fluke, a delegate originally selected by Belgium was unable to attend and Henri LaFontaine was substituted.[44] Otlet was also a delegate. The minutes of the meetings are fascinating reading for anyone interested in bibliographic problems. Should the service being planned be on cards or in published volumes or both? How should the catalog be classified? Billings opposed Otlet on the subject of the Dewey system. Should the councils subordinate to the central council recommended for editing and publication of the catalog be set up by country or by subject? There was considerable division of opinion on this. It was pointed out that small countries would have difficulty assembling a commission to embrace all the sciences. On the other hand a division by the sciences would not take care of the area of overlap in such sciences as chemistry and physics.

Part of the administrative structure was roughed in at the first conference. The Royal Society was asked to set up a committee to which the conference might refer all matters upon which it could not agree, such as classification, or on which more information was needed. Nations represented at the conference were given until January, 1898, to indicate what they were doing toward setting up a participating unit.

Two additional international conferences were needed, one in 1898 and one in 1900, to complete the organization and plans for producing the catalog. The expanded Dewey classification was rejected and another, which its enemies called a poor imitation, created especially for it.[45] It was to cover seventeen branches of science. The enterprise was to be governed by International Convention; administered by an International Council; operated by an International Central Bureau aided by Regional Bureaus in the participating countries, which would supply references; and advised by International Committees of Referees for each of the subjects included.

The financial arrangements were complicated. On paper the enterprise was dependent upon subscriptions to the service held by participating countries and the project was to proceed no further than the amount of these subscriptions warranted. However, in order to get the project started and to provide a legally responsible agent to make printing contracts and the like, the Royal Society assumed the role of an unlimited liability company, and loaned the project money at four per cent interest. It secured approval of the British government to act in this capacity, and was even granted one thousand pounds a year for five years "to make good to the Royal Society a part of any loss which may be incurred by the publication of the proposed Catalogue."[46]

Although this framework for the catalog was agreed to by the delegates, there were many of considerable stature in the bibliographic world who vigorously disparaged it. The classification schedules were attacked alike by Deweyites and scholars favoring no particular scheme. Among the former were Julius Victor Carus and Haviland Field.[47] In this country, open letters were published in *Science* from scientists including H. Carrington Bolton, Franz Boas, and W. J. McGee, all of whom disliked the proposed classification.[48]

When the first annual issue covering the seventeen branches and appearing in twenty-two volumes finally appeared the reception was mixed. Attention was called to serious omissions which were especially noticeable in those subjects for which other bibliographic services such as the *Concilium* existed, with which comparison could be made. In the case of zoology, it was particularly unfortunate that that part of the catalog was always behind schedule. In 1906, the *Zoological Record* was amalgamated with Volume N, Zoology. This improved the quality of the work but did not eliminate the lag in publication.

Inherent defects in the organizational structure soon began to show up. The Central Bureau, finding that the system of having Regional Bureaus send in references was beset with delays and hazards, urged that arrangements be made with authors and publishers to report on their writings as issued. However, for this there was no operating mechanism.

By 1914 the *International Catalogue* was deeply in the red financially and from two to three years behind in production. The *Catalogue of Scientific Papers* in that year published the first volume of the author catalog for the period 1884–1900 and was completing the fourth volume of the subject index. Announcement was made that the remaining volumes of the latter would not be published for lack of funds. The project's great benefactor, Dr. Ludwig Mond, alone, had contributed £19,836 17s 6d to the enterprise from 1901 until his death in 1909.[49]

The Brussels Institute grew steadily although slowly in influence and substance. LaFontaine received the Nobel prize for peace in 1913. The International Office of Bibliography's Répertoire comprised nearly thirteen million cards by 1914.

It is probably impossible to over-estimate the effect of the First World War on these attempts to organize bibliography. However, there is danger of attributing to it particular results which were at most only hastened by it. The destruction of scholarly communication was a body blow to all three enterprises.

However, events prior to the outbreak of hostilities, described in investigations made by committees appointed after the war to survey the three situations, show that in every case if the organization had continued along the path it was following it would probably have collapsed because of its own weaknesses.

In the case of the *International Catalogue*, it did not render prompt service and could not do so with the existing set-up. It provided subject-indexing when abstracting was wanted. Even the President of the Royal Society, Sir Joseph Thomsen, a physicist, frankly admitted before the conference held in 1920 that he never used it but preferred abstract journals for his own work! Because of its form it was difficult to use. The financial responsibility was inequitably distributed.[50]

In the case of the Brussels Institute, its plans and promises so far exceeded its ability to produce tangible results that it generated distrust. It acquired a reputation for inefficiency,[51] which the impassioned refutations of champions such as Ernest Cushing Richardson could not dispel.[52]

The *Concilium's* card distribution system was placing such a filing burden upon users of the service that many were turning to the abstract journals which were becoming increasingly prevalent.[53]

After a thorough investigation of the status and potentialities of the *International Catalogue*, the International Council, in 1922, voted to end the project. Published volumes covered the literature through 1914. The Royal Society acted as receiver to close out the accounts, but little of the indebtedness was cleared so that in 1935 the Society wrote off £14,000 in bad debts.[54] Apparently, at least some of the participating nations thought that the British government would make good the loss.

The Brussels Institute not only had its physical plant partially destroyed but also lost the financial support of the Belgian government. The Répertoire was still intact but the wartime accumulation of entries constituted a formidable filing arrearage for which no staff was available.[55] It reorganized in 1924, accepting as members specialized scientific international associations and national associations of an encyclopedic character.[56]

When Haviland Field died in 1921, the National Research Council of the United States and the Rockefeller Foundation were asked to investigate the status of the *Concilium*. It found that accumulated debts probably exceeded the amount which could be realized if the building, equipment, and cards were liquidated. A five-year arrangement was made whereby the Council and the Swiss Society of Natural Sciences administered the project and the Rockefeller Foundation cleared obligations, including partial return to Mrs. Field of some of the fortune her husband had poured into it, and took care of current expenses. It was hoped that at the end of that time the organization would be self-sustaining or would receive international financing.[57] Neither of these hopes materialized. The Foundation withdrew support in 1926. Although the *Concilium* did not cease publication until

1940, so many institutional subscriptions had been withdrawn that collapse was certain.[58]

Tragic though these events seemed for international bibliographic organization, there were momentous post-war developments beginning which held great promise for the future. The newly formed League of Nations was influenced, Pafford reports, by the International Institute of Bibliography at Brussels to set up an International Committee on Intellectual Cooperation which made the organization of sources of information its first concern. That first committee was a remarkable group of subject specialists, perhaps the best known of whom were Gilbert Murray, Einstein, Millikan, and Madame Curie.[59] The approach was understandably that of organizing the literature by subject fields. Early in its work, the Committee recognized its need of technical advice from bibliographers and librarians. It therefore set up an advisory sub-comittee to "find the best practical methods" of preserving "knowledge accumulated in the past" and of disseminating it rapidly in the future."[60]

In 1924 the Sub-Committee recommended that the Brussels Institute be assisted to establish "exhaustive alphabetical and methodical catalogs: (a) concerning bibliographical publications (periodicals or not, bibliography retrospective or current, and both primary and analytic); (b) concerning the history of the production and sale of books, as well as the history and process of every means of reproduction; (c) concerning publications on libraries and archives, places of preservation for books and written documents; (d) concerning publications on the organization of intellectual work and scientific cooperation."[61]

An agreement was finally signed by the League and the Institute providing, among other things, for "the development of an alphabetical catalog by authors' names on the lines of a collective catalog of the great libraries of the world, indicating where any particular work can be found," and systematic catalogs for bibliography and the organization of scientific work and intellectual cooperation.[62] Article 3 of the agreement provided that the order in which the work would be undertaken would be fixed by agreement. It was here that negotiations broke down. Two factors undoubtedly influenced this: (1) the Brussels Institute had at this time little about it to inspire confidence in its future; and (2) the League and the Committee were in the midst of negotiations with the French government looking to the setting up of an International Institute of Intellectual Cooperation in Paris.

The attitude and action of American librarians had a considerable influence on developments at this time. A prevalent distrust of international cooperative bibliographic enterprises hitherto manifested by the library world was subsiding. As an indication of this the A.L.A., in 1922, was able to appoint a Committee on Bibliography to provide a channel for participation "in the growing movement to get together all going enterprises in bibliography, whether theoretical or applied, for practical cooperation."[63] Ernest Cushing Richardson became chairman of the Committee, and sought to bail out the Brussels Institute by finding a common ground on which the League and the A.L.A. could work for that end. He succeeded in this, but was unable to complete negotiations between these two and Brussels. The A.L.A. backed the League and the new institute and remained aloof to the documentalists.

The paths of the Brussels Institute, the League Committee, and the new International Institute of Intellectual Cooperation separated. The latter, the I.I.I.C., was really an operating agency for the old League Committee, almost entirely financed by the French and housed by them in Paris. Its purpose was to encourage, coordinate, and promote in innumerable ways intellectual cooperation through existing agencies. From the standpoint of contributing to international bibliographic organization, it was a hope and a delusion. The sections on scientific relations which devoted the most attention to bibliography stimulated many excellent bibliographies, abstracting journals, and reviews. However, it proved easier to encourage production than to coordinate it into anything remotely resembling organization.

I am not trying to disparage so noble and relatively successful a venture as the I.I.I.C., but if history is to serve us, we must be candid. The bibliographic world was out of hand and no existing body had the wisdom or the strength to whip it into shape. The specialization of the intellectual world had compartmentalized it. Furthermore, the activity within the specialties was so tremendously accelerated, not only by the war but also by the compound cumulation which is a natural factor of intellectual activity, that even an international body created for the purpose could not keep track of what was going on. The picture became increasingly confusing. The International Union of Academies aided by the I.I.I.C. tried to take a census of bibliographic work in progress throughout the world in the social sciences and the humanities, but after a few years gave up "in despair" over the size of the task.[64]

In 1927, an International Library and Bibliographical Committee was created during the golden jubilee conference of the British Library Association. The inclusion of "Bibliographical" in the titles appears to have been wishful thinking on the part of one delegate.[65] The purpose of the organization was "to select the place for international library conferences and, with the cooperation of local committees, to prepare programs for such conferences, and to make investigations and recommendations concerning international relations between libraries, organizations of librarians and bibliographers, and other agencies."[66] The International Federation of Library Associations grew out of the Committee's work, the latter continuing as the executive body.[67]

The chief contribution of I.F.L.A. to the international organization of bibliography has been to provide an international meeting ground for librarians schooled in differing traditions, documentalists, and bibliographers. Such cross-fertilization, of course, contributes to the most elementary steps in international organization of bibliography. The exchange of information on techniques, processes, devices, equipment, training, current work, and common problems is instrumental in attempts being made to standardize forms, methods, processes, nomenclature, etc.; to revise policy; and to revamp professional education.

The union of librarians and documentalists was strengthened by the establishment of joint I.F.L.A.-F.I.D. committees on standardization, on special libraries and information bureaus, and on cataloging rules.[68] The annual meetings of the International Library Committee regularly heard reports of the bibliographic work of the I.I.I.C.

As far as I have been able to discover at this point, the body which did most to maintain focus on international organization of bibliography, particularly during the 'Thirties, was the resuscitated Brussels Institute (with a general secretariat at The Hague)—first as the International Institute of Documentation and then as the International Federation for Documentation. It accomplished this chiefly: (1) through the direct effect which the doctrines of its founders had on the thinking of individuals in many countries—Donker Duyvis,

A. F. C. Pollard, Bradford, Lancaster-Jones, our own Richardson, and many more; (2) through its affiliated national sections—such as the British Society for International Bibliography, the Dutch Institute of Documentation, the Swiss Association, and the French Committee; and (3) through its international meetings which in the 'Thirties became annual events and at which both individual and group plans for bibliographic organization were presented, discussed, and developed.

It was at these meetings that Bradford evolved some of his proposals for complete documentation of scientific literature. It was here that Pollard gave his critique of H. G. Wells's *World Encyclopaedia* and brought forward a plan for organization of subject bibliography in a World Bibliographic Repertory using the U.D.C.[69]

There are elements in the inter-war years which distinguish thinking, planning, and activity in the field from the attempts made prior to World War I. I would not venture at this point to establish their relative order of importance.

In the first place, the development of new devices and equipment for recording, storing, sorting, selecting, and reproducing recorded information occupied the attention of many who hoped they held the solution to the problem of bibliographically harnessing the tremendously increased volume of material. The potential of the devices could not be realized without suitable techniques and staff trained in those techniques. Therefore, interest and work increased in this area.

In the second place, there was a shift of emphasis from the single great international tool such as the *International Catalogue* and the Répertoire Universel, or from the single great international information bureau to national bibliographic organization as the fundamental unit of international organization. For years, scattered and partial understanding of this need had been recognized. Frank Campbell was a voice crying in the wilderness of the 1890's.[70] The Brussels Institute recognized and stressed the need for current national bibliography, as did others, and tried to utilize for its central service the existing bibliographic services of the various nations in which it had members. The new emphasis was focused upon a closely knit, smoothly coordinated, national system. As the concept grew it looked like a kind of managerial heaven in which the sum of the parts equaled a whole, operating simultaneously with ease and efficiency. The friction in the mechanism came from the grit of certain questions which popped up whenever a plan was presented. A basic and ever-recurring one was: *did* the parts equal a whole; that is, if all the existing bibliographic services in a nation were coordinated into a perfectly meshed national bibliographic system and those national systems into a universal system, would everyone be able to find what he needed from man's record? Informed persons were sure this would not be possible, but that was not a constructive answer. The full answer must be in terms of what proportion of a national whole the existing national bibliographic resources, if unified, would equal? At this point someone was sure to ask what the nature of a national whole was.

Nobody could answer these questions. When attempts were made to prepare answers, it was quickly found that relatively little information existed. Thus a supplementary activity of the managerial approach to bibliographic organization soon claimed a major share of the time, thought, and resources of those working for the international organization of bibliography. This activity was the supplying of data of all kinds about informational resources—what they were, where they were, how good they were, how they were operated, *ad infinitum.* There were surveys made, statistics gathered, directories published, costs analyzed, time and motion charted, bibliographies of bibliographies of bibliographies compiled. So much was done that the bibliographic control of the literature of bibliographic control became a major obstacle to the international organization of bibliography.

When World War II came, the emphasis on national organization of bibliography, in spite of all the hazards of further compartmentalization inherent in it, proved to be a bulwark which protected the progress, slight as it was, toward the international organization of bibliography. When the war ended, much of the thinking and planning of the 'Thirties seemed to have been strengthened, clarified, and sustained by the ordeal of fire and sword. Plans, experiments, surveys held in abeyance during the war were dusted off and re-examined in the light of experience.

Perhaps the major obstacles to the development of at least some of these were the new dimensions of the bibliographic world. The twenty thousand volumes purporting to be additions to the sum of human knowledge published annually in Joseph Henry's day were beyond estimate by the early 1930's when Bradford found 750,000 *worth-while* original scientific papers in 15,000 periodicals.[11] The list of 36,000 scientific periodicals listed in *A World List of Scientific Periodicals* in 1934 reached an estimated 50,000 in 1948.[72] The editor of *Chemical Abstracts* noted an increase of 106 per cent in the literature of chemistry alone between 1944 and 1949.[73]

Not only has the literature increased out of all proportion to anything previously known, but its character has been greatly altered, particularly by the war. The periodical was superseding the book in science and technology before World War I. The latest war made the near-print research report pre-eminent in the same fields.

This change of character, in turn, has added not only to the number of titles issued, but has greatly increased the difficulties of locating them for purposes of bibliographic recording. On top of that, the hopes raised in the 'Thirties by the development of mechanized devices were dashed during the war years when it was conclusively demonstrated that only what was put into the machine could be pulled from it and that the road leading to the knowledge and technique needed to do that was long and rough.[74]

Miss Ditmas has summed up the situation accurately in the following:

"The position had been reached where almost every scientist and technician agreed that something should be done but nobody could decide on the exact course of action or, if they agreed on the course of action, they could not put forward concrete proposals for implementing it. . . . It began to be realized that the problem was not only that of recording the information so that the research worker might know what had been written, but also that of creating some device by which the required data might be located and selected from the records. Luckily in this particular respect the advance in mechanical apparatus makes it possible to operate large-scale schemes in spite of the prevailing shortage of man-power. Nevertheless the central problem remains; no machine can, by itself, make the initial record and classification and, unless methods of co-operation can be improved, a large amount of important material will go unrecorded and be lost to sight."[75]

It was into this appalling post-war bibliographic chaos that the United Nations Educational, Scientific, and Cultural Organization was born. Almost before it had uttered its first cry of life it was confronted with hopes, plans, and projects in all conditions of health and maturity.

Dr. Evans has related the story as follows:

"When the sages were gathered in London in the summer of 1946 to draft plans for the program of UNESCO, to be considered at the first General Conference of that organization later in the same year, they made numerous proposals which came from meetings organized upon the basis of common professions or interests. Now the remarkable thing about these meetings is that one after another they recommended that UNESCO should give attention to the bibliography of the literature in the field of their interest."[76]

UNESCO profited from the experience of the pre-war International Institute of Intellectual Cooperation by centralizing the handling of bibliographic matters in a Libraries Division under which was an office of Research Library and Bibliographical Development. To this agency fell the unenviable task of sifting the proposals for bibliographic work submitted to it while trying to develop a program for furthering the international organization of bibliography. This is a difficult undertaking. Mistakes have been made and progress has been slow. UNESCO is proceeding along cautious lines. It brings together for exchange of information, consultation, and planning those bodies engaged in similar types of bibliographic work in similar fields throughout the world—for example, those interested in problems of abstracting the literature of medicine and biology.

It is encouraging closer union between the two international groups most directly concerned with international bibliographic organization—I.F.L.A. and F.I.D. The first joint international meeting of the two agencies will be held in Paris next November.

It is following the pre-war pattern with respect to providing information and data required in organizing bibliography both internationally and nationally. It is currently engaged in ascertaining the present state of bibliographic work throughout the world. To do this requires surveys of various kinds, preparation of directories, bibliographies, and other compilations of information. Rather than doing the work itself, UNESCO is making arrangements with appropriate national and international groups. For example, the Library of Congress has prepared several studies on a contract basis,[77] and the International Federation for Documentation last year published a *List of Current Specialized Abstracting and Indexing Services*, with financial aid from UNESCO.[78]

How successful UNESCO will be in improving the present state of bibliography few would prophesy. There are reasons for thinking great strides will be made either directly under its auspices or simultaneously with it and because of it. Two of these reasons are that: (1) there seems to be a deeper understanding among scholars and librarians alike of the importance of organizing bibliography; (2) there seem to be more individuals and groups in a position to do something about the present chaos who want, and are trying, to do something about it. The question is whether this maturity and the action it is generating will arrive in time and with sufficient power to mobilize the intellectual record in such a way that man can use it to fortify himself against a chaos far more terrifying than that which presently exists in bibliography.

REFERENCES

1. U.S. Library of Congress, *Antecedentes bibliotecológicos interamericanos e internacionales; recopilados para la Asamblea de Bibliotecarios de América, 12 de mayo a 6 de junio de 1947, Washington, D.C.* (Washington, 1947). Pp. 140.

2. Thomas Coulson, *Joseph Henry, His Life and Work* (Princeton: Princeton University Press, 1950), p. 3.

3. *Ibid.*, p. 203.

4. The Smithsonian Institution, *Annual Report of the Board of Regents . . . 1851 . . .* (Washington: A. Boyd Hamilton, 1852), p. 22.

5. Coulson, *op. cit.*, p. 204. See also British Association for the Advancement of Science, *Report . . . 1855* (London: John Murray, 1856), p. lxvi.

6. The Royal Society of London, *Proceedings . . . 1862* (London: Taylor & Francis, 1863), p. 286.

7. The Royal Society of London, *Proceedings . . . 1864* (London: Taylor & Francis, ?), pp. 497–98.

8. The Royal Society of London, *Proceedings . . . 1866* (London: Taylor & Francis, 1867), p. 271.

9. The Royal Society of London, *Proceedings . . . 1869* (London: Taylor & Francis, 1870), p. 103.

10. The Royal Society of London, *Proceedings . . . 1870* (London: Taylor & Francis, 1871), p. 114.

11. The Royal Society of London, *Proceedings . . . 1886* (London: Harrison & Sons, 1887), p. 379.

12. The Royal Society of London, *Proceedings . . . 1874* (London: Taylor & Francis, 1875), p. 61.

13. The Royal Society of London, *Proceedings . . . 1876* (London: Taylor & Francis, 1877), p. 339.

14. The Royal Society of London, *Proceedings . . . 1882* (London: Harrison & Sons, 1883), p. 305.

15. The Royal Society of London, *Proceedings . . . 1887* (London: Harrison & Sons, 1888), p. 191.

16. M. B. Iwinski, "La Statistique internationale des imprimés ... ," *Bulletin de l'Institut International de Bibliographie* (Brussels), 1911, p. 58.

17. American Association for the Advancement of Science, Committee on Index-

ing Chemical Literature, "Report . . . , "*Proceedings* . . . *1883* (Salem: Salem Press, 1884), XXXII, 147–48.

18. American Association for the Advancement of Science, Committee on Indexing Chemical Literature, "Report," *Proceedings* . . . *1904* (Washington, 1905), pp. 575–78.

19. Frank B. Rogers and Scott Adams, "The Army Medical Library's Publication Program," *Texas Reports on Biology and Medicine* (Austin), VIII (summer, 1950), 275.

20. J. H. McNinch, *Historical Outline of Indexing Publication in the Army Medical Library* (photostatic copy of a memorandum sent to Dr. Luther H. Evans, September 26, 1949), pp. 3–4.

21. The Royal Society of London, *Proceedings* . . . *1888* (London: Harrison & Sons, 1889), p. 51.

22. The Royal Society of London, *Proceedings* . . . *1889* (London: Harrison & Sons, 1890), pp. 455–56.

23. The Royal Society of London, *Proceedings* . . . *1893* (London: Harrison & Sons, 1894), p. 378.

24. H. Carrington Bolton, "An International Index to Chemical Literature," *Journal of the American Chemical Society* (Easton, Pa.), XV (1893), 574–79.

25. "Proceedings of the Congress on Chemistry Held in Chicago, Illinois, August 21 to August 26, 1893," *Journal of the American Chemical Society* (Easton, Pa.), XV (1893), 309.

26. American Association for the Advancement of Science, Committee on Indexing Chemical Literature, "Report," *Proceedings* . . . *1894* (Salem, 1895), XLIII, 172.

27. H. Van Laer, "Des mesures destinées à faciliter aux chimistes et techniciens l'accès rapide de toutes les publications qui les intéressent," *Congrès international de chimie appliquée, Compte-rendu* (Brussels, Gustave Deprez, 1894), pp. 1–6.

28. Herbert H. Field, "The Bibliographia Zoologica," *Library Journal* (New York), XX (December, 1895), 29–30; Société Néerlandaise de Zoologie, *Compte-rendu des séances du troisième Congrès international de zoologie, Leyde, 16–21 Septembre, 1895* (Leiden, E. J. Brill, 1896), pp. 88–93.

29. Information throughout pages 34–35 drawn from: "Chronologie des principaux faits relatifs au développement de l'Institut International de Bibliographie," *Bulletin de l'Institut International de Bibliographie* (Brussels), XII (1907), 31–46; and "Résolutions des congrès internationaux," *Bulletin de l'Institut International de Bibliographie* (Brussels), XII (1907), 47–60.

30. Samuel C. Bradford, "Fifty Years of Documentation," *Documentation* (London: Crosby Lockwood & Son, Ltd., 1948), p. 96.

31. The Royal Society of London, *Proceedings* . . . *1895* (London: Harrison & Sons, 1896), p. 113.

32. F. Donker Duyvis, "The International Federation for Documentation," *Journal of Documentary Reproduction* (Chicago), III (September, 1940), 176.

33. International Federation for Documentation, *Bulletin de l'Institut International de Bibliographie* ..., Vols. I–XVI (1895–96—1911) (16 vols. in 15; Bruxelles: Institut International de Bibliographie, 1895–1911).

No bulletins were issued for the seventeenth and eighteenth years, 1912–13. After the publication of the nineteenth and final volume of this series of bulletins in 1914, five occasional bulletins of information were issued at irregular intervals, from September, 1923, to November, 1925, as Publications of the Institute, Nos. 124, 139–41, and 145. In 1931 the publication of a regular series of bulletins was revived under the title "Documentatio universalis." These three series of bulletins are entered separately in Library of Congress catalogs.

International Federation for Documentation, *Revue de la documentation* ("Review of Documentation"), Vols. I—— (1934——) (La Haye). Vol. II, No.3—Vol. XIII issued as the federation's Publication No. 174. Volumes I–V (1934–38), *I.I.D. Communications* ["Quarterly communications," "Communications trimestrielles," "Dreimonatliche Berichte"]—Vols. VI–XIII (1939–46), *F.I.D. Communications.* Volumes I–IV (1934–37), published under an earlier name of the federation: International Institute of Documentation.

34. Donker Duyvis, *op. cit.*, p. 179.

35. Samuel C. Bradford, "Introduction," *Documentation* (London: Crosby Lockwood & Son, Ltd., 1948), p. 9.

36. E. M. R. Ditmas, "A Chapter Closes: Bradford, Pollard and Lancaster-Jones," *College and Research Libraries* (New York), X (October, 1949), 332. For a discussion of the difference between bibliography and documentation see Lancaster-Jones's editorial in the *Library Association Record*, December, 1931, pp. 424–25.

37. J. H. P. Pafford, *Library Cooperation in Europe* (London: Library Association, 1935), p. 24. J. G. Pearce, "A National Intelligence Service," *Association of Special Libraries and Information Bureaux, Report of Proceedings of the Third Conference Held at Balliol College, Oxford, September 24–27, 1926* (London, 1926), pp. 118–21.

38. P. Bourgeois, "National Collaboration as a Step to International Collaboration," *Aslib Proceedings . . .* (London), I (August, 1949), 144.

39. E. M. R. Ditmas, "Co-ordination of Information: A Survey of Schemes Put Forward in the Last Fifty Years," *Journal of Documentation* (London), III (March, 1948), 210–11.

40. Cyrus Adler, "The International Catalogue of Scientific Literature," *Science* (New York), N.S., VI (August 6, 1897), 190.

41. A. F. C. Pollard, "The Disordered State of Bibliography and Indications of Its Effect upon Scientific and Technical Progress," *British Society for International Bibliography, Proceedings*, IV (1942), 41–42.

42. John S. Billings, "A Card Catalogue of Scientific Literature," *Science* (New York), N.S., I (April 12, 1895), 406–8.

43. Adler, *op. cit.*, p. 31.

44. The Royal Society of London, *Report of the Proceedings at the International Conference on a Catalogue of Scientific Literature Held in London, July 14–17, 1896* (n.p., n.d.), p. 1.

45. International Catalogue of Scientific Literature, *Memorandum of the Systems of Classification and Registration Proposed by the Committee of the Royal Society* (London, 1898). Pp. 7.

46. The Royal Society of London, *Year-Book . . . 1914* (London: Harrison & Sons, 1914), p. 178.

47. J. Victor Carus, "On the International Catalogue of Scientific Literature of the Royal Society" (trans. from *Zoologischer Anzeiger*, No. 566), *Science* (New York), N.S., IX (June 16, 1899), 825–35. "The International Catalogue of Scientific Literature" (letter from Herbert H. Field), *Science* (New York), N.S., X (August 4, 1899), 133–43.

48. "The International Catalogue of Scientific Literature," (letters from H. C. Bolton and W. P. Cutter, W. J. McGee, and Franz Boas), *Science* (New York), N.S., IX (June 23, 1899), 867–71; N.S., X (July 14, 1899), 48–50; N.S., X (August 11, 1899), 173–74.

49. The Royal Society of London, *Year-Book . . . 1914* (London: Harrison & Sons, 1914), p. 178.

50. International Catalogue of Scientific Literature, *International Conference,*

4th, London, 1920, Report of the Proceedings . . . To Consider the Future of the International Catalogue of Scientific Literature, Held in the Rooms of the Royal Society, September 28 and 29, 1920 (London, 1920?). Pp. 104.

51. H. W. Wilson, "The Brussels Institute," *Library Journal* (New York), LII (September 16, 1927), 855.

52. Ernest C. Richardson, "The Brussels Institute Again!" *Library Journal* (New York), LII (September 1, 1927), 795–801.

53. Roger C. Smith, *Guide to the Literature of the Zoological Sciences* (Minneapolis: Burgess Publishing Co., 1945), pp. 24–25.

54. Dorothy Stimson, *Scientists and Amateurs* (New York: Schuman, 1948), p. 231.

55. Richardson, *op. cit.*

56. Donker Duyvis, *op. cit.*, p. 181.

57. National Academy of Sciences, *Report . . . 1922* (Washington: Government Printing Office, 1923), pp. 33–34.

58. Smith, *op. cit.*, p. 25.

59. Pafford, *op. cit.*, p. 317.

60. League of Nations, International Committee on Intellectual Cooperation, *Minutes of the First Session* (Geneva, August 1–5, 1922), p. 16. (C711.M423.1922. XII.)

61. *Ibid.*, pp. 58–59.

62. Ernest C. Richardson, *Some Aspects of International Library Cooperation* (Yardley, Pa.: F. S. Cook & Son, 1928), pp. 111–12.

63. *Ibid.*, p. 116.

64. Waldo E. Leland, "Bibliography and Scholarship," *Inter-American Bibliographical and Library Association, Proceedings of the Second Convention, Washington, D.C., February 23–24, 1939* (New York: H. W. Wilson Co., 1939), pp. 31–32. "Catalogue des bibliographies courantes des sciences cultivées par les corps savants affiliés à l'U.A.I.," *Insitut International de Coopération Intellectuelle, Bulletin des relations scientifiques* (Paris), III (August, 1928), 130–31.

65. International Library Committee, *Actes ... 2ᵉ session ... Rome ... 1929* (Uppsala: Almquist & Wiksells, 1931), p. 36 (Publications, Vol. I).

66. International Library Committee, *Actes ... 1ère session, 1928* (Uppsala: Almquist & Wiksells, 1931), pp. 13–14 (Publications, Vol. I).

67. International Library Committee, *Actes ... 3ᵉ session ... 1930* (Uppsala: Almquist & Wiksells, 1930), p. 36 (Publications, Vol. II).

68. F. Donker Duyvis, "Relations avec la Fédération Internationale des Associations de Bibliothécaires," International Federation for Documentation, *XVIᵉ Conférence internationale ... Paris, 4–9 Novembre, 1946, Comptes-rendus des travaux* (Paris: Comité Français de la Documentation, 1946), p. 28.

69. A. F. C. Pollard, "The Mobilization of Knowledge and the 'Permanent World Encyclopaedia' of Mr. H. G. Wells," International Federation for Documentation, *14th Conference, Oxford and London, 1938, Transactions . . .*, II (The Hague: Central Secretariat, 1938?), C161-C167.

70. Frank Campbell, *The Theory of National and International Bibliography, with Special Reference to the Introduction of System in the Record of Modern Literature* (London: Library Bureau, 1896). Pp. 500.

71. Samuel C. Bradford, "The Extent to Which Scientific and Technical Literature Is Covered by Present Abstracting and Indexing Periodicals," *Association of Special Libraries and Information Bureaux, Report of Proceedings of the Fourteenth Conference . . .* (London, 1937), pp. 59–67.

72. R. S. Hutton, "Preparatory Notes for Working Parties in Section I," *Royal Society of London, Scientific Information Conference, 1948, Report and Papers Submitted . . .* (London, 1948), p. 673.

73. E. J. Crane, "Scientific Publication Now Very Active," *Revue de la documentation* (The Hague), XXVI, Fasc. 2 (1949), 50.

74. Mortimer Taube, "Memorandum for a Conference on Bibliographical Control of Government Scientific and Technical Reports," *Special Libraries* (New York), XXXIX (May–June, 1948), 155–60.

75. E. M. R. Ditmas, "Co-ordination of Information: A Survey of Schemes Put Forward in the Last Fifty Years," *Journal of Documentation* (London), III (March, 1948), 220.

76. Luther H. Evans, "Bibliography by Cooperation," *Bulletin of the Medical Library Association* (New York), XXXVII (July, 1949), 199.

77. Kathrine O. Murra, *Sources of Information for Fundamental Education with Special References to Education for Literacy: A Preliminary Report* (Washington: Library of Congress, 1948), pp. 81, 123. UNESCO/Library of Congress Bibliographical Survey, *Bibliographical Services, Their Present State and Possibilities of Improvement: Report Prepared as a Working Paper for an International Conference on Bibliography* (Washington, 1950), pp. 42, 67.

78. International Federation for Documentation, *List of Current Specialized Abstracting and Indexing Services, Prepared . . . for the International Conference on Science Abstracting, UNESCO House, Paris, 20 to 25 June, 1949, Convened by the United Nations Educational, Scientific and Cultural Organization* (The Hague, 1949). (Publication No. 235). Pp. 23.

THE FUNCTIONAL APPROACH

FUNCTIONAL APPROACH TO BIBLIOGRAPHIC ORGANIZATION: A CRITIQUE AND A PROPOSAL

MORTIMER TAUBE

O UR first effort in this paper must be to clarify the title—that is, for me to tell you exactly what I think it means and for you to accept the interpretation I give to it. Only then can we proceed together to attempt to answer the questions implicit in the title.

Organization is always definable in terms of a purpose or purposes and this is true whether the elements being organized are individuals in the American Library Association, cells in a living body, or books in the collections of a library. Now a discussion of the functions of an organization might be nothing more or less than a discussion of its purposes. Beyond that, a "functional approach" to the study of any organization would be concerned with the particular characteristics of an organization which were designed to make possible the performance of particular functions for the accomplishment of particular purposes. It is this latter interpretation which will set the frame of reference for the discussion to follow. We shall be concerned with the purposes of bibliographic organization, with kinds of organization which have their justification in the achievement of these purposes, with measuring the adequacy of such achievement, and finally with suggesting other forms of organization which might more effectively achieve agreed-upon purposes.

We shall be dealing with two variables: purposes, and organizations for accomplishing these purposes. It should be apparent that these are not independent variables; that the purposes which are set up determine the adequacy of organizations; and contrariwise, the organizational pattern determines what purposes can be achieved. However, this direct functional interdependence of purposes and organization is only theoretical; in practice purposes change more rapidly than organizations, and we are all familiar with rigid organizations which maintain themselves by limiting or even denying the existence of purposes threatening the perpetuation of organizational patterns which have attained the dignity of tradition and the comfort of unquestioned acceptance. When an organization has for years successfully achieved certain purposes, it should not be overthrown lightly by those who confuse an aberrant whim with a new and important purpose. On the other hand, no organizational pattern can be justified by anything other than the purposes it achieves; which is to say that organizations have only a "means" value and organizational values cannot, except in terms of cultural lag, stand against the more real fact of human purposes. In short, in this paper, we shall never say this is a bad purpose because it cannot be achieved by an existing organization, but we may say that this is a bad organization because it cannot achieve this or that purpose.

THE CRITIQUE

In the broadest terms, bibliographic organization has the purpose of making the record of the past or any part of that record a possible factor in present judgment or behavior. We must recognize that this qualification "possible" is the cross which we librarians and information officers must bear, guardians as we are of great masses of organized knowledge which we know should be, but is not, used in solving the day-to-day problems of the market place. But here again we must be careful to recognize that the fault may lie in part with the kinds of bibliographic organization which we create and perpetuate.

In order to decide whether the beam is in our neighbors' eye or in our own, we need to isolate purposes more specific than the general desire to make the record of the past a vital factor in present action. Hence, we will consider first a specific type of bibliographic organization which within recent months has been urged upon us—comprehensive current national bibliography—and question whether or not important scholarly, scientific, or broadly human purposes exist which would justify the organization of recorded information into comprehensive current national bibliographies.

We are fortunate in having at hand two excellent studies on this matter prepared by the UNESCO/Library of Congress Bibliographical Survey, *Bibliographical Services, Their Present State and Possibilities of Improvement*, and the Appendix *Notes on the Development of the Concept of Current Complete National Bibliography*, by Kathrine Oliver Murra, hereafter referred to as the Working Paper and the Working Paper Appendix. The Working Paper, although it seems to lack a general conclusion, is, to my mind, an elaborate argument for the basic necessity and desirability of current complete national bibliographies as the *sine qua non* of adequate selective or subject bibliographies and of international bibliographic organization. The Appendix to the Working Paper is a witty and slightly scolding history of the failure to achieve current national bibliographies during the period 1844–1939. Apparently, it is designed to point up the shortcomings of bibliographic activity which must be remedied if the bibliographic millennium emphasized in the Working Paper is to be attained. The bibliographic organization which will constitute the millennium will have as foundation stones current complete national bibliographies; the totality of such stones, nothing more nor less, will make up current complete universal bibliography, and cross-sections of the stones will give us international subject bibliographies. Do I hear a mocking voice insisting that one can't get blood from stones—that what students, scientists, scholars, and men of affairs need are adequate subject bibliographies, and that current complete national bibliographies and current complete universal bibliography are both will-o'-the-wisps that have no function beyond the professional purposes of their sponsors? But perhaps we have been betrayed here by an unfortunate metaphor. If we had called current complete national bibliographies the cells and current complete universal bibliography the living body, perhaps we could not brush aside so easily the claim that only when such a body has developed is it possible to attain also the special subject bibliographies and indexes which are the life blood of intellectual endeavor. The Working Paper tells us that for both current complete national bibliographies and current complete universal bibliography "all that is needed is the technique—and the necessary cooperation." To be sure—but as the man said, "if I had some bread I could make a ham sandwich if I had some ham." For what is this but an admission that the preparation of a current complete national bibliography awaits both the knowledge of how to do it and the desire to see it done? Of these two lacks, the latter is the more serious. For if the purpose were important enough, we could not long be held back by the lack of technical skill to create the organization necessary to the purpose. This demonstration of valid purposes, the functional approach, is missing from the Working Paper. Purposes are mentioned but only briefly and almost incidentally.

"The primary purpose of current comprehensive bibliography is to provide the prospective users of publications, and others interested in them, with a complete account of what publications are available in the category covered by the particular bibliography, and with certain basic information regarding those publications. This information usually includes the originating source (typically the publisher) from which the publications may be procured. Indications of content (literary form or subject-content) have come to be regarded as an essential part of the information provided."[1]

Later, this account is expanded under the heading "Use: Relationship to Selective Bibliography," and we are told:

"Current comprehensive bibliographies are widely used by those who are concerned with a variety of subject-content. Such are booksellers and librarians, on behalf of the service to their users. In bookshops and libraries, also, current comprehensive bibliographies are frequently consulted by individual inquirers who lack other means of identifying publications. . . .

"Furthermore, current comprehensive bibliographies are extensively used as sources for compilations of retrospective selective bibliographies."[2]

Having made its point with scrupulous honesty, the Working Paper goes on to destroy it, by pointing out that the dependence of subject bibliography on current complete national bibliographies would involve delay, limited access, inadequate selective mechanisms, and excessive costs. What then remains is a statement that current complete national bibliography is important to book sellers and librarians. We need not concern ourselves with book sellers. What they really need, they will get; so current complete national bibliography is reduced in essence to a tool for librarians. This, of course, should be a matter which is clear to all of us from our own experience. We know that we need current complete national bibliographies and we are all familiar with the important function they perform in the internal economy of the library. But do we know any segment of the library's users who need current complete national bibliographies as the chemists need *Chemical Abstracts* or as the people who work in my own organization need *Nuclear Science Abstracts?* The question is rhetorical. Whereas the Working Paper recognizes that this situation exists in fact, it does project an ". . . ideal rela-

1. The UNESCO/Library of Congress Bibliographical Survey, *Bibliographical Services, Their Present State and Possibilities of Improvement* . . . (Washington, 1950), p. 19.

2. *Ibid.*, p. 21.

tionship between current comprehensive bibliography and not only selective bibliography in general, but current selective bibliography in particular. Again it needs to be pointed out that none of the reasons given above for the small amount of service which current comprehensive bibliography now renders to current selective bibliography results from essential characteristics of bibliography itself, but only from characteristics of the vehicles and methods which it employs."[3]

The ideal current complete national bibliography would include not only publications of the book trade but documents, pamphlets, maps, music, newspapers, periodical articles, and documentary sound recordings and films. It would have a complete analytical index, including even "the subject analysis of government documents and the contents of newspapers"; and this analytical index would provide an instrument for appropriate selection from the current complete national bibliography by those who are concerned with selective or subject bibliographies. Now, what is wrong with this prospect is not that it is ideal, but that it is completely out of focus. It is as though one were to go from Washington to Chicago by going due north from Washington to the pole and coming down between the 87th and 88th meridians. Functionally, the picture is inverted; instead of being offered a bibliographic organization directly serving our special purposes, we are asked to create a universal bibliographic organization in which all special purposes are sublimated. We are promised that ultimately our special purposes will be served more quickly and more cheaply than is the case now; but what assurances have we—what evidence is offered that this will be so? Does it follow from the essential characteristics of bibliography itself that it is so? I think, and I shall attempt to exhibit more concretely in what follows, that such purposes cannot be served by universal organizations; that universal bibliographic organization can be nothing more than the sum or product of special (i.e., subject) organizations. Further, I think that in this matter librarians have been misled by the universal acceptance of the elements of descriptive bibliography and have concluded erroneously that it is possible to create a universal system of subjects which will be satisfactory to all specialists.

We began this discussion by asking if there existed important scholarly, scientific, or broadly human purposes which would justify

3. *Ibid.*, p. 23.

the organization of recorded information into current complete national bibliographies or into current complete universal bibliography. We have learned that even those who most strongly urge this type of bibliographic organization upon us admit that it has only an indirect function with reference to the purposes we believe to be important. We have questioned whether or not there is any reason to suppose that special purposes are best served by the creation of general organizations. We have answered this question in the negative and we now turn for additional evidence to a discussion of two existing forms of universal bibliographic organization; namely, the classification and subject heading systems used in libraries.

In the opening section of his *Annual Report* for 1943, Archibald MacLeish, then Librarian of Congress, spoke of the Library as being ". . . the editor and to an extent the arbiter of a basic classification of knowledge which is used over a considerable portion of the earth." The classification of books by librarians, whether it is done in terms of the Library of Congress system, the Dewey system, or any of the official systems is, *prima facie*, an activity which proceeds from a concern with knowledge as a whole to particular determinations of the divisions, parts, sections, sub-sections, items, etc. making up the universal system. If now we take a functional approach to universal classification systems considered as methods of bibliographic organization, we discern a conflict between universal and special purposes. All of you are familiar with the recent discussions—sometimes amiable—sometimes heated—concerning the proposed classification of the Army Medical Library. In its simplest terms the issue, as I understand it, lay between preserving the integrity of the Library of Congress system as a classification of books in general and creating for the Army Medical Library a special classification which would be specifically designed for the needs of modern medicine without regard for any general organization which might constrict and deform the organization best suited to such needs. There is no question here of the gain or loss from having two systems of classifying the literature of medicine in the two collections. For if it is argued that the Army Medical Library should have accepted the limitations of the "R" schedule in order to preserve and enhance a basic pattern of unity with the Library of Congress, it can also be argued that the Library of Congress should have accommodated itself to the needs of the Army Medical Library and made whatever changes were necessary in its over-all classification in order to adopt as its own the special classification developed for the Army Medical Library. In other words, there might have been unity at a price neither side was willing to pay, and both sides were correct in deciding that the price of unity was too high. The specialist saw no point in sacrificing his special interests to an alien unity; the arbiters of a universal system felt that they could not betray their responsibility to knowledge as a whole for the assumed needs of a special discipline. It is not necessary for us to decide the merits of the case—we are required only to recognize that the issue was real—that both sides recognized the conflict between special and general interests and that neither side thought the best way to serve a special interest lay in subordinating it to a general organization.

Even within the structure of the Library of Congress itself, this conflict between general and special interests is a constant and recurring phenomenon. Special consultants in various fields have found that the library classification brought together unrelated materials and tore asunder materials which "naturally" belonged together. Much more serious is the feeling of some of the special divisions that the general cataloging and classification system neglects and subverts their special interests. Many of these divisions have set up special collections and special bibliographic keys not provided by the general bibliographic organization of the Library. The degree of unification to be achieved in the Library of Congress is a matter of internal administrative policies, but the reality of the problem is additional evidence that the specialist is not content with the by-product of a universal organization.

Within the past few years, several agencies of the Federal Government (Central Air Documents Office, Research and Development Board, Office of Naval Research, etc.) have felt the need for special classifications and have found the Library of Congress system unsuited to their purposes. There is no point in the Library of Congress being defensive about this, or rising to protect the integrity of its classification system. What is required is the recognition that the Library of Congress system, for all its complexity and detail, is not a tool for specialists but a general system for the non-specialist's approach to knowledge as a whole.

At the risk of paradox, we may say that the excellence of a general classification system derives from its special purpose, namely to serve the general reader with regard to the totality of knowledge which is his heritage. I need not remind this audience that the great development of library classification systems in this country occurred concurrently with the great development of the public library and the open-shelf system. The patron of the public library was the "common man," the citizen of the republic of letters to whom all knowledge was to be made available. To be sure, there have always been attempts to classify knowledge; but library classification became a major factor in bibliographic organization only when it became a specialized tool for the modern *public* library. This conclusion is reinforced when we note that Europe, which had an older tradition of scholarly and specialized libraries, did not in general adopt the classification systems developed by the great American general librarians.

There is, of course, one obvious exception to this generalization. The International Institute of Bibliography, now the International Federation for Documentation, has long been the advocate of a universal classification system. In fact, the Working Paper Appendix, following Schneider, to whom it makes reference, attributes the failure of the Institute, in large measure, to its excessive preoccupation with the Universal Decimal Classification. Schneider says: "It aims—and all other purposes are secondary to this one—to raise the revised Dewey classification scheme to the status of a universal classification scheme; as though, if that were done, the 'Grail of Bibliography' would be found."[4] And the Working Paper Appendix finds that one of the weaknesses in the "bibliographical world in the period 1908–1920 which . . . prevented steady planned progress and eventual realization of both current complete national bibliography, and universal bibliography for the major disciplines at least," can be seen in retrospect to have been the fact that "the International Institute was becoming more and more absorbed in the dissemination and perfection of the Universal Decimal Classification until cooperating with the Institute was to become, in the minds of many, synonymous with accepting the U.D.C."[5]

It is not necessary to be a supporter of the U.D.C. in order to recognize that these criticisms of the International Institute assume incorrectly that the development of a universal classification system was some sort of unfortunate appendage to what might have been the beginning of effective national and universal bibliographic or-

4. Georg Schneider, *Theory and History of Bibliography*, trans. Ralph R. Shaw (New York: Columbia University Press, 1934), p. 287.

5. The UNESCO/Library of Congress Bibliographical Survey, *Bibliographical Services, Their Present State and Possibilities of Improvement, Appendix: Notes on the Development of the Concept of Current Complete National Bibliography*, by Kathrine Oliver Murra (Washington, 1950), p. 12.

ganization. On the contrary, the International Institute was quite correct and even far-sighted in recognizing that a universal bibliography to serve scholars was unthinkable without a universal system of subject analysis and organization. If a universal classification system is a chimera, then national bibliography and universal bibliography are likewise chimeras. The Working Paper Appendix itself notes that the International Committee on Intellectual Cooperation of the League of Nations rejected the proposal of one of its sub-committees to prepare "exhaustive and alphabetical catalogs . . . because agreement could not be reached on the scheme of classification to be used. It was the consensus however that a catalog by authors' names was of little use to scholars who needed to know what had been published on a given subject."[6] Hence it would seem to follow that from the standpoint of subject specialists there is not much purpose to bibliographic organization which has no subject key—and that, if the International Institute is to be criticized by those who accept the idea of universal bibliography, it must be on the grounds that the Institute advocated the wrong or an inadequate subject key and not on the grounds that it thought that a universal subject key of some sort was required.

It will be recalled that the ideal national bibliography described in the Working Paper had a complete analytical subject index. Our next problem must be to consider whether an alphabetical arrangement of subjects offers a more real possibility of universal bibliographic organization to serve all specialists than does a systematic or classified arrangement of subjects.

We may grant at once that the unsystematic character of an alphabetical index makes it seem plausible that it might succeed in gaining universal acceptance whereas a classification system always presupposes decisions concerning the structure and organization of knowledge which are susceptible to disagreement—sometimes of a very violent character. But this plausibility is specious. In the first place, unlike a classification system, an alphabetical index is limited in usefulness to those to whom the language of the index is native or very familiar. The fact is that the Library of Congress classification system and the Dewey system have proved useful beyond the country and language of their origin, but I know of no similar extension of an alphabetical index. This means that if alphabetical indexes were to be the key to our national bibliographies, we should have no universal subject key to universal bibliography. But if the U.D.C.

6. *Ibid.*, p. 17.

has failed (and in this judgment I but follow the supporters of universal bibliography) and if a universal alphabetical index is impossible because of the barrier of diverse languages—then a general subject key to universal bibliography does not appear to be a realistic goal.

Moreover, even at the national level and without the complication of diverse languages the idea of a complete alphabetical index to current complete national bibliography is not realistic. You will recollect that we are concerned primarily with the services of general bibliographic organizations to special disciplines. Thus, unlike the apocryphal farmer who, having seen a camel, said "There ain't no such animal," I, having seen and even tried to use the Library of Congress catalog, would admit its existence. If size and expense are no deterrents, it is possible to make a complete alphabetical subject guide to the totality of materials to be included in an ideal current complete national bibliography. But I find myself unable to make any realistic estimate of the annual size of such a compilation. I can take *Chemical Abstracts* and add it to the *New York Times Index*. Then I add the totality of the Wilson Company's publications, minus duplications and foreign items but increased by more specific and detailed indexing, then the American sections of *Quarterly Cumulative Index Medicus*, the *Bibliography of Agriculture, Public Affairs Information Service*, etc. etc. At this point I can envisage an annual publication about the size of the catalogs of the British Museum, but this I will admit is just a vague idea of something huge and threatening. I think that we shall have to turn to the advocates of current complete national bibliography and of analytical indexing and ask them to tell us in more specific terms how big the thing will be.

These advocates might reply that it wouldn't matter if it were as big as a battleship providing everything in it were neatly ticketed in alphabetical order. But such an answer, if it were made, would indicate a failure to realize that, at some point, change in quantity becomes qualitative. We don't have to go to Hegel or Marx for this idea. Trust-busting is an American tradition—bigness is a qualitative evil, requiring a stultifying apparatus and a monolithic organization. There is a point at which the very size of an index will make it so difficult to use as to warrant bibliographic trust-busting—but probably we shall never know exactly where such a point is until someone tries to complete an ideal current complete national bibliography with its analytical index.

Quite apart from this question of size, the choice of the index headings to serve general and special purposes remains as the bête noir of alphabetical indexing.

In a recent paper I argued for the use of the most specific headings possible in cataloging library materials. It has since been pointed out to me by experts at the Library of Congress that the degree of specificity a library should seek to attain in subject cataloging varies as between a general and a special library—that a heading which is specific enough for the Library of Congress is too general for the Department of Agriculture or the Army Medical Library. The difference in specificity can be seen by examining some of the cards which the Library of Congress prints from copy supplied by special libraries. In many cases, the Library rejects the subject headings supplied by the special library and supplies its own headings. Now, in the case of general libraries which supply copy for the Library of Congress printed cards, the rejection by the Library of Congress of a supplied heading is complete—the card as printed has only the Library of Congress heading. But when the Library of Congress rejects a heading supplied by a special library, it prints the rejected heading along with its own heading because the Library of Congress officially recognizes that the purposes of a special library may require a degree of specificity in indexing not necessary or desirable for its own general purposes. In short, the distinction we discerned between general and special classification systems also exists between general and special collections of index headings. And we conclude that there cannot be one subject key to bibliographic organization which would serve the librarian, the general reader, and all specialists.

THE PROPOSAL

What conclusion must we as librarians and information officers draw from this analysis, assuming that it is correct thus far? Are we back now with the separate, overlapping, duplicating bibliographic services—a chaos of conflicting organizations and purposes from which current complete national bibliography and current complete universal bibliography, with the special services based upon them, were to rescue us? I think there is no doubt that this is the case. But if we are to emerge with more than a negative result, we must at least propose a pattern of bibliographic organization which offers more promise than the patterns we have rejected.

Almost from the beginning of man's literary record, four methods of organizing information have been employed exclusively—classification, alphabetical order, chronology, and location. A national bibliography makes use of alphabetical order, chronology, and place of publication in its main arrangement, and may employ alphabetical order or systematic classification in its subject key.

Of these four methods, chronology and location are usually used to indicate the scope of a bibliography, whereas alphabetization and classification have been for two thousand years the principal methods of organizing units of information. In the face of this long history, it seems almost bumptious to introduce at this late date a new method of bibliographic organization. But the fact is that the use of machine techniques in recording and searching for information carries with it the requirement that information be organized in new ways which are suitable for machine handling. The machines we speak of —I.B.M. machines, Rapid Selectors, Univacs, Eniacs, etc.—are elaborate adding machines. They are machines that can react to the presence or absence of a hole, or a dot, or a magnetic impulse hundreds of thousands of times per second. And the answers they give are based on the combinations of such reactions.

If then these machines are to be used effectively in the general field of recording, searching, and collating information, the units of information must be so designed that they can be combined with significant results. The technique of developing categories of information which can be combined much as we combine numbers, or black and white dots, I call, for want of anything better, bibliographic coordination.

Both classification and alphabetical indexing are instruments which make it possible to find a particular item of information in an organized system of information. Classification reaches a particular item through the device of subordination and division, i.e., phylum, class, order, family, genus, species, sub-species, etc. Alphabetical indexing employs a system of specific names or items which being arranged alphabetically can be used by anyone who knows the alphabet and the term or name used in the system for the information wanted.

As contrasted with these established methods, the method of bibliographical coordination proposes that particular items of information be found at the intersection of general categories or, put differently, by combining items in different categories.

Consider, for example, a two-dimensional system of coordinates, x, y. Any point in this two-dimensional field is defined as some value of x and y, i.e., if we combine a value of x with a value of y, we can specify any given point in the field defined by x and y. Suppose now that the coordinates are taken to represent categories of information rather than mathematical quantities. In personnel work, where such schemes are strongly established, the categories might be "age" and "education." It should be noted that whereas the values along the "age" axis are still numerical, the values along the "education" axis may be numerical (i.e., one year's schooling, two years' schooling, etc.), but they may also be qualitative (i.e., primary school, high school, college, etc.). Other dimensions can of course be added, i.e., sex, nationality, etc. Once a personnel office has recorded all its candidates in terms of categories which it regards as relevant, it can develop simple mechanical methods for finding a given candidate of any specified sex, age, nationality, education, etc. It should be noted that, in principle, the desired information is found by combining a particular sex with a particular age, level of education, etc.

This same system of recording and finding information can be used in bibliographic organization, but its use requires first a recognition that we cannot construct a system of coordinates for knowledge in general out of which we can get any conceivable fact or piece of recorded information. In order for the method of bibliographic coordination to work in any field, it must be possible to isolate that field and to analyze it completely into a finite system of categories or coordinates. The number of categories in any system does not matter, but the point of intersection, or the combination of an item in one category with an item in any other, must be an intelligible combination.

The Technical Information Service of the Atomic Energy Commission is now developing, on an experimental basis, systems of categories for two different special fields. One of these fields is quite simple and has only three categories; namely, facilities, processes, and program data. The first category, facilities, will contain a list of all major facilities owned and operated by or for the AEC; the second category, processes, will contain a list of the major processes of interest to the AEC from the mining of ore to the final products of its activity; the third category, program data, will contain items such as design, cost, chronology, purpose, level of operation, etc. It can be seen that from any amount of information, records, publications, etc. organized in this way, it will be a simple matter to find all the information about any item in any category or any combination (or intersection) of items in two or three categories, i.e. the cost of a facility for a certain process, or the design of another facility for another process, or the date a process was begun at a certain facility, etc. etc. The other field in which we are experimenting with bibliographic coordinates has more dimensions, but is still relatively simple and presents few difficulties. We intend to organize the literature on nuclides by means of the following categories: elements, isotopes, properties, applications, reactions, radiations, and experimental techniques. Now it may be that we shall learn as the experiment proceeds that these categories are not adequate and that others need to be established; but the mark of success will be that every important fact in the literature to be organized can be exhibited as a combination of items in one or more of the categories.

If we compose these two relatively simple fields, we can see that the use of the category program data in the fields of nuclides would lead to nonsense, e.g., the cost of construction of an element. On the other hand, some categories such as elements, applications, etc., might be used in a number of fields, i.e., metallurgy, medicine, etc.

The system of bibliographic coordination is functional because the categories of any discipline will reflect the basic interests and purposes of those concerned with that discipline. Further, the chance of wasteful overlapping or duplication is minimized. Duplication is never absolute, it is always a matter of degree. When we talk of the duplication between *Chemical Abstracts* and *Physical Abstracts*, we do not mean that one is an exact replica of the other but only that some part of one is repeated in the other. However, if a specific category had been worked out for one field, no one would be silly enough to work out the same category for another field; he would use the one already available. If two fields had all categories in common, they would be the same field and again no one would do over exactly the same thing which had already been done and was available for use.

The system of bibliographic coordination has three major advantages over the systems of classifying and indexing. In the first place, a system of bibliographic coordination is designed for machine sorting and collating. In fact, it is the very existence of machines capable of manipulating multiple concepts which makes it possible to analyze fields of information into categories, leaving to the machine the problem of combining the categories in order to achieve specific headings. Secondly, once the categories have been determined, the actual indexing of material in any particular field would be very simple. The indexer would not have the problem of designing particular specific headings which would sum up the particular contents of the item being indexed. He would merely indicate that there was, or was not, information falling in the various categories. Finally, the system of bibliographic coordination would, if properly set up, disclose to the searcher more information than had been put into the system. It has become fashionable to state that we can get nothing more out of machines than we put into them. This is like saying that since mathematics is tautological there is never any more in the conclusion than there is in the premises. It is certainly true that when we add a column of figures with an adding machine we get an answer that we did not know even though the answer was implicit in the column of figures. Similarly, in the system of bibliographic coordination, by combining various categories, we may get information which, although implicit in the system, was never explicitly recognized.

Any system of names or related facts can be considered or used as a category, e.g., the names of the elements, the names of places, the time series, the names of diseases, the parts of the body or of the bone structure, the names of plants, etc. etc. Within special sciences, categories of various kinds exist and are used—the step from the use of categories to the use of the method of bibliographic coordination consists of determining the totality of categories required to organize all the relevant information in any particular field. There is thus indicated a method of approach to the international organization of information which can be pursued not through national bodies, but through international scientific societies. Perhaps UNESCO, in addition to its concern with national bibliography, can encourage such societies to develop and standardize various categories, especially those which might have applications in fields other than the one for which they were first devised. For the use by biologists of categories developed by chemists and vice versa is not duplication but mutual aid.

If we were to build special sets of bibliographic coordinates for special disciplines in this manner the general form of bibliographic organization would be a collection of chapter headings and each chapter would be analyzed by the method of bibliographic coordination for machine sorting and collating. As we have said, this system is functional because the categories of any discipline will reflect the basic interests and purposes of those concerned with that discipline. The development of categories for special disciplines and experiments in the combination of categories opens a whole new field for bibliographic exploration and conquest.

CLASSIFICATION AS THE BASIS OF
BIBLIOGRAPHIC ORGANIZATION

JESSE H. SHERA

CLASSIFICATION . . . is the highest function of the librarian's work, calling into play every faculty and every attainment of knowledge."[1] Thus did Ernest Cushing Richardson, a half-century ago, address the students of the New York State Library School. But this was no hortatory injunction admonishing the youth of "Albany" to "mind" their *Cutters* and their *Deweys*. On the contrary, Richardson was merely voicing the esteem with which the act of book classification has long been regarded by practicing librarians in general and catalogers in particular. Today this touching faith in the efficacy of subject classification as it has been traditionally applied to *books* is beginning to weaken, for there can no longer be any doubt that library classification has failed, and failed lamentably, to accomplish what it was designed to do. If present methods of library classification are obsolete, and I submit that they are, what has been the reason for their failure? Is classification *out* as a bibliographic technique? Has classification anything to contribute to the new and improved methods of bibliographic organization, and if so, *what kind* of classification will it be? What lines of investigation must be pursued before classification can be made to meet the needs of bibliography? In short, has the profession merely been guilty of misusing a very effective instrument for the improvement of its bibliographic services? These are the major questions to which we shall here address ourselves—let us begin by examining the record.

THE HISTORICAL DEVELOPMENT OF CLASSIFICATION

The theory of the organization of knowledge, from Plato to Henry E. Bliss, has been founded upon four basic assumptions: First, that there exists a *universal* "order of nature" that, when discovered, will reveal a *permanent* conceptual framework of the entirety of human

1. Ernest Cushing Richardson, *Classification, Theoretical and Practical* (3d. ed.; New York: H. W. Wilson Co., 1930), p. 42.

knowledge; second, that the schematization of that order is a hierarchy of genus and species, class and sub-class, that progresses downward from general to specific, from terms of maximum extension to those of maximum intension; third, that the principle of *differentiation* that operates throughout the hierarchy is derived from the *likeness* or *unlikeness* of the properties or attributes of the component units of the classification; and fourth, that these properties or attributes partake of the *substantive nature* or physical properties of the units being classified: an intrinsic part of the unit itself, permanent and unchanging, an essence that resists alteration by the external environment, and denies all consideration of the fortuitous or accidental. Such are the four pillars upon which, for centuries, classification systems have been erected. The superstructure might vary in form and intricacy of detail as man's knowledge of his environment broadened, deepened, and became more mature, but the fundamental assumptions, whether specifically expressed or merely implied, have remained essentially the same. Whatever its form or its function the completed edifice always lay within the shadow of the Aristotelian predicables of *genus, species, differentia, property,* and *accident.*

The concept of classification as a *hierarchy* was probably the first to develop historically; at least that is the opinion expressed by Durkheim and Mauss in a monograph on primitive forms of classification published at the beginning of the present century.[2] Observation of the classification of primitive peoples discloses that they closely reflect the social organization of the tribe. The first "classes," then, were classes of men, and the classification of physical objects was mainly an extension of previously established social classification. The hierarchy of type and subtype in logical classification, "for which neither the sensory world nor our own minds offer us a model,"[3] parallels the hierarchical pattern of earlier forms of social organization; hence all objects, both animate and inanimate, in the environment were classified as belonging to this or that clan, phratry, or other kinship group.[4]

As early as the fifth century B.C. these basic assumptions that are

2. Émile Durkheim and M. Mauss, "De quelques formes primitives de classification," *Année sociologique,* VI (1901–2), 1–72.

3. *Ibid.,* p. 6.

4. See also Emile Benoit-Smullyan, "The Sociologism of Émile Durkheim and His School," in Harry Elmer Barnes (ed.), *An Introduction to the History of Sociology* (Chicago: University of Chicago Press, 1948), p. 516.

today the accepted foundations of logical classification, had begun to crystallize, and in the work of Plato is found their earliest mature expression. Plato was the first writer known to us who began his treatment of classification with the philosophical assumption of the unity of all knowledge, and then went on to postulate its parallelism with a universal and permanent "order of nature." To Plato philosophy represented the unity of knowledge, for philosophy was *One*, and all ideas ultimately merged into a single concept of the *Good*. The basis of the Platonic classification was perceptual, for he divided the universe into two worlds—the visible and the intelligible, the former being composed of things or their images, the latter of conceptions and ideas. Basically, then, the Platonic concept was dichotomous, but it was the Neo-Platonist, Porphyry, who, in his famous *Tree*, has given us the most picturesque example of binary classification. Further, the *Tree of Porphyry* added to the dichotomy the principle of *gradation by specialty*, the progression downward from terms of greater to less extension and successively increasing intension.

To the philosophical bases of classification the Middle Ages added little that is relevant to our present purposes except by an insistence upon a theological orientation, to reaffirm the doctrine of the essential unity of knowledge and to demonstrate how the focus of thought about the organization of knowledge can be altered in response to current changes in the philosophical climate of a period or an age. With the Scholastics came a further reconsideration of classification, this time in terms of a pedagogic order as typified by the *Trivium* and *Quadrivium* of the curriculum of Medieval universities. Here again one finds a manifestation of the influence that shifting patterns of philosophic thought exert upon the organization of knowledge. More important, it furnished the philosophic foundation for the classification devised by Konrad Gesner for the organization of his *Pandectarium sive partitionum universalium*, considered by Edwards to be the first bibliographic system, and certainly the greatest early attempt to relate the subject arrangement of books to the educational and scientific consensus of the day.

Of all the precursors of science by far the most significant figure, from the standpoint of the magnitude of his contribution to bibliographic organization, was, of course, Sir Francis Bacon. Admittedly his scheme, derived ultimately from the Trivium and the Quadrivium, and based upon the human faculties of Memory, Imagination, and Reason, rests upon a subjective foundation, and his selection of the "faculties of the rational soul" is entirely arbitrary. But he argued successfully for the unity of knowledge, "the divisions of [which] are like branches of a tree that meet in one stem,"[5] and it is not excessive to say, as does Berwick Sayers, that "almost every scheme of classification from the seventeenth century to the present has been affected in a greater or less degree by . . . Bacon."[6] From Memory Bacon derived History and its subordinate disciplines, from Imagination came Literature and the Creative Arts, and from Reason, Philosophy and the Rational Sciences. Here, at least, is at work a principle of division that can be recognized and appreciated. In effect, Bacon is saying that the senses are the portals of the intellect. The impressions received by these sense perceptions pass into, and are fixed in, the memory just as they occur. These perceptions are then processed by the intellect in one of three possible ways. It may merely enumerate or rehearse them; it may create fanciful representations of them; or it may analyze and classify them. "Therefore, from these three fountains—Memory, Imagination, and Reason— flow these three emanations—History, Poesy, and Philosophy; and there can be no others."[7]

Today a scheme that implies that the human intellect exercises its several faculties as isolated operations, and that rather arbitrarily distributes the fields of knowledge among its three major branches, does violence to our concept of the organic unity of knowledge. But at the time it was devised it represented a real advance over the earlier theories of classification, differed fundamentally and in detail from all preceding schemes, and in the prominence which it accorded History was especially radical. When Diderot and d'Alembert were, in the eighteenth century, preparing their great encyclopedia they could devise no better arrangement for its organization. Bacon's scheme influenced the early classification system of the Bodleian Library. Thomas Jefferson founded upon it the classification for his own books and from this it was absorbed into the plan of book arrangement at the Library of Congress, where it was employed, with modifications, for almost a century. In inverted form it was used by William T. Harris, from whom Melvil Dewey took it for his own

5. Quoted by Henry E. Bliss, *The Organization of Knowledge and the System of the Sciences* (New York: Henry Holt & Co., 1929), p. 316.

6. W. C. Berwyck Sayers, *A Manual of Classification* (2d ed.; London: Grafton, 1944), p. 107.

7. Quoted by Robert Flint, *Philosophy as scientia scientiarum* (Edinburgh: William Blackwood, 1914), p. 106.

Decimal system. Its broader outlines can be vaguely discerned in the system devised at the turn of the century by Martel and Hanson for the Library of Congress. So influential has been Bacon's thinking in the development of library classification that, if present library practices continue, it will have to be understood by students of librarianship for generations to come.

Hobbes followed Bacon in distinguishing historical and descriptive knowledge from the theoretical and philosophic, though he did not make this the basic division of his system. For present considerations he is important first because he carried the principle of binary division throughout, and second because he was the first really to approach the order of modern science. Kant, like Plato, distinguished between rational and empirical knowledge, and followed Hobbes in his dogged insistence upon dichotomy.

However, as we recognize today, any valid classification of knowledge should represent a synthesis of the component parts with respect to the significant central concepts, the content, the scope of each, their relationships to each other, and their interdependencies. This kind of structure was approached by Hegel, in whose schematism the whole of reality was conceived as being in the Absolute Idea, of which all phenomena, all concepts, and all sciences were component parts. But Hegel achieved this synthesis and unity from a metaphysical rather than from a natural and empirical orientation.

Our modern concept of the hierarchy of the sciences, and the principle of filiation, in which each science in the series is dependent upon those that precede it but not upon those that follow, derives from the work of Auguste Comte. He declared the fundamental order of knowledge to be one of decreasing generality and increasing complexity, and that this order was coincident with historical development and pedagogic sequence. His series began with mathematics, progressed "downward" through astronomy, physics, and chemistry, to its termination in "Social Physics," or sociology, of which he is said to be the founder. Certainly he at least raised the social sciences to a new level of importance by his recognition that there is no generic difference in the desirable methodology of the social sciences that might distinguish them from the other disciplines, even though the problems of the sociologist are made more difficult because of the great complexity of the phenomena with which he deals and the lack of means for the adequate measurement of these phenomena. Comte further held that there are three stages of intellectual advance—the theological, metaphysical, and scientific—through which must pass the proper development and education of the individual, the various realms of human knowledge, and the general process of social evolution. None of these stages can be eliminated, though intelligent direction, or lack of it, may respectively accelerate or retard it. Each is a necessary antecedent to the one that follows. Spencer largely demolished the theory that the sciences have developed historically in the order assigned to them by Comte, but though he argued for the unity of knowledge, he failed in his attempt to deny Comte's principle of filiation, a doctrine that was even more positively justified by Lester F. Ward. Thus, in the sequence of its component disciplines and in the hierarchical pattern of its organization, modern schematisms of the organization of knowledge are still dominantly Comtean.

THE DEVELOPMENT OF LIBRARY CLASSIFICATION

At the close of the nineteenth century, when librarians began to think seriously about the problem of the arrangement of their book stocks, these were the major threads that had been conspicuous in the fabric of classification theory—dichotomy, the unity of knowledge, the hierarchical order, the principle of filiation, and gradation by specialty. If one may learn anything from such a cursory examination of the history of classification it is that every scheme is conditioned by the intellectual environment of its age or time; that there is not, and can never be, a universal and permanent classification that will be all things to all men; and that each generation may build upon the work of its predecessors, but must create its own classification from the materials that it has at hand and in accordance with its own peculiar needs. History does not deny the doctrine of the essential unity of knowledge, but it does affirm that man's perception of the nature of that unity is conditioned by the maturity of thought at any given period.

The early systems of library classification may here be dismissed briefly since, in most instances, they were purely utilitarian and without philosophic foundation. In the main they were either one of two types or a combination thereof: (a) arrangement by fixed location and (b) grouping by broad subject divisions of literature. Like the scheme of Brunet and the Paris Booksellers (which consisted of five main classes: Theology, Jurisprudence, Arts and Sciences, Literature, and History) they were a convenient and often arbitrary sequence designed without reference to the interrelationships of the subject disciplines. Despite the impact of Bacon's thinking upon the philosophers of the Enlightenment, practicing librarians of the period conservatively adhered to an arrangement of books as physical objects rather than attempt to organize knowledge itself. As long as stocks of books remained of a manageable size, and they were relatively well known to those who would use them most frequently, such an arrangement was practicable enough. As early as 1627 Gabriel Naudé had rejected the order of nature as an appropriate basis for bibliographic classification—". . . since the order of Nature which is always uniform & like her self, not being to be exactly imitated, by reason of the extravagancy & diversity of Books, there onely remains that of Art, which every man will for the most part establish according to his own fancy, and as he finds best to suite his purpose."[8]

The rapid growth of libraries and the multiplication of printed materials during the nineteenth century brought to practicing librarians a new awareness of the need for better methods of book arrangement. They began to think in terms of a system that would not only serve as a location guide to the titles in their collections, but by its logical arrangement would bring together related materials in such a way as to be a positive aid to the user in his pursuit of subject knowledge, and reveal to him in an orderly fashion the resources of the library in the several disciplines represented in its collections. In such terms did the practitioners of library economy affirm their faith in law and order and proclaim their essential kinship with the new spirit of scientific inquiry.

Quite naturally, then, the history of modern library classification is a story of adaptation of existing philosophical systems to library materials and needs. Early in the nineteenth century Thomas Jefferson had turned to Francis Bacon for the philosophical basis for a book classification that was adopted by the Library of Congress. Melvil Dewey, in the Amherst chapel on that bright Sunday morning, as he listened to President Stearns and pondered the beauties of the decimal system, bethought himself of Harris' "inverted Baconian" and adopted it as the framework of his own scheme. The Expansive Classification of Charles Ami Cutter, especially in the evolutionary or developmental pattern of its subordinate classes, shows the influence of Comte and Spencer. The work of Martel and

8. Gabriel Naudé, *Instructions Concerning Erecting of a Library*, trans. John Evelyn (Cambridge: Houghton Mifflin Co., 1903), pp. 134–35.

Hansonn, in spite of their intention to give primacy to the book as a practical base rather than to any theory of knowledge, closely follows, in general outline, the Cutter Expansive. Hence it is heavily indebted to the nineteenth century philosophers, is indirectly derived from Brunet, and even the Baconian influence is not entirely absent. The Universal Decimal was, of course, derived from Dewey, but its makers strove to achieve added dimensions, depth, and flexibility by the use of certain signs of association to indicate relationships and points of view. The result was not improvement but greater complexity and a serious magnification of the weaknesses inherent in the parent scheme. Similarly, other bibliographic systems had their own philosophical antecedents (Bliss, for example, is heavily indebted to Comte), and though their authors might insist that they had been busying themselves with a classification of printed materials rather than an organization of knowledge, the fact remains that in reality they were merely adapting the former to the latter, with such tinkering with notation, provision of form categories, and other relatively minor adjustments as would make their efforts more nearly adequate to library conditions and needs.

Today, under the impact of a rapidly growing volume of graphic records, and the appearance of new forms of publication, traditional library classifications are becoming hopelessly inadequate. No amount of basic revision or tampering with their organic structure can save them from this failure. As guides to the subject content of the library they are essentially meaningless. Even librarians, who are best qualified to interpret them and to exploit their virtues, use the notation only as a guide to location, and largely ignore the interdisciplinary relationships that they were designed to reveal. Yet, as their efficiency has declined, the cost of their maintenance has increased until at least one major research library has abandoned subject classification of its book stocks and has turned to other and more promising forms of bibliographic organization.

But it must be emphasized, and it can scarcely be said too strongly, that the failure of contemporary library classification to achieve its purposes is not because the classification of knowledge has no place in bibliographic organization, nor is it because the men who made these schemes were fools. Dewey, Cutter, Martel, and the others were groping for the application of a principle that we now know to be an established fact—*that classification is basic to bibliographic organization*, and that in large measure the success of our attempts to organize the graphic records of our civilization will depend upon our ability to devise systems for the ordering of those records in such a way as to maximize their social utility. This can be done only when we have adequately studied the different ways in which all such records are used by recognized groups within the society, and when we have analyzed the internal conceptual arrangement of such records in order to adapt any possible classification scheme to the *existing structure of thought* rather than to some abstract universal "order of nature" encompassing all knowledge.

CLASSIFICATION AS AN INSTRUMENT OF BIBLIOGRAPHIC ORGANIZATION

The failure of our present systems of book classification in no way condemns the act of classification as a fundamental bibliographic technique. Book classification, as we have used it in the past has failed for two reasons: one, because it has been based upon the book as a physical entity without taking into consideration the inherent character of the book as a composite intellectual product; two, because of limitations arising from the properties of our hierarchical systems of classification. Jevons was right, for library classification as he knew it, was indeed "a logical absurdity."[9] By this he meant, of course, that the content of books is poly-dimensional, which is logically incompatible with the traditional hierarchical schematization of knowledge which is a linear progression from general to specific. The book, then, as a physical unit, and irrespective of the dimensions of its content, must be forced into a mono-dimensional system in which it has only linear position. This limitation alone destroys most of the utility of traditional book classifications as instruments for the effective subject organization of library materials. Almost two decades have passed since the investigations of Grace Osgood Kelley demonstrated with a reasonable degree of certainty that the library classification reveals only a relatively small proportion of the total resources of the collection in any given subject.[10]

9. "Classification by subjects would be an exceedingly useful method if it were practicable, but experience shows it to be a logical absurdity. It is a very difficult matter to classify the sciences, so complicated are the relations between them. But with books the complication is vastly greater, since the same book may treat of different sciences, or it may discuss a problem involving many branches of knowledge" (W. Stanley Jevons, *The Principles of Science* [London: Macmillan, 1887], p. 715).

10. Grace O. Kelley, *The Classification of Books: An Inquiry into Its Usefulness to the Reader* (New York: H. W. Wilson Co., 1937). Pp. 200.

Her results did not so much as hold out the hope that the classification made available even the most important portions of the library's holdings. Yet, we still pursue the same practices in bibliographic classification, not for any doubt as to the validity of her findings, but largely because we have not known exactly how to remedy this situation.

Classification, then, can achieve its fullest purpose as an instrument of bibliographic organization only after the *idea* content of the book has been dissociated from its physical embodiment—its codex form. Once this has been achieved, and the thought unit, rather than the fortuitous manner of its publication, is the subject of classification, the old limitations of library classification will be abolished, the organization of knowledge itself will become the paramount consideration, as it always should have been, and the results of bibliographic systematization will become more accurate and usable.

As this conference progresses it will grow increasingly apparent that, if bibliographic organization is to attain its highest degree of efficiency, traditional library methods and techniques may largely be discarded in favor of an entirely new array of tools—indices, subject bibliographies, annotations, abstracts, micro-photographic processes, mechanical sorters, electronic devices, and combinations of the foregoing. For all of these the physical form of the graphic record, in its original state, is inconsequential. Book stocks, and other library materials, can hereafter be arranged in any way that is convenient and efficient, without jeopardizing the availability of their intellectual content.

But if these new tools promise emancipation from many of the ills that beset traditional library classification, they do not foretell the demise of classification itself as an important bibliographic mechanism. No device can be better than the classification system through which it operates. An index, by virtue of the nature of its terminology, is in effect itself a concealed classification. Systematic arrangement is essential to the utility of the index, the bibliography, and the abstracting service. Microphotographic processes relate mainly to the improvement of physical accessibility. In and of themselves they do not contribute to the solution of content accessibility, but only intensify the problem by expanding the bibliographic resources available to the individual scholar. Mechanical sorters and electronic "brains" stand or fall on the relative effectiveness of the coded classes through which they must operate. Of all the new instruments now at our command, classification is for them the most fundamental. We say that they are machines that "think," but in reality they only respond in a limited way to the impulses or stimuli that activate them. They cannot think for themselves; the responsibility for the cerebral operations is still human.

From these new implements for the bibliographic organization of graphic materials will arise a completely new concept of classification that is entirely alien to those of us who have been accustomed to thinking in traditional library terms. We stand at the threshold of a reorientation of the idea of classification. Even a cursory examination of the history of the classification of the sciences emphasized the extent to which any attempt to organize knowledge is conditioned by the social epistemology of the age in which it was produced. This dependence of classification theory upon the state of the sociology of knowledge will doubtless be even more strongly confirmed in the future. Here, then, is an implicit denial of Bliss' faith in the existence of a "fundamental order of nature," a rejection of the belief that there is a single, universal, logically divided classification of knowledge. Ability to develop a universal scheme for the ordering of all human experience implies the ability to prognosticate all possible future knowledge, to foretell what man may learn before he has learned it, to diagram all possible relations of all possible knowledge, and so to stabilize the intellectual processes of society to the point of stagnation. For it is by the grouping and regrouping of his data that the scholar discovers new relationships, new approaches to old problems, and new areas for exploration.

Further, if classification is relative to the task to be performed and to the inherent nature of the tools by means of which it is to be achieved, one need no longer adhere to a blind devotion to the Aristotelian predicables and the necessity for a hierarchical structure of knowledge. To assert that classification is founded in philosophical consideration is not to deny that it is also highly utilitarian. If we would make of it something more than a speculative indoor-sport, played according to established and inviolable rules, we must not hesitate to alter the principles upon which it has for so many centuries been established. To free classification from the straightjacket of the hierarchical order is to endow it with new meaning, deeper significance, and far greater potential utility.

A NEW ORIENTATION FOR CLASSIFICATION

Alfred North Whitehead, arguing for a referential classification, as derived from projective geometry, has condemned Aristotelian logic in terms that are suggestive of a completely new orientation of the organization of thought.

"It is well-known that Geometry can be developed without any reference to measurement—and thus without any reference to distance, and without any reference to numerical coordinates for the indication of points. Geometry, developed in this fashion, has been termed 'Non-metrical Projective Geometry.' Elsewhere I have termed it, 'the science of cross-classification.' Aristotle's science of classification into genera, and species, and sub-species, is the science of mutually exclusive classification. It develops Plato's suggestion of a science of 'Division' . . . Aristotelian Logic, apart from the guardianship of mathematics, is the fertile matrix of fallacies. It deals with propositional forms only adapted for the expression of high abstractions, the sort of abstractions usual in current conversation where the presupposed background is ignored."[11]

Whitehead goes on to assert that there are two Orders, the Observational and the Conceptual (Plato again!), and that the former is invariably interpreted in terms of the concepts supplied by the latter. Since Observational discrimination is not dictated by the impartial facts, no scientific schematism is valid that is based upon the independent individuality of each bit of matter. Classification, then, need not be a process of atomization; its component units may be a single fact, idea, or concept, or any constellation thereof which is consistently used as a unit. Classification can be synthesis as well as analysis, and its cohesive force any meaningful relationship that serves the immediate purpose irrespective of whether that relationship be expressed in terms of generic properties, function, or any other unifying principle that expediency might dictate.

This pragmatic approach to classification through meaningful units of knowledge must be based on a recognition of the obvious truth that any single unit may be meaningful in any number of different relationships depending upon the immediate purpose. *Thus it is the external relations, the environment, of the concept that are all-*

11. Alfred North Whitehead, *Adventures of Ideas* (New York: Macmillan Co., 1933), pp. 176, 196.

important to the act of classifying. A tree is an organism to the botanist, an esthetic entity to the landscape architect, a manifestation of Divine benevolence to the theologian, a source of potential income to the lumberman. Pragmatic classification, then, denies the existence of the "essence" of tree, for each of these relationships owes its existence to different properties of the tree. Relationship is not a universal, but a specific fact unique to the things related, and just as these relations reveal the nature of the relata, so the relata determine the character of the relationship.

This new approach to classification must begin, then, with the isolation and identification of these units which will comprise the new schematism for any field, after which they must be precisely defined. For to maintain the relativity of the classification process is not to suggest that its nomenclature can afford to be muddled and confused or its component categories indiscrete. Therefore semantics lies at the base of all classification, and the standardization of terminology is a prerequisite to its success. The need for such standardization is emphasized by the results of two tabulations recently made at the Graduate Library School. In the first the subject headings used in the card catalogs of nine industrial relations libraries were analyzed to determine the uniformity of subject entry among the several cooperating institutions involved. Of a total of 938 headings, of which 218 (or 23 per cent) showed significant alternative forms, 57 per cent were unique to one library; 17 per cent were used by only two libraries; 9 per cent by but three institutions; 7 per cent by four; only 10 per cent were common to five or more libraries.[12] A similar dispersion was evident from an analysis of the concepts appearing in the indices of three general textbooks in bacteriology, in which, from a total of 2,256 concepts, 66 per cent were unique to one text, 23 per cent were found in only two, and only 11 per cent were common to all

12. The libraries of the industrial relations centers were situated in the following universities: Chicago, Cornell, Michigan, Princeton, Queens, Stanford, Illinois, Washington, and California at Los Angeles.

No. of Libraries	No. of Headings	Per Cent
1	532	57
2	158	17
3	82	9
4	66	7
5 or more	100	10
Total	938	100

three.[13] In other words, there was substantial agreement about only one-tenth of the terms used in each case. Yet in the terminology of two areas as compact and closely integrated as these one might expect to find a relatively high percentage of agreement. But one must emphasize that this same standardization of terminology is not a responsibility of the librarian-classifier alone; it is also an obligation of the subject expert in the discipline itself. The maturity of an area of knowledge is reflected in the degree of standardization of its nomenclature. In physics, chemistry, and the other precise sciences such agreement is relatively high; this is, in fact, the very source of their precision. In sociology and economics such consensus is lamentably lacking with disastrous consequences for communication within the disciplines. Speech is in itself a form of classification and the problems of communication and classification are essentially one. Nomenclature, then, is a responsibility that the subject specialist cannot afford to delegate to other hands, or abrogate as being unworthy of his labor. Indeed it is one of the most profitable tasks for groups of subject specialists to undertake. The resulting classification of concepts and the freedom to manipulate such concepts in newly-devised schematisms would contribute most notably to both the advance and the synthesis of knowledge.

If utility is the primary objective of classification, it logically follows that the most useful classification will be one so specific to a given situation that the groupings will be meaningful in the relevant context or relationship. To emphasize and clarify this essential proposition it may be well to return to the example of the tree. To the landscape architect the red-twigged, or red-osier dogwood (*Cornus stolonifera*) is a very useful and important plant. In a classification appropriate to his needs, then, it would appear in terms of its relation to the cluster of properties evinced by the other plant materials at his disposal, its habit of growth, the character of its fruit and

13. The three texts used were: Arthur T. Henrici, *The Biology of Bacteria* (Boston: D. C. Heath & Co., 1948); Fred W. Tanner, *Bacteriology* (New York: John Wiley & Sons, 1937); Martin Frobisher, *Fundamentals of Bacteriology* (Philadelphia: W. B. Saunders Co., 1949).

No. of Texts	No. of Concepts	Per Cent
1 text only.........	1,488	66
2 texts.............	520	23
All 3 texts.........	248	11
Total..........	2,256	100

leaves, its appearance during the several seasons of the year, the type of soil it requires, the geographic localities to which it is native, etc., etc. By contrast, however, the forester will have no traffic with this beautiful plant, but considers it quite disrespectfully as being only a weed-tree. In his classification, then, it appears only with reference to its undesirable properties, to those characteristics which deny it economic value to the lumberman, and to the means for its effective eradication. Obviously these two points of view are so divergent as to deny the possibility of effective reconciliation in any sort of universal schematism that would serve the needs of both the landscape architect and the forester.

As early as 1890 William James attained this same point of view by applying to the problems of classification and nomenclature his own philosophy of pragmatism. He held that concepts are created by human beings in the pursuit of some particular enterprise or end. They are segments of human experience, which itself is never static, endowed with names and fashioned to suit human purposes. But these concepts become fixed and immutable in the thought processes of the human intellect, because only by reference to their stability are we able to deal with experience intelligibly. When we conceive of paper as an appropriate writing surface we fix that one fact about paper. But such a concept is of our own making, an instrumentality fashioned to a particular need; it does not mean that paper is *essentially* something to write upon. James insists that there is no property absolutely essential to any one thing. During the act of writing the writer conceives of paper as a surface upon which he can write. But if the paper is being used to ignite a fire, it is held to be a combustible substance. Thus, the same paper may be regarded in an indefinite number of ways. To quote James directly:

"[The paper] is really *all* that it is: a combustible, a writing surface, a thin thing, a hydrocarbonaceous thing, a thing eight inches one way and ten another, a thing just one furlong east of a certain stone in my neighbor's field, an American thing, etc., etc., *ad infinitum*. Whichever one of these aspects of its being I temporarily class it under, makes me unjust to the other aspects. But as I always am classing it under one aspect or another, I am always unjust, always partial, always exclusive. My excuse is necessity—the necessity which my finite and practical nature lays upon me. My thinking is first and last and always for the sake of my doing, and I can only do one thing at a time. . . . All ways of conceiving a concrete fact, if they are true ways at all, are equally true ways. *There is no property AB-SOLUTELY essential to any one thing.* The same property which figures as the essence of a thing on one occasion becomes a very inessential feature upon another."[14]

James admits that this denial of the existence of an 'absolute essence is repugnant to logic, which maintains that there must be for every thing a core that constitutes its essence and of which its other characteristics are merely properties. The essence of the thing, then, would be that which gives it its name. The thing *is* paper, and its rectangularity and combustibility, etc., are but accidents or properties. But this attitude itself derives from our practical need to name things in order to expedite communication. So habitual has become this practice of naming that the name comes to stand in our minds for what the thing really is. We traditionally think of water as *really* being a union of hydrogen and oxygen atoms in the ratio of two to one, but water is no more H_2O than it is something to drink, or something to bathe in, or something to keep flowers fresh. To conceive of it in terms of its chemical formula is useful in certain circumstances, but in other frames of reference it is more useful to regard it from a totally different standpoint. No one conception invariably represents its reality independent of a particular purpose. *"This whole function of conceiving, of fixing, and holding fast to meanings has no significance apart from the fact that the conceiver is a creature with partial purposes or private ends."*[15]

If we accept this application of James' pragmatism to classification, and agree that every separate frame of reference accentuates only a part of the totality of attributes of the object with which it deals because only that part is relevant to the specific purpose, it therefore follows that every special classification system devised for the use of a special group should be erected upon a framework of such *properties*, rather than upon the *actual* or *essential* objects that substantively fall within its orbit of interest. These properties are permanently a part of the frame of reference to a much greater extent than the alleged *essence* or substantive matter of the objects

---

14. William James, *The Principles of Psychology* (New York: Henry Holt & Co., 1890), II, 333 (italics his). The sequence of the quotations has been reversed.

15. *Ibid.*, I, 482 (italics his). See also Edna Heidbreder, *Seven Psychologies* (New York: Appleton-Century Co., 1935), pp. 182–83.

themselves. Such properties rather than the essential objects them-selves should, therefore, become the axes of their respective special classification schemes. Furthermore, those properties relevant to more than one field would serve as axes common to a cluster of re-lated schematisms, and from these would emerge the bases for cross-referential classifications that would contribute to inter-disciplinary integration.

HABITS OF USE AS THE BASIS OF CLASSIFICATION

All this not only denies the validity of universal classification and the necessity for a hierarchical gradation, but it also reemphasizes the basic preeminence of function, the importance of the external fac-tor of habits of use in like situations and as applied to identical ma-terials in unlike situations, and the great need for the pragmatic study of the units used in any given subject field at any given time. Hence flexibility in classification will be achieved by providing *mul-tiple approaches* to the relata rather than, as is the practice in con-temporary classification, the provision of multiple or alternative *locations* for the individual units. The growing need for special schemes of classification is emphasized by the proliferation of such classifications among special librarians who have been forced by cir-cumstances to devise their own schemes, largely independently and without any guiding principles for the formulation and ordering of their endeavors. All this might seem to suggest the necessity for constant and continuing reclassification—anathema to all library classifiers and administrators. But since it now seems established with relative certainty that the vitality of most of our research literature is almost wholly ephemeral, and as the new tools for bib-liographic organization are inherently flexible, new systems of classi-fication can be introduced without recourse to reclassification of the older, and hence less used, materials.

If one grants that this new concept of classification is grounded in pragmatism, it becomes axiomatic that the study of *habits of use* is requisite to the act of classifying. At the present time our knowledge of the uses to which literature is put, and the demands made upon bibliographic resources by those who consult them, are lamentably fragmentary. One cannot talk intelligently about the problems of classification or devise effective schemes for the several branches of knowledge until he can answer with some degree of certainty the question: how does any consultant search for and use the literature that theoretically is at his command? To this the users themselves can give no valid answer. Conjecture and generalization based upon subjective opinions are not enough. Yet the responsibility for the development of a body of specific factual knowledge of these habits of use belongs to the librarian. Already some progress has been made through the studies of citation analysis in the fields of the physical sciences and the humanities, but much more remains to be done. At the moment the case study approach would seem to be the most promising, but it is the obligation of graduate study in librarianship to devise more adequate techniques and effective procedures than have been heretofore available for scholarly investigation in this all-important area. But whatever techniques of research may be brought to bear upon these problems, it becomes mandatory that we know what classification is supposed to achieve and how, why, and by whom it is going to be used.

TECHNOLOGICAL DEVELOPMENTS AND CLASSIFICATION

But even were it possible at this moment, with a snap of the fingers, to solve all these problems of theoretical classification, and to devise as many varying schemes of classification as needs and purposes demanded, there would still remain the enormous task of their application to a body of recorded materials that is increasing at a truly alarming rate. No one knows with any degree of certainty the number of bibliographic units that are extant today. Estimates of book production from the invention of printing in Europe vary from fifteen to twenty million titles. Similarly the volume of periodical articles for the same period would surely be counted in the hundreds of millions, and the volume of ephemera would be truly astronomical. Even though much of this increasing mass is unworthy of subject analysis, to organize even a usable portion of it is a task that far exceeds the capacities of our traditional methods. Gesner's dream of a universal world bibliography grows more faint with each passing decade. In the United States Patent Office alone some three million patents must be arranged so that their patentable properties may be approached by structure, function or effect, and the "art" involved. The present provision of some 43,000 categories is already proving inadequate to patent-searching needs. Classification problems of a similar magnitude are beginning to confront American industry, and other agencies engaging extensively in research.

To meet this problem we have begun to consider seriously the possibilities for the development of new tools which will perform more rapidly, more effectively, and at lesser cost the bibliographic operations traditionally the function of the card catalog, the index, and the "published" bibliography. These mechanical electrical and electronic machines, with the exception of the Shaw Rapid Selector, were mainly designed for purposes other than bibliography, and hence require modification and adaptation to meet peculiar bibliographic needs. But all of them, including the Rapid Selector, necessitate the use of a code, either mathematically or phonetically expressed, for their operation and hence their success or failure largely rests upon the virtues of the classification system through which they operate.

What, then, are the improvements in our classification methods that these machines make possible? The advantages to be derived from the separation of the intellectual content of the book from the book as a physical entity have already been suggested. This does not imply, of course, that the book cannot be considered as a whole—indeed, for some purposes, the book is still most effectively used as a whole—but separation into its component concepts will be practicable when appropriate to specific requirements. The inherent flexibility of these machines, in conjunction with this reversion to the organization of knowledge as distinct from the organization of physical units, i.e., books, periodicals, whether bound or unbound, pamphlets, and the like, will make frequent reclassification and the use of multiple classifications economically practicable. The unitary approach provided by such devices automatically permits of change, expansion, new orientation, and unique approaches to classification. The classifier of the future, then, need not desert philosophy for purely utilitarian ends, but he may easily do so whenever such departures seem desirable. He will no longer be tied to the shibboleths of universals and permanents. Finally, these machines will facilitate and make economically feasible large concentrations of bibliographic activity in strategic centers in which truly expert bibliographic services can be performed for those agencies which are quite remote from areas of library concentration.

PROBLEMS OF PERSONNEL AND MANAGEMENT

But there are certain practical considerations that must not be neglected in the full flush of our enthusiasm for these new bibliographic potentialities. The expense will be great, for the cost of these machines will be high and the skills requisite to their development and use cannot, and should not, be bought cheaply. Subject knowledge is essential, for we are not here concerned with generalities and superficialities, but exact specialties based on a thorough understanding of problems, needs, and points of view in the component fields. Not only is such work completely valueless if it is done without care and understanding, but it might seriously jeopardize the entire future of bibliographic organization. This will mean coordination of economic as well as bibliographic resources, a social responsibility that cannot be neglected by state and federal government and the many public and private agencies that would profit thereby. In terms of social costs and values the effective bibliographic organization of knowledge is a bargain. But we must first "educate" the public to the social importance of bibliography and the effective organization of knowledge. This will be no simple task but it is fundamental to our success.

Let no one be deceived into thinking that our present antiquated and disorganized bibliographic methods are either economical or efficient. The *American Library Directory* for 1948 lists over 11,000 libraries in the United States, of which some 7,000 are public libraries; 1,500 those of colleges and universities, including about fifty large research libraries; and the remaining 2,500 largely special libraries of varying kinds. Every day, in these libraries, many of the same books are bibliographically described, cataloged, classified, and otherwise prepared for the use of patrons in an unending procession of duplication and waste, the cost of which no one has yet been able even to estimate. Yet the price that society pays for these "hidden" expenditures cannot be rationalized by the mistaken belief that much of our cataloging must necessarily be unique to the institution by which it is performed. Centralization and coordination might appear to demand a high initial outlay and an impressive continuing expenditure, but it would represent a marked advance both in economy and efficiency over the traditional procedures to which we have for so long been accustomed.

This is not an argument, as one might at first suppose, for a simple extension of the services now offered to libraries by the card distribution systems of the Library of Congress and the H. W. Wilson Company. Such action would only perpetuate the existing weaknesses of our obsolescent methods of bibliographic analysis. What is necessary is a coordinated attack upon contemporary bibliographic problems by groups of skilled subject bibliographers who have been adequately trained in the new theories of classification, and prepared to translate these theories into effective operations. The results might then be transmitted to the cooperating libraries as continuing services and special bibliographic investigations.

CONCLUSIONS

In conclusion, what are the possible implications of these new approaches to classification for the future of the technical processes? To put it bluntly, are catalogers confronted by technological obsolescence? The answer is emphatically in the negative, for *catalogers* are not obsolete even though their present *methods* are becoming so. Classification is central and basic to the whole problem of bibliographic organization, and far more fundamental than it has ever been to present library practice. The mechanization of bibliographic organization does not imply the degradation of catalogers and bibliographers through subordination to the machine. The objectives of this mechanization are the expedition of our mental processes, not a substitution for them. Machines can process great quantities of material at high speeds, but the results they produce can never rise above the skill that has entered into their design and manipulation. As instruments of classification they are bound by the binary principle, they have not advanced beyond the dichotomy, they cannot devise new relationships or exercise judgment in selection. In short, we must do their thinking for them, and this will demand a higher level of skills, including subject knowledge and research ability, than catalogers have been called upon to exercise in the past. Freed from the drudgery of descriptive cataloging and the largely arbitrary pigeonholing of books into an artificial classification scheme, catalogers can anticipate the opportunity to become true subject specialists in bibliography and the organization of knowledge.

To the library schools this means that classification, more than ever before, will be vital to the curriculum, that there will be a continuing demand for students trained in the bibliography of subject specialization, and that there must be both planning for and continuing research in (a) the techniques for identification of concepts of knowledge and the ordering of those concepts, (b) the changing contexts of meaningfulness, and (c) the varying and shifting patterns of use.

Specifically this means, among other things—

1. A series of studies of existing classifications, their weaknesses and virtues for specific purposes.

2. The development of new classification schemes, with a reexamination of the principles upon which they might be based.

3. Experimentation in the construction of varying conceptual frameworks upon different axes of reference.

4. The content analysis of the research literature of varying fields for the identification of terminology and concepts currently in use.

5. The careful scrutiny of subject headings in the light of such analyses.

6. The development of adequate techniques for measuring the effectiveness of all forms of classification and subject entry.

7. Study of the dispersion and concentration of materials in varying schemes of classification, and the interpretation of the results of such findings in terms of utility to the library user.

8. The precise measurement of costs of varying kinds of classification as related to the production of bibliographic values and the improvement of bibliographic functions.

Admittedly, librarians may not find immediate satisfaction in the freedom from traditional routines that these new forms of bibliographic organization promise, and they may feel very alone and helpless in an almost unexplored land, where the terrain can be but dimly seen, the landscape is strewn with strange and weird excrescences of the machine age, the atmosphere is apparently inhospitable, and where the few inhabitants communicate in a queer, unintelligible tongue. But I am convinced that the soil is fertile, the waters refreshing, the natives friendly, and that here is a country that promises to yield a rich return to those adventurous souls who love the spirit of exploration, find pleasure in the exercise of a little imagination, and are not averse to a great deal of hard work.

COLON CLASSIFICATION AND ITS APPROACH
TO DOCUMENTATION

S. R. RANGANATHAN

A TRADITION has been established in this Conference. A person who comes from outside the United States and speaks from the platform first expresses his thanks for a foreigner having been permitted to take part in the Conference. In conformity with that tradition I should begin by conveying to you the thanks of the Indian Library Association. But I propose to break that tradition. For I hold that library service, bibliographic organization, and library classification recognize no national or political boundaries. They are international. The library profession is international. Bibliographers and documentalists are international. As a librarian and a classificationist, I belong to the world and not merely to any particular country.

INTRODUCTION

Let me thank you however for the great mental stimulus I am receiving at this Conference. This is the most technical, earnest and busy Conference I have ever attended. Librarianship has gone through several stages. It is now entering a stage in which documentation service is dominant. The distinguishing feature of this stage is that micro-units of thought, embodied perhaps in an article or even in a paragraph, have to be isolated and brought to the notice of the right reader without any loss of time. We have had an exhaustive analysis of the possible forms which bibliographies can take. Another paper traced the history of the attempts at exhaustive documentation in the past. We had a penetrating paper which laid bare the difficulties in the classification required to make documentation effective. We were taken to the brink of water and left to drink by ourselves. We were taken to the very threshold of solution but not into it. We also had a very learned and scholastic paper on the history of classification. We have also had interesting discussion on the distinctive problems which are met in particular sectors of knowledge.

1. ENUNCIATION OF THE SUBJECT

The subject assigned to me is in a sense a much narrower one—a humble one. I am going to deal only with the making of the machine tools, so to speak, needed to make documentation service effective. Whatever our objective is, whatever be the mechanism set up, it all depends on the machine tools that are available for work. We had read in the history of the Second World War that what gave a start to Hitler was his accumulation of machine tools years in advance. The delay in the advance of the Allies was also said to have been due to our not having paid sufficient attention to this problem of machine tools. I remember how in the middle of the war many young boys, commonly known as Bevin Boys, were trained and drafted into the machine-tool industry. It is only then that the tide turned in our favor. So it is in every walk of life. So it is in documentation service also. What are the machine tools needed for documentation service? How are they to be forged? How are they to be used? How are they to be altered to suit changing conditions? These are the questions that I propose to discuss. It is in the design of the machine-tools needed to face the eruption in the field of knowledge that the Colon Classification shows the way. I shall attempt to indicate the way it shows.

1.1. FIRST PURPOSE OF CLASSIFICATION

Let me begin from the very beginning. Let me state some of the assumptions which have been elaborated so often elsewhere. The business of the librarian and the function of library tools are to help every unit of thought-energy to reach its destiny. What is its destiny? It is to enter into the minds of thinkers, stimulate them, and create more of thought-energy. The thought-energy produced at any one place or at any one time must be made to reach thinkers who can resonate with it, no matter where they live, no matter how distant they are from the source, and even those thinkers who are yet to be born. But thought-energy is intangible and even more intangible than electrical energy. How is it to be carried across space and time? Humanity has devised a method. It transforms thought-energy into a material—a portable material—which we call books, periodicals, articles, and so on. Reading materials are really thought-cells even as we have electricity in the form of dry-cells. We have to transform the thought-cells at the other end into a form that can be consumed with ease. One of the steps in this process is to arrange the thought-cells in a series which is most efficient and helpful. We want machine-tools to arrange them in this way.

1.2. CLASSIFICATION AS TRANSFORMATION

Let me try to bring out the difficulties of this problem by a change in analogy. Thought is multi-dimensional. But we are one-dimensional beings—that is, we still prefer all things to be handled to be arranged in one-dimension. We want to have them arranged in a line, say from left to right. Even while thinking, we think serially; we speak of "one at a time." This means that classification is essentially a transformation of a many-dimensional universe into a uni-dimensional, uni-directional one. The machine tools are expected to perform this transformation.

1.3. FIELD OF KNOWLEDGE, AN INFINITE UNIVERSE

We shall get another view of the problem by yet another change in analogy. Classification has to face the field of knowledge. Its machine tools should be designed to suit this function. Classification should throw into a helpful order all kinds of specific subjects which are thrown forth by the field of knowledge from time to time. The field of knowledge is an infinite universe. So we do not know all its specific subjects. It is an infinite universe of unknown and unknowable entities. There is therefore an element of uncertainty. Any specific subject may crop up in any corner of the field of knowledge and at any depth. The machine tools of classification should be such that it can keep step with them unerringly and instantaneously. A study of the tactics of the field of knowledge is necessary to enable us to forge the machine tools needed to set up counter-tactics to checkmate them.

1.4. FOUR MAJOR FACTORS

The following table is a brief résumé of the tactics, the corresponding counter-tactics, and the machine tools by which we implement them. Incidentally they also introduce the terminology developed in the study and application of the Colon Classification. The table enumerates four major methods by which the field of knowledge may throw forth new specific subjects.

2. BREAKING RIGIDITY IN NOTATION

It is the notation which forms the machine tool. It is by the design of variegated machine tools, or notation, that classification is enabled to stand up to the tactics of the field of knowledge. Rigidity in nota-

tion is fatal to classification. It is only by breaking rigidity in notation that classification can survive and escape being snowed under
by the downpour of specific subjects in the field of knowledge. The
whole history of classification is a history of breaking rigidity. From
the Vedic period, through Aristotle and Bacon, down to the middle
of the 19th century the number of specific subjects was too small to
make itself felt by classification. However, in practical daily life,
even that number was inconvenient and so recourse was had to nota-

TACTICS OF FIELD OF KNOWLEDGE			COUNTER-TACTICS OF CLASSIFICATION		
Diagram	Name	Result	Focus	Notation	Result
1	Denudation	Subordi- nated classes or chain of classes	Sharper focus	Decimal- fraction notation	Infinite hos- pitality in chain
2	Dissection	Co-ordinate classes or array of classes	Additional focus	Octave no- tation	Infinite hos- pitality in array
3	Lamination	Composite- class	Compound focus	Faceted notation	Infinite hos- pitality in facets
4	Loose-as- semblage	Combina- tion-class	Complex focus	Phased no- tation	Infinite hos- pitality in phases

tion. Things, ideas, persons, specific subjects—entities, in short—
were all represented by numbers. Their relative order was indicated
and their arrangement was mechanized by the ordinal numbers into
which their names were translated. Since integers lent themselves
to use both as cardinal and ordinal numbers, it was integral ordinal
numbers that were first resorted to. This was all right so long as
as all the entities were known at the very beginning.

2.1. RIGIDITY OF CONSECUTIVE INTEGERS—GAP NOTATION

But when applied to specific subjects in the field of knowledge, the
use of integral ordinal numbers for the notation introduced an element of rigidity. For, it was not possible to enumerate exhaustively,
at the time when the classification was designed, every possible specific subject—past, present, and future. If the specific subjects actually known at the time were thrown into a more or less helpful order

and then represented by the consecutive integers 1, 2, 3, etc., and if a new specific subject took shape demanding, as its helpful place, a place between two of the known specific subjects, the notation was too rigid to accommodate the new subject in accordance with this claim. This rigidity was first broken by the simple device of numbering the known specific subjects, not by consecutive integers, but by non-consecutive ones leaving a reasonable number of unused integers between them—by gap-notation, so to speak.

2.2. RIGIDITY OF GAP NOTATION—DECIMAL FRACTION NOTATION

But the field of knowledge soon outwits even the cleverest guess about the gap that should be left between any two integers brought into use at the time of designing the classification. It often happens that certain gaps do not get filled up at all, while certain others soon get glutted and it is in these glutted regions that newer and newer specific subjects come up. Indeed, the rigidity of gap-notation can be easily seen by a theoretical approach. The field of knowledge is infinite. It is ever active. It is indeed a dynamic continuum. It is a finite universe in which all the entities are not known at any moment, nor are they knowable. It follows from this that an infinity of specific subjects can crop up in the future between any two consecutive ones known at present. This is a result of a well-known mathematical postulate concerning infinite aggregates and continua —a postulate stated by mathematicians during the last century but enunciated from trans-intellectual considerations by the Vedic Seers of yore. The postulate is, if infinity is taken away from infinity the remainder is still infinity! The greatest forward step in classification was taken less than a century ago by one whom I always call the "Father of Modern Librarianship"—Melvil Dewey. He broke the second rigidity in notation. He broke it by abandoning the use of integers altogether and introducing pure decimal-fraction-notation. It is a great pity that this master-stroke was light-heartedly ignored and the rigid, primitive, gap-notation of integers was adopted by the most influential scheme of classification in existence—the Library of Congress Classification—which has all the influence, resources, and backing of a mighty Government. The world is all the poorer for this. But it is never too late to mend. I need not dilate before this learned audience how a decimal-fraction-notation provides for infinite hospitality.

2.3. RIGIDITY OF ONE-FOLD HOSPITALITY—OCTAVE NOTATION

But the way in which new specific subjects are created by the field of knowledge is neither simple nor single. A specific subject which is subordinate to an existing one may be formed. With equal fecundity a specific subject co-ordinate with an existing one may also be formed. In other words, notation has to provide for hospitality in chain as well as hospitality in array. The decimal-fraction-notation assures us of infinite hospitality in chain. It cannot, however, handle hospitality in array. The Decimal Classification felt over-powered by the demand of the array for infinite hospitality. It had only 9 digits—1, 2, 3 . . . 8, 9—at its disposal. It made the best of the situation to respect the Canon of Exhaustiveness. It denoted the first eight subjects by the first eight integers and used the digit 9 to represent all the other classes of the array, jointly but not severally, without distinguishing them—the so-called "minor authors," "others," "miscellaneous" and so on. This was somewhat like a person who had only 9 chairs at his command and therefore asked all late-comers after the eighth to sit all together on the ninth chair! The fact is that hospitality of notation has to be two-fold—in chain and in array. One-fold hospitality is rigid. This is the third rigidity in notation which needed to be broken. The Octave Notation of the Colon Classification broke it. The first eight classes are represented in the usual way by the first eight integers. The ninth class of the array is represented not by 9 but by 91, the tenth by 92, and so on until we get 98 for the sixteenth class. Again the seventeenth class of the array is represented not by 99 but by 991, etc. One can easily see why this notation is called Octave Notation. One can also see that the Octave Notation provides infinite hospitality in array. This is secured by giving up 9 as a number to denote by itself any class. It is by sacrificing its normal use. It is by sacrifice that we gain the Kingdom of God!

2.4. RIGIDITY OF DECIMAL CLASSIFICATION—FACETED NOTATION

But this does not bring us to the end of rigidity in notation. Consider the specific subject "Emotion in old people." This is really a composite subject—composed of the 'psychology of old people' on the one hand and the 'psychology of emotions' on the other. It is a specific subject of two facets—Entity Facet with 'old people' as its Focus and a Problem Facet with 'emotion' as its Focus. Neither the decimal-fraction-notation nor the octave notation can always by themselves represent a multiplicity of facets. Even if we manage to represent it in the first design, the rigidity of the notation soon disables us from meeting a new related specific subject like "Anger in octogenarians." We may easily satisfy ourselves that if in the notation the Entity Facet comes last, we can by adding an extra digit represent "Emotion in octogenarians" but not "Anger in octogenarians." On the contrary, if the last facet of the notation is Problem Facet, we can by the addition of an extra digit represent "Anger in old people" but not "Anger in octogenarians." This is the rigidity of the Decimal Classification. It is experienced almost at every point in that scheme. An important contribution of the Colon Classification is that it broke this—the fourth kind of rigidity. This it manages to do by faceted notation. It makes its notation represent the transition from one facet to another—in the example given, from the Entity Facet to the Problem Facet by inserting the connecting symbol ":" (colon) whose ordinal value is defined to lie between those of zero and one. We have:

| S18:5 Emotion in old people | S188:5 Emotion in octogenarians |
| S18:54 Anger in old people | S188:54 Anger in octogenarians |

It can be seen that in a faceted notation—in the Colon Classification —a class number can grow not only at its end but also at the end of each of its facets. It is well known that in the Decimal Classification the class number can only grow at its end. A decimal number is like a coconut palm tree. It can only grow at the top. But the Colon Number is like the banyan tree which can grow in all directions simultaneously.

Here is another subject with three facets. "Political history of the United States in 1950's." Most of the specific subjects are really multi-faceted. The Decimal Classification has no mechanism to meet them. Such subjects lead either to cross-classification or to inconsistency in placing. Merrill has cleared the ground in his *Code for Classifiers*. His brain power and time need not have been wasted over it if the Decimal Classification had had faceted notation.

It is on account of the great service rendered by this little symbol ":" (colon), which claims to be treated as no more than a bigger zero, that I called this scheme the Colon Classification out of sheer gratefulness. It can handle any number of facets. Engineering and Sociology have five facets. Theoretically we can speak of infinite hospitality in facets.

2.5. RIGIDITY OF COLON CLASSIFICATION—OPTIONAL FACETS

But there is a rigidity which develops here. This will be experienced not so much when we classify macro-units of thought embodied in books and treatises, but only when we classify for documentation service—when we classify micro-units of thought embodied in small articles or announcements of considerable intension. Here it is found as impracticable to anticipate all possible facets which a specific subject can present, as it is to anticipate all the possible specific subjects which may appear at any time. It is again found that even if we can enumerate all the facets, and provide for them in the facet-formula, the class numbers of specific subjects in which most of these facets are vacant will present an irritating collection of connecting symbols. It is to break this rigidity in notation that we are now engaged in developing the concept of Optional Facets. The results of our investigation are appearing regularly in the *Abgila*, which is the quarterly organ of the Indian Library Association.

2.6. RIGIDITY OF FACET FORMULAE—FUNDAMENTAL CATEGORIES

What little work we have done till now on the Optional Facets has disclosed a sixth kind of rigidity in notation. That concerns the order of facets in facet-formulae. In the published editions of the *Colon Classification*, the facet-formulae give only compulsory facets. They are few in number. In most cases they throw the facets in an order which was found to be the most helpful by all classes of readers. However, in documentation-classification which calls for many facets, it is conjectured that it may prove to be dangerous to fix the order of all facets rigidly. An attempt to break this rigidity has led us to realize that all possible facets of all possible specific subjects can be regarded as manifestations of one or another of the five Fundamental Categories—Time, Space, Energy or Action, Matter, and Personality. We have provisionally conjectured that it will secure great freedom if we use different connecting symbols for the facets which are respectively manifestations of these five Fundamental Categories. We have proposed the use of

. (Dot)   as the connecting symbol to precede Time Facet;

. (Dot)   as the connecting symbol to precede Space Facet;

: (Colon)   as the connecting symbol to precede Energy Facet;

; (Semicolon) as the connecting symbol to precede Matter Facet; and

, (Comma)   as the connecting symbol to precede Personality Facet.

We have fixed the ordinal values of these connecting symbols to fall between zero and one in such a way that the following is an ascending sequence:

$$\text{o} \quad . \quad : \quad ; \quad , \quad \text{I}$$

It is not possible to go here into all the details of this proposal. They are all fully discussed in the *Abgila*.

2.7. AN EXAMPLE

Let me demonstrate with a concrete example, viz., "Painting of iron signboards on the highways in the United States in 1950." Here

'1950' is the Focus in the Time Facet
'United States' is the Focus in the Space Facet
'Painting' is the Focus in the Energy Facet
'Steel' is the Focus in the Material Facet

Of what fundamental category is 'signboard' a manifestation? Surely, it is not Time, Space, or Energy. It cannot be Matter either. No doubt, 'steel' was rightly regarded as a manifestation of Matter. But 'signboard' is something more than mere 'steel.' Steel has been impregnated with something intangible to make it a 'signboard.' 'Signboard' is indeed a manifestation of personality. You see what I mean by the term Personality. Perhaps some of you may think of a better term to denote this intangible, subtle, unanalyzable, holistic, fundamental category. But let us provisionally agree to denote it by the term 'Personality.' 'Highway Engineering' is a manifestation of a still higher order of the fundamental category 'Personality.' Indeed it is the basic manifestation of Personality, the Basic Class, the Basic Focus—which alone gives a meaning to all the other digits in the class number and all the other terms in the name of the specific subject.

The translation of the name of the specific subject is now very simple. As a preliminary step, we shall re-arrange the terms—the substantive terms, which alone count—in the name of the specific subject as suited to the syntactical arrangement of the elements in the Colon Language and insert the appropriate connecting symbol before each substantive. To throw them into proper relief, I am enclosing each substantive within square-brackets.

[Engineering] [Highway] , [Sign-board] ; [Steel] : [Painting]
. [United States] . [1950]

Here is the translation into the Colon Language—the Colon Number—the Class Number: D411, 95; 8:5.73.N50

2.8. THREE OTHER RIGIDITIES—UNSCHEDULED MNEMONICS, PHASE ANALYSIS, SIGNATURE DIGITS, AND PRIMORDIAL SCHEDULES

There are three more rigidities that have to be broken. Time does not allow me to deal with them. I can only say that they are being broken by concepts of Unscheduled Mnemonics and Phase Analysis, discussed in *Colon Classification*, Edition 3 (1950) and *Prolegomena to Library Classification* (1937), and the concept of Signature Digits and Primordial Schedules being now developed in the *Abgila*. We shall be helped in the construction of Primordial Schedules if we can be furnished with the schedules and subject headings worked out for narrow subjects by the industrial and other special libraries concerned.

3. AVOIDANCE OF THE DEBACLE OF DUNKIRK

All this may look complicated. So are the machine tools of today. The complication of machine tools is not their creation. It is the creation of the work to be done by the machinery which are fitted with them. So also the complication of a classificatory notation is not its own creation. It is the creation of the work to be done by the class numbers. That work is now very involved. Documentation service is responsible for that complication. Progress in modern thought cannot be made adequately and efficiently, it is agreed by those engaged in research and creative thinking, unless expeditious, exhaustive, and exact documentation service is done by the library profession, for alphabetical arrangement cannot produce such a service, and systematic, fully expressive, co-extensive, individualizing, daring class numbers alone can do the job. It was indeed pathetic to hear some librarians proposing to leave the trench, as it were, to give up classification altogether, and to put their faith back in alphabetical arrangement, though it is more than seventy years since Melvil Dewey put that controversy to rest. The debacle appears to include even a serious proposal to revert to arrangement of reading materials in accession order and to deny open-access— the greatest human contribution of the library profession by our immediate predecessors to the fullest satisfaction of all the Laws of Library Science. This reminds one of Dunkirk. No, no! We ought not to desert in that way. We must be manly enough to face the difficulties thrown on us by documentation service and by the demands of industrial libraries and fundamental research.

4. NEW FUNCTIONS OF CLASSIFICATION

We should also remember that the purpose of a classificatory language has been widened during our life-time. It was merely the mechanization of arrangement when Dewey started it.

4.1. SERVICE TO CLASSIFIER

Now it has to serve many other purposes. It has to help classifiers by its facet- and phase-formulae in finding out quickly and unerringly all the foci in a piece of writing, by a systematic process which reduces flair to a minimum. The way in which the facet- and phase-formulae throw forth and make visible the pattern of thought in a piece of writing reminds one of an experiment in Sound associated with Chladni's figures. These formulae put the reading material on the rack and make it confess all its foci. In other words, classification has to canalize the process of discovering the full content of a piece of writing.

4.2. SERVICE TO REFERENCE LIBRARIAN

It has to be of similar and equal help to the Reference Librarian in helping a reader to enunciate his own requirements exactly and exhaustively.

4.3. SERVICE TO INTERNATIONAL COMMUNICATION

Lastly, the latest purpose to be served by classification, which is now taking shape, is that it should play a vital part in promoting international communication. The importance of this is getting more pronounced day by day. In the last century most of the creative thinking in the world was done only in three languages—English, French, and German. After the First World War, the languages of Eastern Europe have also come forward. Today the countries of Asia are reviving rapidly. That will add many more languages. The output is going to be enormous. No individual can cope with them unless documentation service of a high order is done and unless all nascent thought is featured and arranged in terms of an international, artificial language of ordinal numbers—in terms of a universal classificatory language which can be handled as an efficient tool by reference librarians and with whose aid they can find for every reader every nascent thought he needs and find for every nascent thought that person who can carry it still further.

5. MACHINERY FOR SEARCH AND MINUTENESS OF CLARIFICATION

No doubt classificatory work of this high order should be entrusted only to men of great ability. No doubt humanity cannot spare enough of such persons to appoint classifiers in each of the myriads of libraries in the world. But it is not necessary. There is nothing gained by a thousand people classifying copies of the same material at the same time. Classification is an impersonal process. It can be done centrally. It ought to be done centrally. I go a step further. Economy will require not only that classification should be done centrally but that even the housing and the service of materials of advanced and sparsely-used nature should be done only in a few centers. No doubt the search should be done by machinery to save time. This machinery should be coupled with the machinery for teletyping so that any inquirer may get his service without any delay at whatever distance he may be from the central depository from which this high-level service is rendered. We as librarians have to remember one thing. We should not be under the illusion that because machinery will be brought into use we can revert to alphabetization and say good-bye to classification. Machines may do things quickly. But they cannot do anything more than that for which we design them. Machinery for documentation service can help us only in the measure of the code we use—the degree to which we carry the subject breakdown and the thoroughness of the classification we use. In fact I feel that the advent of machinery is going to stimulate classificatory thought, emphasize the importance of analytic-synthetic classification, and direct research into the foundations of such a system of minute classification. Indeed, the machinery for search will ever continue to challenge us with the words: "Be minute, be more minute, be most minute."

THE SUBJECT APPROACH

THE HUMANITIES: CHARACTERISTICS OF THE LITERATURE, PROBLEMS OF USE, AND BIBLIOGRAPHIC ORGANIZATION IN THE FIELD

CARL H. KRAELING

WITH your indulgence I would describe the situation in which you and I find ourselves here today by paraphrasing a popular quotation and making it say, "Some aspire to bibliography and others have bibliography thrust upon them." You, I take it, are those who aspire to bibliography and I commend you most heartily for those worthy aspirations. I am the one who has bibliography thrust upon him, not indeed in the sense that I feel at all constrained by the kind invitation to speak to you here today, but in the sense that as a worker in the records of human enterprise and self-expression, I am compelled to make bibliography, and to use bibliographic services and controls. It is good that we should get together here, and I for one cherish the opportunity to express to you who are bibliographically minded by choice and aspiration the sincere thanks of those of us who are bibliographically minded only of necessity for the tremendous services you are continuously performing in our behalf.

If I appear here today as a representative of the Humanities, it is only as a worker in a few of the more remote disciplines of that vast field and if I speak on problems of bibliography it is only as one who has had the opportunity to serve on one or another library committee, who has associated with library folk and found them altogether enjoyable people, who has browsed about in the literature of bibliography a bit as any amateur might do, and who has asked a few questions of those who know the subject intimately. I sense from all this the seriousness of the situation in which we find ourselves bibliographically speaking. I see very plainly the enormous increase in the demand for bibliographic services that libraries are being asked to meet. I see the tremendous complexity of the apparatus necessary to meet those demands. I realize the pressure under which libraries are to reduce the high costs of administering bibliographic controls and performing bibliographic services. I see how the great dreams of national and international unification and standardization that, if realized, would solve so many of our bibliographic problems seem to become less and less possible of fulfillment as the volume of the material increases and as the urgency of the immediate needs crowds the service of the long-range objectives out of the picture. This situation, I take it, is not without some bearing upon my presence here this morning. If I understand the matter correctly, you are trying through us representatives of the humanities, the social sciences, and the natural sciences to get to the grass roots of the situation and to get a down-to-earth view of the subject, and if that is what you want I think it would be most ungracious of us did we not try to oblige.

With the topic assigned to me, I plan to take a certain degree of liberty, for as I see it, there are fundamentally three questions you would ask me as the representative of the humanities:

1. What kind of an animal is the humanist anyway? How does he work bibliographically and how did he get that way?

2. What kind of material does the humanist work on? How does it organize itself in his own thinking and what is his understanding of its variables as they affect the bibliographic problem?

3. If the humanist were to stop thinking about himself and his material and would think about the bibliographer and the bibliographer's problems, what suggestions might he have to make about the bibliographic handling of his materials so that the bibliographer might be able to help him the better and also help those who might also be concerned with his material?

Now there are two ways to approach the first two questions, the statistical and the experiential. I am sure there should be statistics on the humanists and I know that there are statistics on the representatives of other disciplines, but I have no statistics for the humanists and could not be expected to supply them without sending out a questionnaire, which I did not do, so you will have to be satisfied with the experiential approach, and as I have said before, the range of my experience is limited to a few of the more remote disciplines, such as classics, archaeology of the ancient world, ancient art, Biblical literature, and perhaps a bit of Byzantine art and history.

Now bibliographically speaking the humanist is, no doubt, a bothersome type of animal. He is brought up with and never loses a special sense of reverence for a body of material that is his subject matter. This material is that of the authors, composers, artists, artisans, statesmen, politicians, philosophers and prophets, and the small people whose lives, works, creations, and interrelations he studies. This material is the humanist's pride and joy. He lives for it and in it. Not only that, but he never gets away from it. The scientist, though brought up on and continuously using a body of traditional material, soon learns to take his knowledge to the laboratory, to test it by the experimental procedure, and to launch out into new experiments that apply or extend his body of information. The social scientist has society as his laboratory and is early taught to supplement his reading with the collection of new statistical information. Of course both the new experiment and the new statistical information wind up by presenting bibliographic problems, but the fact is that in the course of his experimental operations the scientist develops a different slant on his printed or recorded material. It is a repertory of information rather than a part of his flesh and blood. I am not saying this to belittle the scientist, social or natural, or the humanist, but to describe a peculiar facet of the humanist as a bibliographic animal. Bibliographically speaking he is the world's prize introvert. Try to get him to do without a telephone or give him insufficient shelf-space for his growing collection of books and you have offended not him but the sanctity of his gods, be they Homer, Augustine, Spinoza, or Firdausi. At least that is the way he puts it. This is bad enough for his Dean or administrative officer, but potentially much worse for his bibliographic associates on the library staff, for whom not to be able to supply the means of obtaining a missing bit of information is *lèse majesté* of the highest order.

Still, as a bibliographic animal the humanist is not such a bad workman. He has been brought up in a good tradition, bibliographically speaking, and knows his way around. Let us follow him briefly in the course of his humanistic development.

When the young humanist, and for that matter the budding social and natural scientist, first meets up with bibliography it is in the form of that list of Supplementary Readings that he finds at the end of each chapter of his high school text-book. At this point his bibliographic problem is simplicity itself. The list of readings is there, the authors are clearly indicated, and the demand for them from the library will not be very great, for what the student does not understand at this time is why more than one person should have to write about the same subject anyway and what is the use of reading more than one treatment of the same subject, especially when the books referred to in his list of supplementary readings are clearly older and therefore less authoritative than the text before him.

When we next meet the young humanist he is in college, where he is assigned his first term paper on any one of a given list of topics. In this connection he is normally, as we all know, directed by his teacher to the library and told to assemble a bibliography on his subject. This is where the dictionary catalog appears first in his line of vision. At first this is a magnificent discovery and invention, for here are a lot of titles on precisely the subject he has chosen, be it the Pullman strike, Michelangelo, the Roman military machine, or Shelley and the French Revolution. Truly a pearl of great price is the dictionary catalog. But once the slips have been filled out with the titles and dumped on the librarian's desk with a masterful gesture, the difficulties begin. It is not so much that NS 57.44jg is in Room 210 while Zq. 14.56ff is out and won't be due for two weeks and that EF 17.99sq is at the binders, it is rather that of the dozen or so titles that do come under his scrutiny a large number may be quite irrelevant, being either too general or too specific to do him any real service. Usually it takes the help of his professor to put him back on the track of an idea. Here he learns for the first time that books have a double function, to supply facts and to act as triggers for the release of thought, and that exhaustive bibliographies regurgitate the facts *ad nauseam* and tend to produce a disproportionately low number of thought releases.

When we next see our humanist he is in graduate school, where he is a member of a seminar. Here first the problem of the newest information on a given seminar topic presents itself on his horizon. The question is what are the newest slants on the development of wall painting in the post-Pompeian era or what are the newest thoughts on the causes of the Italian Renaissance, or how shall we develop a positive basis for estimating the value of the Chicago criticism of the value of Luke-Acts. It is the contemporary scholarly problem that appears upon the scene here and new bibliographic procedures are necessary to handle that type of problem. Here he learns the value of the contemporary research article, the value of book reviews and of statements on current trends in the development of his discipline. He encounters in this connection the plurality of the sources from which such information can be drawn, namely the journals that associate themselves with or are the organs of scholarly groups cultivating one or another aspect of his field. If he is being guided with discrimination, he will in this connection find himself in the immediate presence of the newest issues of such trade-publications and will be thrown into what are commonly called journal clubs, where the most recent issues of the periodicals in his field are gone over systematically each month in all their parts. If so he will develop a habit that will stand him in good stead during his later years, namely that of studying carefully the reviews and the news and notes sections of scholarly journals and of relying on them to keep him posted.

As we follow our budding humanist we next find him writing a dissertation. Here a new aspect of the bibliographic problem presents itself to him. He is interested for the first time in complete coverage of a topic, for now he is to compose the definitive work on a given subject, and not only does he need to know all that has been said around and upon it, but is clearly out to show up the inadequacies of everybody else. He therefore loves nothing more than to set up straw-men from among those who have approached his problem from opposite angles, to knock their heads together, and to grind them in the dust with his superior intelligence. Aiming at the *magnum opus*, he usually spends an inordinate amount of time going through the history of his subject and comes out with a first chapter on this topic that is quite out of proportion to the rest of his work. This is the occasion for the development of no little amount of bibliographic learning, but the bibliography which he appends to the *magnum opus* is usually not very useful, largely because, having learned of bibliographic procedures only from his own labors, he has no principles of selection and organization and merely packs his list with every book he has ever looked at.

Having done his dissertation our young humanist eventually finds himself teaching somewhere, commonly at an institution with much smaller library facilities and bibliographic resources than the one where he wrote his dissertation. Here one problem with bibliographic overtones immediately presents itself to him. He must teach courses on rather comprehensive subjects and know slightly more than the text-book does about them, but clearly much of the material has not come under his scrutiny, so he has much immediate need for much spot information on manifold subjects. Here he soon learns the value of ready references, but lacking a wide bibliographic knowledge and equipment he falls back necessarily upon the great compendia that are available for the several disciplines of the hu manities, the German *Realenzyklopädieen* and *Handbücher* and the French *Dictionnaires*. These are amazing reservoirs of information, bibliographically and subject-wise, and stand him in excellent stead, especially when they are up-to-date and complete. Caught in the mill of instructional routine and standard instructional materials, the young humanist, however, soon begins to yearn for release in the shape of contact with new and unfamiliar materials. So he applies for grants in aid of research to take him where he believes this material is, that is if he can think up an angle on the study of this material that provides a suitable occasion. If the man is bright and his slant is good, he deserves his chance and profits accordingly in his own growth, but you would be surprised to find how many applicants have the most naïve ideas of where to go to look for things. The location factor has not played a part in their bibliographic up-bringing.

When finally the humanist has established himself, he has obtained at least a cursory acquaintance with a wide range of materials. More important from our point of view, he has developed a fine sense of how to find what he needs to know. He knows his way around the better libraries of the country and through their several divisions including the sections on bibliography, and has often a sixth-sense of how to circumvent difficulties and obstacles in the path of the acquisition of the information he needs. This makes him for his own work and for the training of others an excellent bibliographic instrument.

What emerges from this description of the humanist's development for our purposes? The first thing to be said is that the humanist is no slouch when it comes to knowing the literature of his field and being able to marshal it on demand. The corollary is that the better he is as a representative of his subject the less he depends upon the services of others for his bibliographic purposes. For, fundamentally, he is an individualist in bibliography and for the solution of the bibliographic problems in his field is of small real comfort to the professional bibliographer. This is not because he is not systematic. I know few people in my fields who do not keep systematic files of some kind for their own bibliographic use. It is rather that he works bibliographically primarily for his own purposes and from hand to mouth. Bibliography remains in many respects a personal matter, namely the matter of his own need and his communication of bibliographic material to others. What he loses in comprehensiveness by this means he gains in selection, for clearly it is the more recent and the more useful material that he hands on to his students and puts in his books.

By not including the humanist himself out, as our Pennsylvania Dutch friends would say, of this "subject" approach to bibliographic organization, I may have taken some liberties with the topic set for me, but I believe that he is a definite factor in the subject category, and in describing him I have already paved the way for part of the answer to the second of my two questions, namely: "What kind of material does the humanist work on? How does it organize itself in his thinking and what is his understanding of its variables as they affect the bibliographic problem?"

Here the first part of the answer must now be evident. It is an authoritative body of material representing the sum total of the things men have written and done and fashioned, seen as witnesses to the development of the race in its epic struggle to achieve higher ends. Much of this material, of course, is of interest also to the social scientist, and the humanist welcomes his participation in its use, but their objectives and in part their media of study will in some measure at least be distinct. For this body of material the humanist requires vast reservoirs of factual information. These are in the first place the great collections of texts, be they the scores of the world's great music, the editions of the world's poets, novelists, historians, and philosophers, the tremendous *corpora* like the Patrologies Greek, Latin and Oriental, the Teubner and Oxford series of classical authors or the *Acta Sanctorum* and Mansi's *Conciliorum Collectio amplissima* or the *Monumenta Germaniae*. On the other hand these reservoirs include collections of representations of objects, be they the archaeological publications of individual sites, the *Corpus vasorum antiquorum*, the *Corpus Inscriptionum Graecarum et Latinarum*, Rodenwaldt's *Antike Sarkophagreliefs*, Wilpert's *Mosaiken und Malereien*, or Garrucci's *Storia del'arte cristiana*. This whole body of material is sacred to the humanist. It is the body of his original sources.

To this body of first-hand material we must add as the second element of the humanist's equipment the vast array of recorded critical and interpretative opinion. The critical literature begins, of course, with the ancient commentators, whether Poseidonius commenting on Plato's *Timaeus* or Servius on Virgil's *Aeneid*, and extends to our most recent critics in the *Saturday Review of Literature*. The interpretative literature is of two kinds, the synthetic and the analytical, and embraces everything up to Toynbee's *Study of History* on the one hand and the newest dissertation on the pronominal suffix in the Ugaritic language on the other.

To the basic materials and the works analyzing and synthesizing them, we must add as the third element of the literature of the humanities that representing in one way or another the groups which handle the materials and analyze or synthesize them. Here I would list first of all those works that apply to specific groups among the people who concern themselves with the material, whether text-books for grade, high school and college or professional instruction, or popularizing media such as Durant's *Story of Philosophy* or the most recent anthology of Shakespeare put out for the Book-of-the-Month Club. Next I would group here all the media that people use to approach the material, the catalogs of MSS and special collections, the dictionaries, handbooks, encyclopedias, *Reallexika*, and introductions, no matter how many volumes they contain. Finally I would group here the professional literature of the organizations and individuals that concern themselves with the humanistic disciplines, the *Proceedings* of the learned societies and the foundations, the professional journals, the biographies of the scholars, and the history of scholarly activities in the more recent periods.

This is one way of describing and grouping the materials of the humanistic field. Probably the grouping is utterly useless, but I have given it because the analysis seems to represent the humanist's approach as I see it.

Now all this vast body of printed material has, like that of all other disciplines, certain variable features that make it distressingly difficult to handle from a bibliographic point of view. So far as the humanist's basic materials are concerned, they represent series that are open at the near end and God willing will never close. So far as the humanist's ocean of critical and interpretative production is concerned, this has in it tides and currents that shift with the times, and plenty of dead water left between the currents at all times. So far as concerns the material that reflects our own professional approach to our subject matter, this is subject to the greatest fluctuations and changes. Partly this is because the personnel changes and the organizations through which it works change. Partly it is because educational theory and procedure change. Partly it is because in a rapidly changing world the things we want to know most directly are quite different from the things we used to want to have most immediately at our finger tips.

Beset by all these variables, it is almost impossible for the bibliographer to keep solid ground under his feet and to keep abreast of the most recent developments. The question whether a first novel by a new author belongs merely to modern fiction or also to literature cannot be answered save in terms of long perspective. The question at what point works of criticism and interpretation are to be relegated to the body of historical material instead of being carried along as part of the scholar's working equipment involves a fielder's choice. How to keep up with the changing agencies of the humanistic field and with its changing practical application is an endless task because things do not actually stay put. The surprising thing is that our bibliographers are so close on the heels of the developing pattern in all these areas and don't fall as far behind as we might expect.

But still other variables must be mentioned. One of them is the misfortune that has overtaken the humanities in recent times. At one time, as you know, they were the pride and joy of Maecenases, of Cardinals and princelings and crowned heads who supported them with their accumulated wealth. The last great splurge of such support by private wealth came in the twenties of this century. Since then the humanities have again donned the mendicant's garb that they wore in the early middle ages, but they have not found it easy to keep their eyes from wandering to the spectacle of the opulence of their brethren in the social and natural sciences, who, having found practical ways of demonstrating their value for contemporary civilization, have inherited the world and no small part of the wealth thereof in comparison. To the relative pauperization of the humanities we must add the destructive effects of the wars through which we have lived, wars which made possible tremendous forward strides for science and gave it almost oracular prestige, while destroying so much of the material of humanistic effort and dislocating so much of the traditional pattern of humanistic relationships. The dislocation of relationships will ultimately be seen to have been highly salutary, but the immediate effects upon the material and the media for its professional use, especially as they effect bibliographic hopes and prospects, are devastating.

Clearly it would be of the greatest utility for bibliographic purposes if the materials of the humanist's knowledge, the literature of his analytical and synthetic activities and the instruments of his professional work, were all nicely packaged and co-ordinated. During the past century humanists were well on their way toward such packaging and co-ordinating, but there is scarcely a major organizing operation in the spheres of my acquaintance that has not either broken down completely or is being held together only with the greatest difficulty. Most of the great *corpora* remain torsos and their continuation is highly problematic if not impossible. The Vienna Academy at one time began a series of authoritative text editions of the Greek Church Fathers and many volumes have been issued. That the series will ever be finished is most doubtful. The Prussian Academy once inaugurated a *Corpus Inscriptionum Graecarum*. It is a massive work and has done a great service. Of course it has become antiquated by recent discoveries. After the last war a continuation on a more modest scale was inaugurated in the form of the *Supplementum Epigraphicum Graecum*. This was supposed to take in all the new material. It too has died. Before the last war the Italian Government began a lavish edition of the wall paintings of Pompeii and several fasciculi actually appeared. That it will ever be completed may be doubted. The *Corpus Vasorum antiquorum* sponsored by the International Union of Academies was the first undertaking begun on an international base. All the several countries were to publish their own holdings in Greek vases, but in a form homogeneous with that of other countries and as part of a series. Several parts have appeared, but that the *Corpus* will ever be complete is at least questionable. Everyone grants the need of a new Du Cange, the dictionary of mediaeval Latin. There has been much discussion about it at international congresses, but that the old one will be replaced is an almost forlorn hope, and so it goes on down the line. Torsos, fragments, beginnings but no completed products or products so organized that they could be kept up to date. The difficulties are largely financial, but also in no small degree the result of individualism and ineffective national and international organization.

Faced with this kind of situation institutions whose scholars have sensed the larger needs and requirements tried to make up by individual effort for deficiencies in the work of the field as a whole. Harvard University through Dumbarton Oaks, a research institute devoted to Byzantine art and civilization, began trying to assemble in its "Archives" a collection of pictures and information concerning all monuments of Byzantine art and architecture. The Oriental Institute of the University of Chicago began collecting an Archaeological Corpus for the ancient Near East along similar lines. Princeton has for years been compiling an Index of Christian Art. Yale has been collecting a great Cross-Cultural Index. All of these could be important tools of humanistic research and reservoirs of bibliographic information. Some of them are still being carried on and will succeed. The most successful to my knowledge, because best organized and most immediately ancillary to an immediate local interest, is the Princeton Index of Christian Art. Others have folded up. I fear there are analogies in many fields of humanistic effort. The fact is that generally speaking private institutions are unable to support under present circumstances bibliographic undertakings that service a discipline or a field. Meanwhile conditions in the field as a whole steadily deteriorate, to the great disadvantage of those bibliographically minded.

We are in a particularly bad way, for instance, as regards the tools of disciplines, especially where new fields of inquiry open up. Let me mention specifically grammars and chrestomathies and dictionaries of ancient languages. It may seem hard to believe, but there are literally dozens of ancient languages, long familiar or recently come within our purview, for which we have either no adequate grammars or no dictionaries, and the chances are that we won't get them. Take the Hittite language as an example. We now have a grammar but we have no dictionary. We have tried for years, but nobody wants to finance a Hittite dictionary. Why a Hittite dictionary? Yes, why? It seems quite irrelevant to the problems of an atomic age, but are we really to give up all normal cultural pursuits and accept the thralldom of the atomic age and its abbreviated time perspective or is it still of importance that we concern ourselves with the best that man has done and can do and be? If it is important, how can we keep our Hittite specialists sufficiently competent to write a dictionary and at the same time sufficiently aware of the necessity of making their learning contribute also to the further development of human civilization to convince people that their labors should be supported? And what agency has that sense of responsibility for the humanities and that gift of strategy in the discharge of such responsibility to strive for the simultaneous achievements of both of those ends? Until we have the answers to these questions not only the bibliography of the humanities, but the humanities themselves are subject to the severest kind of limitation.

If I have adequately described the peculiarities of the material with which the humanist is concerned and the circumstances in which he finds himself with respect to it, it is high time for me to go on to the third of the questions I have raised, namely the question: "If the humanist were to stop thinking about himself and his material and were to think about the bibliographer and the bibliographic problems, what suggestions might he have to make about the bibliographic handling of his material so that the bibliographer might be able to help him the better and also help those who might be concerned with his material on a non-professional level?"

The answer might have several parts. In the first place, I think, the humanist would want and need to have both the bibliographer and himself know the situation in greater detail. The important fact to note in this connection is that whereas there are already national agencies that take some immediate interest in the bibliographic problems of the natural and the social sciences, there is as yet, apart from such a forum as this and apart let us say from the American Bibliographical Society and the American Documentation Institute, no similar agency in the humanities. This may be typical but it is also something that will not be remedied until someone points up the problem, so that the agencies that should be charged with the responsibilities might be alerted and so that the necessary financial support for the work of such agencies might be mobilized.

To point up the bibliographic problem in the humanities, in my estimation, we need to have someone or some group undertake a full-scale analysis of the situation. This would undoubtedly be a labor of some years but it would pay for itself over and over again in showing up precisely where the problems lie and how confused the situation is. What group or individual could and should undertake and sponsor such an effort I would leave to persons like yourselves to judge. From my point of view it should be a group that can enlist the co-operation of humanists to the extent necessary, but should not be made up basically of humanists.

What such an investigation would find we can prognosticate at least in part, namely an excessive fragmentation of the bibliographic procedure with resultant loss of that effectiveness that Verner Clapp was making a part of the definition of bibliographic pattern.

Every humanist knows how multiple are the controls which he himself has to utilize to keep abreast of his subject or to find what he wants to know. Some of these media of bibliographic information on recent literatures are old-established and are doing excellent service. For philology the German *Philologus* and the *Philologische Wochenschrift* are irreplaceable. For archaeology the *American Journal of Archaeology*, the *Revue Archéologique,* the *Jahrbuch des Deutschen Archaeologischen Instituts* are basic. For Byzantine studies the Greek *Epeteris tēs Etaireias tōn Byzantinon Spoudōn,* the *Byzantinisch-neugriechische Jahrbücher*, and the *Byzantinische Zeitschrift* are fundamental. For the history of art the *Art Index* is a necessity; for Biblical studies it is the *Revue Biblique,* the Italian *Biblia*, and the German *Theologische Literaturzeitung*. But in no one discipline is the coverage by any one of these instruments complete. There are dozens of sources of possible bibliographic information on modern professional literature in each field instead of one or two. As an example let me tell you merely about the effort of one institution to keep abreast systematically of the literature in its field. The field happens to be that of Byzantine studies and the institution Harvard's Dumbarton Oaks. Here, for ten years through the indefatigable efforts of the lamented Robert Blake of Harvard there has been kept an index of new publications on Byzantine topics. The card file is extensive and each card is duplicated. The one file contains the cards listed alphabetically according to author. The other arranges them according to the subject matter, but there is also a file that shows from what sources the information about the bibliographic item comes. You would be surprised to see how many periodicals and serials must be scanned and have been scanned regularly by Robert Blake to make this catalog possible. They number up in the sixties.

This situation is by no means unusual, as every one of you probably knows by experience. One has only to go to the bibliographic section of a well-organized central research library and see how many bibliographic helps have to be kept on hand for each of the different fields. How we get that way is not hard to understand. The multiplicity arises in part from national needs and language preferences and in part from the individualism of the humanistic scholar and the agencies through which he works.

Clearly, then, the humanist thinking for and with the bibliographer must in the second place support the general thesis of a reduction in the number of bibliographic controls for a given field, and it may be that with the financial difficulties in which he at present finds himself and his periodicals, he would welcome further suggestions of how this simplification could be accomplished. I know for a fact that one of our own learned journals in this country is so heavily committed to keeping its readers informed on the newest publications and discoveries that it ceases to provide any satisfaction to its editor as a vehicle for the publication of original contributions to learning. Too much of the income and too large a share of each issue is mortgaged for reporting at second hand.

At this point a third suggestion might be proper to a humanist trying to think with the bibliographer. It is that he should strive through the national organization of scholars representing his own field to organize a standard annual bibliographic listing of at least the newest publications of his discipline. Our learned societies in the humanities, I fear, have been so pervaded by the individualism of humanistic learning that they can think only of discharging the necessary routine business of the organization, and then of providing the individual scholar with a chance to read a paper, and finally of publishing such a paper if it is any good. It is not safe to generalize, and there are undoubtedly exceptions to the rule. But so far as my knowledge goes, there is at present apart from the natural desire to perpetuate themselves nothing in the life of the American learned societies that shows a recognition of and a willingness to assume active responsibility for the continuous administration of the field. The study of the bibliographic situation in the humanities suggested above could be of great help by pointing out to the disciplinary groups their responsibility for the organization of the bibliographic controls within fields. The humanities and the national organizations representing the several disciplines of the humanities have today a co-ordinating agency in the American Council of Learned Societies, which is analogous to the SSRC and the NRC. I see no reason why it could not act as a forum for the discussion of such questions, as clearing-house for suggestions on the distribution of responsibility in one discipline or the other, and why through it the several societies could not establish such standards of bibliographic organization in the several disciplines as would make the bibliographic material more useful and make easier its co-ordination with similar national efforts in other countries. What is needed here more than anything else, in my humble judgment, is an impulse toward concern of scholarly groups not with making more bibliographies but with the fundamental problem of bibliography, its simplification and standardization.

The suggestions I have made to this point concern themselves largely with the question of keeping up with the newest material in the fields. There are still other matters of concern to bibliographers about which the humanist might also do some reflecting. I am thinking in this connection not so much of the most recent publications but of the means of access to the great body of primary source material that is the backlog and the mine of humanistic effort. What is it that should be knowable about this material and how can it be made knowable to as large a group of interested persons as possible?

The first thing to be said in this connection is that we should not try to know everything or even too much. There are too many risks involved in omniscience. I recall a story, probably apocryphal, that was current in Washington right after the war. During the war, you will recall, we found ourselves bibliographically illiterate about many parts of the globe in which we were suddenly seriously involved, and so the OSS without previous training went to work to compile bibliographies on all and sundry countries of the world for ready reference of Washington officials. One young man was set the task of making a bibliography on Afghanistan and came up with a finished product that was duly mimeographed and distributed. Included in his exhaustive all-knowing treatise was one title representing the work let us say of Mildred Smith. The title of her book was "How to make an Afghan." The moral of the story is very plain. Bibliographers must be discreet and know where to draw the line.

The second thing I have to say concerns the unusual demand. I know that all of us, professional bibliographers in particular no doubt, are plagued with the "crank" who dogs our footsteps and plagues us with sudden and unexpected demands for the means of access to the most abstruse information imaginable. We have to be polite, of course, and we are polite and it is always important to distinguish between the honest inquirer and the mugwump, which name I apply to the person educated beyond his intellect. The honest inquirer I am always happy to serve as best I can, but the mugwump is already suffering from indigestion of facts and should be discouraged from gorging himself with more. I wish someone had discouraged Dr. Velikowsky in his younger years. It would have saved us a great deal of trouble. Be that as it may, the point is that we can't let our understanding of what should be bibliographically accessible and knowable be determined by the demands for the abnormal.

To put the matter positively, what should be knowable through bibliographic controls as regards the material of the humanities should be limited, in my humble judgment, to certain very practical and concrete things. As regards unpublished materials we should be able to tell what and above all where they are. As regards published materials we should know through bibliographic tools the basic facts about the languages, cultural geography, and political units of the world from prehistoric times to the present; we should be able to identify persons and what they have written or done or created. We should be able to locate historical events. We should be able to locate ideas. We should be able to locate artistic works of all kinds.

As regards the first of these, the value of knowing where unpublished materials are is obvious. This is what the humanist, lacking the laboratory of the scientist and the statistical yard-stick of the social scientist, needs above all to keep his frontiers expanding. The WPA tackled a really important piece of work when it went to work on local archives back in the 'thirties. A lot more could be done in that area. We need to know much more about the contents of museums and local collections. Indeed we need to encourage the development of regional responsibility for the establishment or the identification of local repositories of cultural materials. Even an index showing merely the location of such repositories and the type of material reposing would be of great value.

As regards the second, the contents of the published materials, the central thing to keep in mind is that the humanities are or should be concerned with the cultural heritage and achievement of man. This means that in the humanities the bibliographic emphasis should be upon the means of access to the most significant elements of man's intellectual, aesthetic, and moral insights. What we must avoid in this connection is the thought that all this can be distilled into a test-tube or an anthology, for our concern with the intellectual, the aesthetic, and the moral achievements of man is worth the effort only if they are seen not as abstractions but as dynamic elements of the cultural process. They can be so seen only in their context, which is the continuum of time and space, and in their relation to the historical persons and groups in whom and through whom they work. Hence we must make provision for a framework of historical and biographic knowledge in planning our essential bibliographic tools.

For what it may be worth I would suggest that the development of bibliographic tools to meet these demands should take into consideration one further practical factor. It is the immediate needs of the persons and communities whom these tools are to serve. We have seen earlier this morning that the humanist is not from infancy a highly developed individual bibliographic instrument. In fact only a small portion of all humanists ever actually achieve that eminence. We should therefore try to gear the organization and distribution of our sources of bibliographic information to the requirements of users of several types at the several stages in which they are when they come seeking information. We might also need to think of gearing our bibliographic information to the greatest needs of the communities that are to be served. Naturally all such accommodations to educational and cultural needs have to be handled intelligently lest they become blocks to growth and progress. In fact it would be well in such an attempt to accommodate to the several levels of need to keep one step ahead of an indicated median. Of course it would be wonderful if a full repertoire of bibliographic information were available everywhere, and eventually our civilization may demand it, which would be more wonderful still. But until that time it is not necessary by bibliographic means to inform every librarian who has a copy of Somerset Maugham's *Of Human Bondage* on his or her shelves that the title is taken from Spinoza, for there might be a lot of other, more important things he or she would need to know or know how to find much more frequently.

How and when we shall achieve the bibliographic organization of the material of the humanist's learning is difficult to see. The humanist through his own learned societies can conceivably help the bibliographer with the listing and organization of the newest contributions in the field of critical, interpretative, and professional literature. But neither the humanist nor the bibliographer nor both of them together can encompass with their own present strength the bibliographic organization of the essential factual content of primary source material of humanistic learning. Here larger resources both of manpower and of wealth must be brought together. The humanities themselves are at present working under a disadvantage in such matters for they have not been able to demonstrate their immediate value to society in the same way as the natural and the social sciences. That being so they cannot expect to find underwriting for their bibliographic needs in the same way as the sciences. But I am inclined to believe that the humanities are due for a re-orientation in some measure at least and that, having hitherto been all too vague in their formulation of what they call "spiritual values," they will in the not too distant future become much more specific and direct, and having been relatively detached and "ivory-tower," they will strive to be much more functional in their relation to the motives and premises of cultural progress. The extent to which they accomplish this is the measure of their ability themselves to clarify the principles of the bibliographic organization of their material and at the same time the measure of their success in mobilizing support for that organization.

To stimulate the humanist in the direction of a clearer understanding of his function in the social process the bibliographer can do much, especially if he presses the humanist to assume responsibility for at least a part of the bibliographic operation and if he requires him to think about the nature of his material from the bibliographic point of view. To assist the bibliographer in his effort to encompass the subject matter of the humanities and to make it accessible, the humanist can do much, especially if he is given the opportunity to set forth the premises of his understanding of himself and of the cultural process. I therefore hope that there will be increasingly frequent meetings of humanists and bibliographers in the future, and that our session here this morning may be a token and an augury of the shape of things to come and a step in the direction of the fuller realization of our several hopes and aspirations.

THE SOCIAL SCIENCES: CHARACTERISTICS OF THE LITERATURE, PROBLEMS OF USE, AND BIBLIOGRAPHIC ORGANIZATION IN THE FIELD

IRENE B. TAEUBER

A MONOGRAPH on bibliography in the social sciences would be a difficult task; a discussion of the problems in a brief paper is presumptuous. Many groups of social scientists have struggled with the problems of literature control. Bibliographies have been planned and a few have achieved publication, although the average duration of life has been brief. The Graduate Library School and the Division of the Social Sciences of the University of Chicago have just made a comprehensive survey of "the desirability and feasibility of an abstracting system for the social sciences" and are exploring further steps and implementation possibilities.[1] In accordance with the recommendations of a meeting of experts on documentation in the social sciences, held in December 1949, UNESCO is creating a coordination committee whose function will be to explore the possibilities for coordinating the work accomplished by various services and to formulate rules on the publication of guides and comparative indexes.[2] A UNESCO-Library of Congress bibliographic survey on *Bibliographical Services, Their Present State and Possibilities of Improvement* has just been issued by the Library as a working paper for an international conference on bibliography.[3] Governments are be-

1. University of Chicago, Graduate Library School and the Division of the Social Sciences, "Bibliographical Services in the Social Sciences," *Library Quarterly,* XX (April, 1950), 79–100. Several working documents were issued and two preliminary reports: Bruce L. Smith, *Proposals for Unified Bibliographic and Reporting Systems for the Social Sciences* (Chicago, 1949); University of Chicago, Graduate Library School, *Bibliographical Services in the Social Sciences* (a report by the Graduate Library School and the Division of the Social Sciences of the University of Chicago, 1949).

2. United Nations, *Catalogue of Economic and Social Projects 1950.* (Lake Success, N.Y., 1950). Pp. xx+515. The projects of the United Nations Educational, Scientific, and Cultural Organization in the field of the social sciences are listed and described on pp. 338–43. The documents prepared for the meeting of the Committee of Experts on Documentation in Social Sciences are listed on pp. 339–40.

3. UNESCO/Library of Congress Bibliographical Survey, *Bibliographical Services: Their Present State and Possibilities of Improvement: Report Prepared as a Working Paper for an International Conference on Bibliography, Appendix: Notes on the Development of the Concept of*

coming concerned over the elusiveness of social science research and social scientists, and several learned societies are searching for feasible solutions to segments of their problems of research and publications control.

The philosopher-scientist of the nineteenth century would have been the ideal savant for assessing the characteristics of the literature of the social sciences, the problems of use, and bibliographic organization in the field. Generalization was his profession, for he built an edifice whose apex was systematic theory. The modern practitioner in a sub-field of the social sciences is perhaps least qualified to seek solutions that embrace all the social sciences. Modern research involves analysis in depth, and thus intensive work on a segment of human culture. The scholar's knowledge of the broad subject field in which he was trained becomes antiquated, his possibilities for maintaining intellectual control of current developments minimized by the inconvenient fact that the pursuit of any given hypothesis carries him beyond the boundaries of his traditional discipline. With specialization within disciplines, the blurring of interdisciplinary lines, and the emergence of social research projects involving psychological, biological, and even physical or chemical aspects, the social scientist becomes less and less competent to assess bibliographic problems other than his own.

Why, then, not refer the problem of bibliography in the social sciences to the librarians, the information specialists, or the generalizers who occupy the proverbial benches of the social sciences in the smaller institutions? Solutions in the sense of outlined projects would be simpler if this were done. The difficulty is that the problems of bibliography in the social sciences are the immensely complicated ones of the social sciences themselves. Solutions that ignored the frontiers of research development and failed to contribute toward that cumulation of knowledge which is essential to scientific advance would merely add further to the number of the bibliographies that appear for a few months or even years and then become items for perusal when a new generation of scholars surveys the history of past attempts at bibliographic control as prelude to new plans and new publications.

This may seem somewhat exaggerated and unduly pessimistic, but after some fifteen years in which I have struggled with both

---

Current Complete National Bibliography, by Kathrine O. Murra (Washington, 1950). Pp. ix+ 67; v+42.

research and bibliography in a field predominantly but not wholly social, that of demography, I have reluctantly reached the conclusion that the problems of bibliography lie basically with the state of the social sciences rather than with the development of the bibliographic art—or is it also science? This personal background is mentioned both as validation of credentials and as precautionary apology, for I shall utilize the population field as major source for illustrations of situations, difficulties, procedures, and requirements.

PREFACE TO BIBLIOGRAPHY

Bibliographic organization is a relatively straightforward technical and administrative job provided certain preconditions exist. The production of a bibliography or an analytical index within a specific field requires a definition of the field to be covered; an agreed purpose in the coverage; and an accepted subdivision into major categories, with conceptualization adequate for analytical classification within the sub-fields. The statement of scope and the canons of selectivity must be capable of sub-formulation into objectively determinable criteria for the actual operations of bibliographic coverage and annotation, citation, or abstract—for unless such objectivity is obtainable bibliography can only choose between an omnibus listing and an evaluated selection whose validity depends upon the judgments of individuals.

Once social scientists have defined their field, subdivided it rationally, developed an analytical classification for research and literature, and determined the purpose for which they wish bibliographic and/or analytical control, the problems of bibliography become those discussed in previous sessions of this Conference, and ably analyzed by Dean Berelson and his associates of the University of Chicago in their report to the Carnegie Corporation.

The difficulties of social science are in part the transitional ones of rapid developments which permeate the field but at divergent rates and with differing degrees of intensity. Learned associations themselves are unstable, with a fragmentation of disciplines and a formation of cross-disciplinary groups to supplement, replace or conflict with the conglomerate associations of yesterday. Functional divisions are compounded by an evolving specialization in substantive analysis for countries or regions and by the approach of area studies to research stature.

Each learned discipline has its related applied field, and in each case the activities in the allied field have involved increasingly sub-stantial analysis until any realistic definition of social research or the social scientist must involve the formerly scorned applied groups. In sociology there is social work; in economics there are the business and the marketing groups; in political science there is public admin-istration; in anthropology there is an applied variant which asserts direct research status in fields relevant to action. Within each dis-cipline, almost within each subdivision, functioning has become dif-ferentiated into social research and the administration of research, the farthest developments here being in the fields of economics and statistics.

The social scientists were once segregated in the college and the university, where research tended to be individual or small group projects with personal responsibility and personal credit. Today they also function in government, where research is a cooperative project in which the specific contribution of the individual becomes merged in the whole.

Nor is this the totality of the difficulties. As our society has evolved in size and complexity, research and data collection has become a necessary adjunct of operational functioning and administrative planning within and outside the government. Labor unions, planning groups, trade associations, business corporations, and applied re-search organizations produce publications which demand biblio-graphic organization, whether the purist would label them as re-search or not. Functioning itself produces by-product data that are often of extraordinary value: the industrial mortality statistics of the life insurance companies and the transportation statistics of the railroads may be cited as illustrative. And often trained social scien-tists are involved in planning the collection, compilation, and analy-sis of these operationally-collected or functionally by-product ma-terials, whether they be data for research or research itself.

There is still another aspect of social science functioning. Social science is taught and social literature written as a contribution to the general education and adjustment of the individual to the society in which he lives. Whether factually accurate and conceptually sound materials written for the enlightenment of students or the general public are research or not may be debatable; the need for their con-trol in a bibliographic system is incontestable.[4]

4. The problem of bibliographic orientation toward method rather than toward sub-stantive content is critical, but too complicated to be outlined adequately in the space avail-able to us here.

Thus the definition of the social scientist and of functioning in the social sciences, and the allocation of individuals or functioning so defined to the proper learned discipline or sub-field thereof, become as difficult as the delineation of fields and sub-fields within the broad contours of social science. There are no concise definitions other than the arbitrary which will find "the social scientist" whose wishes are to be met through the compilation and publication of bibliography.

CHARACTERISTICS OF SOCIAL SCIENCE LITERATURE

With this over-long preface completed, we may now discuss the published product, the "social science literature." Bibliographic problems have been ably discussed in the recent surveys, but all have had to assume that there was a defined field of literature to cover and so have ignored or treated quite cavalierly the core of the problem that has frustrated previous bibliographic attempts and even gone far to perpetuate the collective ignorance that has minimized the cumulative growth of social science research. The problem of the literature may be solved quite simply by defining as the relevant literature that which is included or reviewed in series or periodicals labelled as social science. This, I submit, is to beg the problem of bibliography as a tool for research.

We shall first consider the scientific writings of recognized members of the various social science disciplines. Type, scope, and place of publication are likely to differ sharply according to whether scholars are attached to private institutions, to government, or to business organizations. We shall consider first the contributions of the scholar or group of scholars published by them as individuals. This research may appear as a periodical article, part of a symposium or volume of proceedings, a monograph or a book. The most obvious outlet is the journal of the learned association to which the individual belongs, but if the research is advanced this outlet suffers from major deficiencies. It is usually necessary to indulge in verbalism to explain the problem and its importance, at the same time that the space for methodological and substantive materials is quite inadequate.

The recognized journal outlets are limited, so recourse is had to professional journals outside the general field, particularly for specialized materials. A methodological article may appear in *The Annals of Mathematical Statistics*, while an article on the characteristics of growth among densely-settled and mortality-dominated agrarian peoples may be sent to the *Journal of Geography*. A study of cultural

factors in the fertility of contemporary groups in Nyasaland may
appear in *Africa, Journal of the International Institute of African
Languages and Cultures.* The author whose research involves subject
analysis for a geographic area must choose between the subject journal and the area journal. To secure minimum coverage for population research we find it necessary to cover such specialized journals
as *Tanganyika Notes and Records,* the *Journals of the Royal Central
Asian Society, The Middle East Journal,* the *Journal of the Institute
of Actuaries,* and *Tropical Diseases Bulletin,* to mention only a few
of the English language journals. Then, too, social research may be
relevant to public policy or concern subjects of wide current interest.
If so, it may involve considerable research content and yet be so
written that it appears in *Foreign Affairs, Pacific Affairs, Weltwirtschaftliches Archiv,* or the *Annals of the American Academy of Political and Social Science.* If research has its locale or its data in a definite area, the possible places of publication include the local historical, economic, medical, or general cultural journals. The conclusion is therefore obvious. The periodical literature of social research
is widely scattered. Furthermore, much of it is so written in lay-
man's language that only the expert can quickly determine relevance,
scientific character, and contribution.

Monographs and books are often assumed to be relatively simple
to locate and assess. This is true provided coverage remains within
the orbit of academic research for academicians published in book
form and titled according to the accepted terminology. But significant analysis of limited scope is often included incident to a more
comprehensive topic or research project. Pamphlet publication and
monograph disappear into the yawning chasm of the unprocessed
materials of libraries or those listed by general series only. The symposium and the volume of proceedings are excellent outlets for publications seeking oblivion unless and until bibliographic facilities are
available so that each chapter or research article becomes a separately classifiable contribution. Reviews in learned journals assist
in this problem of books, monographs and symposia, but the learned
journals review selectively from among those central core publications sent to them. In theory the book editor of a learned journal
should select books and monographs for review on the basis of bibliography rather than have the process operate in reverse.

Private or individual publication is only a part of the problem, for
increasingly there is government publication, and in a rather aston-

ishing number of fields the research of government is not only quantitatively larger but qualitatively superior to that done elsewhere. In fact, as governments extend the scope of their functioning and become major sponsors of research and publication the division between governmental and private publication becomes blurred. The library can solve this problem quite simply; a publication issued by a government is a government publication. However, private scholars publish in government journals and scholars in government may secure permission or be requested to publish government-sponsored research outside. This immensely complicated situation with all its implications for the freedom of research is beyond the scope of our discussion here except to stress the relative decline of private research and private publication throughout major regions of the world.

Government publications run the gamut of types: specialized research journals, public information series, monographs, reports, etc. They are issued by local, state, national, and international organizations, the richest research ore being in the national publications. They are sometimes luxurious publications, but sometimes they are a few crudely mimeographed sheets stapled together. And these sheets so seemingly inconsequential often contain the technical statement of methodology or substance for research that is published in more impressive and enduring form only after being so generalized and interpreted as to lose the major portion of its research value.

RESEARCH VERSUS MATERIALS FOR RESEARCH

There is a widely held belief that in the social sciences research is differentiated from data for research, that a bibliography of research can somehow include publications of the higher echelon but exclude those of the lower. With the massive statistical materials on which major segments of economics, statistics, and demography, even political science and sociology, depend, this distinction is a tenuous one. Any given function in statistical research may be distinguished as research or operational, but the classification of publications is quite a different problem.

A national census illustrates the difficulties of differentiating research from the materials for research. The Seventeenth Decennial Census of the United States involved substantial research: in sampling; in sub-regional delineation; in errors of response; in the validation of data through successive enumeration by comparable or divergent techniques. The native censuses taken in selected areas of British East Africa in 1948 will provide data for research, but they are themselves research. National vital statistics systems include increasing amounts of research, in preparation for collection, in collection, and in analysis.

Thus in many research fields within the social sciences the arbitrary exclusion of certain categories as materials for research rather than as research itself may actually exclude primary research publications from social science bibliography. Present systems of listing and review tend toward such exclusion, with consequences that are rather ludicrous. A brief book which was a summary of major tabulations of the Jamaican census of 1943 was "research," reviewed as such in learned journals and listed in bibliography, whereas the census volume itself was ignored except in "source" bibliographies.

The problem of the availability of statistical sources which are both social research and data for social research is one on which constructive action may be expected. The American Statistical Association is exploring the problem, as are regional and international statistical associations, the appropriate groups within the United States government, and the international organizations.

Social science research uses information in addition to the statistical as raw materials for research. The problem of the bibliographic organization of these sources is somewhat removed from the major problem we are considering, but it is one which should be explored by the organized social scientists.

The studies on the characteristics of statistical materials and the problems of their bibliographic organization have a broad relevance for social science bibliography. The conclusion may be stated somewhat categorically as follows: Research bibliography must include the research that accompanies the production and presentation of source materials. And bibliography adequate for research needs must include major sources as well as analyses made on the basis of those sources.

EXISTING BIBLIOGRAPHIC FACILITIES

Bibliographic facilities explicitly organized for the social sciences are severely limited. This fact has been documented in all the recent studies of the subject, as in those of previous decades. There is no bibliographic index of the social sciences, indeed no adequate index of the literature of any major subject field within the social sciences. From a research standpoint the situation for the individual scholar is even more serious than that indicated by the gloomy portrait of services by the University of Chicago group. Listings of articles from social science journals in bibliographic indexes for the general public may be defined technically as bibliographic coverage, but if the classification is alphabetical or geographical or if it involves popular categorization, the location of relevant materials requires scanning the entire list. And scanning is frightfully boring, even aside from the fact that a scholar who scanned all available bibliographic lists would have little time left to accomplish the research which was the purpose of his scanning. A few illustrations may suffice. The *Monthly Check List of State Publications* is alphabetical by issuing department within states listed alphabetically; the Far Eastern bibliography included in *The Far Eastern Quarterly* is alphabetical within countries, separately for articles and books; *Current Medical Literature* is alphabetical by title of journal received within broad medical categories.

Foreign listings or abstracts are particularly frustrating. The conceptions of social science are more theoretical and philosophical than empirical. With notable exceptions, as in econometrics, quantitative techniques have lagged in development and application. Field study and experimentation are less developed. Moreover, completeness, consistency, and accuracy in citation are not continental habits except among the always systematic Germans. Proofreading would appear to be a recent invention not yet generally adopted.

There are exceptions to the general critique of existing bibliographies, but they are in fields tangential to the social sciences or only partially social science: *Biological Abstracts; Chemical Abstracts; Quarterly Cumulative Index Medicus; Bibliography of Agriculture; Psychological Abstracts.* Then there is, of course, that most valuable but seldom mentioned bibliographic tool, the proof sheets of the Library of Congress Card Division.

THE USE OF EXISTING FACILITIES

The existing facilities for bibliographic organization are severely limited if evaluated as tools available for the use of the individual scholar. They are, however, of extraordinary value if centrally utilized for the production of bibliography in a limited field of the social sciences. I can best illustrate this use by describing the production of *Population Index*, which is compiled by professional people with a minimum expenditure of time. Identical procedures might not function adequately in other fields, but comparable procedures of utilization could be developed.

The goal of *Population Index* is the coverage of demographic research, broadly defined to include causes, correlates, and consequences of demographic processes as well as the processes themselves, together with the basic data for research and sufficient of the evaluative, propagandistic, and policy literature to make demographers cognizant of the trends and aware of major sources if they need materials for interpretation or research. There is thus a central core of objectively definable materials surrounded by a broad band of related materials. In general, the rules for inclusion become increasingly more stringent as the peripheries of the field are approached. And, also in general, the rules for inclusion become lenient for areas of the world in which statistical data are inadequate and research fields little cultivated. Essential background materials for demographic research are introduced on an evaluative basis.

The coverage of the population journals and the major social science and other journals which include demographic research relevant to their specialties is done directly on a current basis. A long list of journals is scanned once or twice a year. Current government publications central in the field are received directly or covered systematically in the Library of Congress. The massive current intake of the Library of Congress is checked and the relevant materials abstracted from a daily selection made by the Census Library Project in order to maintain its current reference activities in the Library. This cooperative arrangement is valuable to both participants; the *Index* can expand its coverage of fugitive materials far beyond what would otherwise be possible, and the staff of the Census Library Project can procure citations and annotations from the *Index*.

For books, the galleys of the Library of Congress cards are scanned throughout the classifications for social science, science, law, philosophy and psychology, and medicine. Books obviously in the field as well as the much larger numbers that might include materials are examined quickly for discard, citation only, citation with brief annotation, or abstract.

The independent coverage is supplemented by a systematic utilization of available bibliographic and related sources for fugitive and marginal materials. Official lists of government publications for major countries are basic; these may be the omnibus listings of government printing offices, as our own *Monthly Catalog*, or specialized, as the excellent series of the United States Bureau of the Census or the semi-annual lists of the Public Health Service. *Quarterly Cumulative Index Medicus, Bibliography of Agriculture, Current Geographical Publications, Psychological Abstracts,* and *Biological Abstracts* are covered to yield demographic research in the fields of medicine, agriculture, geography, psychology, and biology respectively. Book reviews, lists of books received, and similar sections of periodicals are scanned. Where possible an adequate review is used as a basis for annotation, with credit to the source. Subject bibliographies are also scanned, particularly those of the International Statistical Institute, the United Nations, and the regional associations.

Population Index is seriously deficient, particularly because the absence of an annual analytical index precludes easy access to the specific materials now buried somewhere within the major subject categories of fifteen volumes. It is generally useful to a research field, though, as well as to students engaged in regional or comparative research in national and international organizations. The critical point to be emphasized here is that a considerable portion of this particular international bibliography is achieved through centralized and evaluative utilization of existing resources. It is not the ideal solution, but it is a feasible one.

THE ORGANIZATION OF SOCIAL SCIENCE BIBLIOGRAPHY

I approach the subject of the organization of bibliography with considerable timidity, but with sufficient conviction to overcome any hesitancies in speaking as an amateur in the presence of professionals.

The organization of bibliography reflects the goal for the final product. The ultimate solution would involve two goals, the one a complete listing of relevant materials with analytical controls of content, the other a highly selective and evaluative survey of major contributions.

The University of Chicago group received its grant from the Carnegie Corporation to explore the need for and the possibilities of an abstracting service in the social sciences. Their studies revealed a widely prevalent need for some service that would permit social scientists to learn of developments throughout the social sciences. Their recommendations for immediate consideration included an abstracting service and a series of bibliographic essays, both designed to contribute toward a balanced professional knowledge throughout the social sciences. They were predicated on the assumption that the major problem for the individual scientist was general cognizance of related fields rather than direct assistance in his field of specialization. The abstracting service and the topical essays would contribute toward lessening the intellectual in-growth that accompanies concentration on a specific research problem. They would, moreover, permit that increasing number of social scientists in operational or administrative positions to remain informationally competent in the social sciences in general and their specific fields in particular.

The present discussion has been oriented primarily toward what the Chicago group envisaged as a longer-range but more fundamental solution: a selectively complete bibliography covering private and government publications of all types, with control of content achieved through an adequately conceptualized analytical classification system or index. This bibliography would function both as locational tool and as basis for more comprehensive informational and evaluative services. Fragmented bibliographic location compounds costs as contrasted to comprehensive coverage at key intake points. With the techniques at present available and to come, citations on any subject and/or area could be procured by mechanical sorting and made available to subject specialists, in our case the social scientists, for further processing and reproduction. This would not be a substitute for existing bibliographies, and particularly not for abstracting services, but it would give to each group the citations to relevant materials outside the central core that could otherwise be procured only incompletely and with great difficulty.

Complete coverage of materials published in the United States would be simplest to achieve, but it is in areas outside the United States where deficiencies in information on literature are greatest. Eventually, comparable national bibliographies for each country or region in the world could solve this difficulty, but the eventuality would appear to be far removed whereas the need is urgent. Hence it is suggested that in its own national interests the United States assume responsibility for complete citation and analytical indexing of the foreign publications that enter this country.

Whatever the stimulus to the organization of planning and operations in social science bibliography, the product that flows from the operations will contribute to the utilization of existing research and the further development of research in almost direct proportion to the validity of the criteria for selection and the classification schemes for the analytical index. Thus for the social sciences we return to the argument with which we introduced the discussion. The problem of bibliography in the social sciences is that of the organization of the social sciences themselves as well as that of bibliographic organization.

The complete or selective analytical index to the social science content of all published literature, or even appreciable proportions of it, may be so visionary as to constitute the imaginative fringe rather than the central reality of the problem of bibliography in the social sciences. This is not necessarily true, for complicated high-speed processing has become reality in the statistical field, with electronic tabulation and computation. The reproduction and transmission facilities of today would have appeared visionary a decade ago, fantastic half a century ago. It is highly probable that concentration of inventive and organizational talents and adequate financing could produce rapid developments in the field of publications control. Such concentration is not inconceivable, for research, including social science research, is recognized increasingly as the basic ingredient in the perpetuation and development of the American economy, the American political system, and the American way of life, whether in peace or in war. International commitments intensify the needs for research and information on all aspects of human cultures. The problem, I suspect, is not that integrated and imaginative planning for global research control is premature but that it is already too late to avert the inherent stupidity of finding ourselves as librarians and social scientists almost as unprepared as we were a decade ago.

THE NATURAL SCIENCES: CHARACTERISTICS OF THE LITERATURE, PROBLEMS OF USE, AND BIBLIOGRAPHIC ORGANIZATION IN THE FIELD

HERMAN H. HENKLE

IT IS necessary at the outset of this paper to give some consideration to what we mean by the term "the natural sciences." The
simplest way to dispose of the question would be to state that
we mean those areas of learning which are called astronomy, physics,
chemistry, geology, botany, and zoology. This is not enough, of
course, because there will be made in this paper some reference to the
application of these areas of human knowledge to such activities as
agriculture, engineering, and medicine. And perhaps we should slip
mathematics into the basket, too, without calling more attention to
it than need be. Whether it is a natural science is debatable. Someone
has said that it is one of the three international languages—music,
drawing, and mathematics. It is not normally referred to as the "science of mathematics," but it certainly has a great deal to do with
the manner in which scientists think and work.

There is need for a closer examination of the matter than this, because it is not possible to understand the characteristics of the literature and problems of use of the natural sciences—more commonly
referred to by the singular substantive "science"—without at least
a measure of understanding of what we mean by the term science.
Science has many definitions. Broadly conceived, it is organized or
systematized knowledge. If one examines the critical bibliographies
in the periodical *Isis*, one gets a view of science broadly conceived.
But even then, not broadly enough for many.

The commonly accepted assumption is that the term science is
closely associated with experimental method, although there are accepted at the same time, within the meaning of the term, such disciplines as astronomy and geology which are largely descriptive and
to which the experimental method has contributed very little. In
spite of these qualifications, the meaning of science in this narrower
sense is the one to which we pay special attention in this paper. We
accept then the interpretation of Harvard's President Conant when

he states "that science emerges from the other progressive activities of man to the extent that new concepts arise from experiments and observations, and that the new concepts in turn lead to further experiments and observations."

SCIENCE IS CUMULATIVE

Aside from the above definition, there are certain general characteristics of science which are closely related to the literature of science and its use. The first of these is that science is cumulative. The fact that science is a progressive activity and that it results in a continuous accumulation of experience affects peculiarly the characteristics and use of scientific literature. Our sense of this fact will be heightened if we consider briefly some examples of this cumulative effect of science. The history of science is filled with fascinating stories which show the gradual unfolding of man's understanding about natural phenomena, and incidents in which the discoveries of some individuals sprang directly from the discoveries of men who had worked before them, and whose work, in fact, could not have been done except by the successful activities of their predecessors.

The first example is drawn from the history of mathematics. The concept that natural phenomena can be measured, one of the motivating forces in modern science, originated far back in antiquity. But refinements in techniques in measurement came slowly. The expression "the next decimal place" has been used to epitomize the progress made in science with each new refinement in instruments and measurement, and in methods of experiment. Thought is rarely given, however, to the recency of the time since which the phrase itself could be used. The idea of decimal fractions seems to have originated in India about the 6th century. It was first effectively set forth in publication, however, in 1585 by the Flemish scientist Simon Stevin. It was refined and supplemented by John Napier thirty years later by his discovery of logarithms. These two concepts contributed immensely to the speeding up of calculations possible in scientific work. It was said that logarithms "doubled the lives of astronomers."

Our next example we take from the field of biology. Biologists once believed, and some continued to believe right up to the time of Pasteur, in the doctrine of spontaneous generation. It was believed that under many circumstances it was not necessary for living organisms to be present in order for living organisms to be generated. Lacking much, if not most, of present day knowledge of living phenomena, and lacking even the now common instrument, the microscope, they could hardly have arrived at any other conclusion. With the invention of the microscope, however, and its increasing use in the second half of the 17th century, more accurate evaluation of the theory became possible.

Even without the microscope the first scientific attack on the question was made in the 1660's by the Florentine scientist Francesco Redi. In a carefully controlled series of experiments, he demonstrated that "the flesh of dead animals cannot engender worms unless the eggs of the living be deposited therein." The theory of spontaneous generation was abandoned, however, with great reluctance. It required the accumulated evidence of many experiments to dissipate acceptance of the theory; and its final downfall came two centuries later only after the careful experimental work of Louis Pasteur.

One is tempted to elaborate on such illustrations and to give many more, but we will limit ourselves to two additional, the first from the field of chemistry. About 1770 Joseph Priestly found that mice living in a closed space gradually spoil the air and die, and that candles under similar circumstances will not continue to burn. He observed that green plants under the same conditions would improve the air up to a certain point until the "fixed air" (carbon dioxide) obtained a certain density. Finally, in 1774 he identified oxygen, which he described as "dephlogistized air." In other experiments about the same time he found that "saltpetric air" (nitrogen peroxide) in the presence of water and free oxygen will absorb the free oxygen and form a simpler oxide which is absorbed by water. The first of these discoveries, namely, of oxygen, enabled Lavoisier during the following years to study the fundamental nutrition of animals and their respiration. The second discovery was used by Fontana in inventing the first eudiometer, an instrument employed in gas analysis.

Our final example of the cumulative nature of science we will draw from the field of physics. Modern medicine is immensely aided by X-rays, and the roentgenologist is often depended upon for accurate diagnosis of disease. But the knowledge of X-rays is little more than a half century old, and their discovery would not have been possible without the scientific experiments of a galaxy of brilliant physicists, beginning with Faraday; including J. J. Thompson, Lord Rutherford, and others; and culminating finally in the discovery of X-rays by Röntgen in 1895.

INTERDEPENDENCE OF THE SCIENCES

The second of the general points to be developed is the interdependence of the sciences. Specialization is a primary characteristic of modern science, not only among the practitioners in the various branches of applied science, but also in fundamental research. Each of the major branches of science—chemistry, physics, geology, botany, zoology—and the major fields of the applied sciences—agriculture, engineering, medicine—continues to generate sub-specialties, giving a semblance of truth to the old gag that "specialization is knowing more and more about less and less." But there is another aspect of modern science that must be taken into account in evaluating the course of development of the sciences and their practical applications. This is the union of two or more sciences to form specialties which bridge the gaps between major disciplines. Biochemistry, biophysics, mathematical biology, medical physics, and other such fields are growing in importance, and illustrate interrelationships of all of the sciences.

These relationships have important bearing on both the content and use of the literature of science, and they must be understood if we are to develop rational plans for the organization of scientific libraries and the bibliographic controls to make them usable. The interrelationships can be illustrated in several ways.

The first example is drawn from a new theory in the field of ornithology. Two years ago there appeared in *Science* a paper by Professor Wolfson of Northwestern University, in which there was formulated the hypothesis that "continental drift was the stimulus for the evolution of the more highly developed forms of migration" among birds. As the basis for his theory, the author showed the close correlation between the migration patterns of such famous travelers as the Arctic tern and the Pacific golden plover and the early drifting of the continents which has been hypothetically described by the geologists. The theory is of interest in demonstrating the interrelationship of two sciences, ornithology and geology, and hence the literature of these sciences, for two reasons.

In the first instance, the ornithologist could not have evolved such a theory without an intensive examination of the literature of historical geology. As a matter of fact, from his firm conviction in his own theory he concluded that certain distributional patterns of bird migration constitute "prima-facie evidence for the drifting of continental masses." In the second instance, in publishing the theory, he excited the interest and observations of scientists from other scientific disciplines, as well as other ornithologists; and their comments indicated that the author of the new theory had not made sufficient use of the literature of paleontology, geophysics, and meteorology, and even of his own field of ornithology.

A second example is provided by a study made at the University of Chicago some twenty-five years ago by the Commission on the Future Policy of the University of Chicago Libraries. In this study, each department of the University was asked to estimate: (1) what percentage of total use of library books by its own instructors and graduate students in the following thirty years was likely to be use of books belonging primarily to each of the other departments and schools in the University; and (2) what percentage of the total use of the department's own books, in the same period, was likely to be by instructors and graduate students of each of the other departments and schools. The results of the study were presented in tabular form.

One of the first conclusions to be drawn from the study was that the overlapping in use between the social sciences and the physical and biological sciences was negligible. The estimate of overlap between psychology in the social sciences, and zoology, anatomy, and physiology in the biological sciences was from five to ten per cent. The estimate of overlap between geography in the social sciences and geology, botany, and zoology in the natural sciences was also from five to ten per cent. These were the only significant estimates of overlapping between the social sciences and the natural sciences.

In the quarter of a century since this study was made, there has been no apparent depreciation in the amount of overlapping between the literature of most of the sciences. For this reason, the estimates of overlapping given in the Chicago study still have considerable validity, in spite of their largely subjective basis, and are reproduced on the following page.

The interrelationship of the sciences is reflected clearly by the journal literature. A study made in 1935 of the periodical literature for the previous five years[1] showed that the literature of biochemistry is scattered through the periodicals of practically every other subject field. Only thirty-four per cent of a total of more than 17,000 papers was contained in journals devoted primarily to the field of

1. Herman H. Henkle, "The Periodical Literature of Biochemistry," *Bulletin of the American Library Association*, XXVII (December, 1938), 139–47.

biochemistry. Eighteen per cent was in medical journals; sixteen per cent was in physiological journals; eleven per cent was in chemical journals; and the remaining twenty-one per cent of the papers in biochemistry was scattered in journals devoted primarily to general science, general biology, botany, agriculture, engineering, and bacteriology, with a trace in the journals of physics and mathematics.

In a more recent study by Fussler on "Characteristics of the Research Literature Used by Chemists and Physicists in the United

INTERRELATIONSHIP OF SUBJECT FIELDS BASED ON ESTIMATED USE BY SPECIALISTS OF LITERATURE IN OTHER SUBJECTS*

Mathematics	—Astronomy (45); Physics (10); Chemistry (5)
Astronomy	—Mathematics (45); Geology (5)
Physics	—Mathematics (10); Astronomy (10); Chemistry (10); Geology (5); Botany (5)
Chemistry	—Mathematics (5); Physics (10); Geology (5); Botany (5); Zoology (5); Anatomy (†); Physiology (5); Physiological Chemistry (15); Pathology (†); Hygiene & Bacteriology (5)
Geology	—Astronomy (5); Physics (5); Chemistry (5); Botany (5); Zoology (5)
Botany	—Physics (5); Chemistry (5); Geology (5); Zoology (15); Physiology (5); Physiological Chemistry (5); Hygiene & Bacteriology (5)
Zoology	—Chemistry (5); Geology (5); Botany (15); Anatomy (15); Physiology (10); Physiological Chemistry (10); Hygiene & Bacteriology (5); Clinical Medicine (5)
Anatomy	—Chemistry (†); Zoology (15); Physiology (15); Physiological Chemistry (5); Pathology (10); Hygiene & Bacteriology (5); Clinical Medicine (20)
Physiology	—Physics (†); Chemistry (5); Botany (5); Zoology (10); Anatomy (15); Physiological Chemistry (30); Pathology (15); Hygiene & Bacteriology (5); Clinical Medicine (20)
Physiological chemistry	—Physics (†); Chemistry (15); Botany (5); Zoology (10); Anatomy (5); Physiology (30); Pathology (15); Hygiene & Bacteriology (5); Clinical Medicine (10)
Pathology	—Chemistry (†); Anatomy (10); Physiology (15); Physiological Chemistry (15); Hygiene & Bacteriology (20); Clinical Medicine (35)
Hygiene and bacteriology	—Chemistry (5); Botany (5); Zoology (5); Anatomy (5); Physiology (5); Physiological Chemistry (5); Pathology (20); Clinical Medicine (10)
Medicine	—Zoology (5); Anatomy (20); Physiology (20); Physiological Chemistry (10); Pathology (35); Hygiene & Bacteriology (10)

* Adapted from Chicago University, Commission on the Future of the University Libraries, *Tentative Report* (Chicago: University of Chicago Press, 1924), Appendix A, Table VI.

† "Indicates a relationship too small to be represented by the figure 5, yet not inconsiderable."

States,"[2] there is detailed analysis of similar data to show not only the percentages of references in each of the major subject classifications with respect to journal titles, but also with respect to the individual references. Fussler shows that even in such fundamental subjects as physics and chemistry there is a similar dispersion of papers in serial publications classified in other subject fields. In chemistry less than one-third, and in physics approximately one-fifth of the journal titles are classified in the respective subjects, although it is shown that this percentage has increased in the forty year period, 1899–1939. Further analysis of the data shows, however, that in 1939, seventy-one per cent of the total references for chemistry and sixty-five per cent of the total references for physics appeared in journals classified in these respective subjects. In spite of this seeming concentration, however, it must be noted that almost thirty per cent of the references in chemistry, for example, are in journals classified in subjects other than chemistry. Further, it must be noted that the problem of library service is greatly complicated by the fact that this thirty per cent of references is scattered through almost seventy per cent of the periodical and other serial titles. Fussler throws light on another interesting aspect of this problem as follows: "There is a consistent and regular decline in the number of references per serial title with but a few minor exceptions. This decline is most conspicuous in the journals pertinent to the major fields in chemistry. . . . The implication is quite clear that, to cover any number of given references, a larger number of titles will be required than was formerly necessary, and the figures do not indicate that a limit has been reached. The situation is undoubtedly a result of the increasing proliferation of journals, many of them highly specialized in character."

PRIMARY IMPORTANCE OF SCIENTIFIC PERIODICALS

A third important point is the primary importance of scientific periodicals. In one of his many stimulating essays, George Sarton has said that "science is progressive and, therefore, ephemeral." It is not surprising, therefore, to find that one of the primary problems in the field of science and the efforts of scientists to push out their frontiers of knowledge is one of communication. It was out of this

2. Herman H. Fussler, "Characteristics of the Research Literature Used by Chemists and Physicists in the United States," *Library Quarterly*, XIX (1949), 19–35, 119–43.

very problem of communication that the scientific journal was born, in the same century that gave birth to experimental science.

Publication of scientific books during the 17th century was fairly active in a number of centers. Books, however, did not serve the need for more rapid communication. The only effective means was through private correspondence; and the exchange of letters between some of the leading scientists of the day, such as Huygens and Boyle, was voluminous. With the establishment of the scientific journal these "communications" could be published and thereby addressed to many scientists rather than to the small circle that could be covered by private correspondence.

The *Journal des Sçavans* was the first scientific journal to be published, the first number appearing on January 5, 1665. Evidence that it served a real need is provided by the fact that similar publications appeared in England, Italy, Germany, and Holland within a short span of years. The Royal Society of London, as a matter of fact, began the publication of its *Philosophical Transactions* less than three months after the appearance of the *Journal des Sçavans*, the first issue of the *Transactions* appearing on March 1, 1665. It was interesting to note that the first of these publications, the *Journal des Sçavans*, became a model for scientific periodicals intended for the broad reading public and the *Philosophical Transactions* came to be, and still are, a standard for publications of scientific societies.

Other journals of both types appeared in quick succession and by the year 1700, more than thirty scientific journals were being published, or had been published, during this incunable period of the scientific journal.

One journal established in the 17th century, the *Philosophical Transactions of the Royal Society*, is still being published in 1950. The pioneer, *Journal des Sçavans*, remained active for almost 130 years, issuing 111 volumes between 1665 and 1792. Almost from the beginning, however, the life span of a large proportion of scientific journals has been short. Relatively few outlive the individual scientists responsible for their founding and editorial supervision. There are, of course, important exceptions other than the two titles just mentioned. A few 18th century journals are still current: *Curtis's Botanical Magazine* (1787), *Annales de Chimie* (1789), *Journal de l'École Polytechnique* (1795), *London, Edinburgh and Dublin Philosophical Magazine and Journal of Science* (1798), and *Annalen der*

Physik (1799). Many 19th century journals are still being published, but of the journals listed in Bolton's *Catalogue of Scientific and Technical Periodicals*, published by the Smithsonian Institution in 1897, fewer than 20 established before 1850 are still alive. Many hundreds of scientific journals have expired within a very few years of their founding.

EXTRAORDINARY INCREASE IN VOLUME OF SCIENTIFIC LITERATURE

This brings us to one of our primary problems, *viz.*, the extraordinary increase in the volume of scientific literature. With respect to the history of scientific literature, and especially with respect to the problem of effective utilization of scientific knowledge, the outstanding phenomenon with which we must struggle is the vast increase in the volume of publications. The Bolton bibliography of periodicals, to which reference has just been made, described 8,603 different scientific periodicals, exclusive of medicine and exclusive of the transactions of learned societies which are devoted primarily to the proceedings of the societies by which they are edited; and many thousands of new journals have been established in the intervening half century.

The issue of the *American Eclectic* for September, 1841, contained a section on scientific journals. A German writer was quoted in protest against the increasing number of scientific journals in Germany. "Most of the natural sciences," he wrote, "have some great journal of undisputed authority, which is conducted by the ablest men in that department, and sought by their fellow-laborers in the same department. . . . Of *medical* journals there are forty-three in Germany. It must be granted that different modes of practice require different periodicals. . . . But forty-three journals are an astonishing number. What physician who practices daily can read them all, and to what physician who does not practice can they be useful? The number of journals in natural science can be justified only by the number of particular departments, which are sufficiently important to have a separate periodical devoted to them."

This finger in the dike did not stem the flood, because the number of scientific journals being published had increased several hundred fold even before the end of the century in which the protest was written. The reason is clear enough; the increased activity in scientific research made comparable increase in the number of journals inevitable, in order to accommodate the number of scientific papers being written.

Hulme, in his *Statistical Bibliography in Relation to Modern Civilization*,[3] gives data drawn from the *International Catalogue of Scientific Literature* to show the number of papers recorded for 1901–1913 in five sections devoted to biological sciences. In round figures, the number of papers were: anatomy, 27,000; bacteriology and serology, 73,000; botany, 85,000; zoology, 101,000; and physiology, 143,000—or a total of 429,000 papers in thirteen years. And the flood had only begun! We need not burden our discussion of this point with too many astronomical figures, but we can quote current statistics for one of this group of subjects—botany. In 1948, according to the managing editor of *Chronica Botanica*, there were being published 2,000 journals "devoted to plants." He estimates that there are at least 100,000 active workers in the plant sciences, a fact which does not portend a decrease of either interest in or production of botanical literature.

CRUCIAL PROBLEM OF RESEARCH

All of these factors—the cumulative character of science, the extensive interrelationships between the sciences, the growth of scientific journals and, above all, the extraordinary increase in the volume of scientific literature—accent the fact that the problems of use of scientific literature lie principally in the areas of use in relation to fundamental research and the technical application of scientific information in the professions. The cumulative character of scientific discoveries means that each investigator must know the latest developments in his field if he is to extend the horizons of knowledge. The complexity of his problem is increased by the constantly expanding boundaries of knowledge, by the voluminous record which he must explore, and by the necessity for taking account of the relationships between his own field of research and other scientific disciplines.

If it were not for the overview we have just taken of the extraordinary increase in the volume of scientific journals, this brief statement of problems would be deceptively simple. Given a situation, however, in which the researcher can hardly become aware of all of the new books and periodicals in his limited field of research, and in

3. Edward Wyndham Hulme, *Statistical Bibliography in Relation to the Growth of Modern Civilization* (London: Grafton, 1923). Pp. 44.

many instances could not read all of them if they were laid before him, the hopelessness of his need to take account of related data in other fields becomes acute. The problem is further complicated by the necessity not only of his watching developments in the forefront of his field, but also by the occasional necessity of his looking backward through the literature to assure himself (and his colleagues) that he has not overlooked some important discoveries that might have antedated his own present investigations. It is hardly possible to overemphasize the fact that his salvation lies in effective organization of scientific data on the one hand and of its literature on the other.

ORGANIZATION OF SCIENTIFIC DATA

The first of these necessities, namely the organization of scientific data, is met in at least some degree in several types of publications. The most direct is the *handbook* in chemistry, physics, and related fields of engineering, giving physical and chemical constants, formulas, equations, mathematical tables, and similar data. There are handbooks for a wide variety of technical subjects, especially for the various special branches of engineering. The best are frequently revised to assure the latest available data. A good handbook, such as Terman's *Radio Engineers* (McGraw-Hill) may have data condensed from two thousand or more technical articles from many different journals. To be useful they must be frequently revised.

Extensive *compendia* of scientific information exist for a number of special fields. Examples of these are the great German Handbücher, such as *Beilstein* for chemistry, *Geiger and Scheel* for physics, and *Abderhalden* for biology, and similar works for various other branches of science and medicine. Another type of compilation is Sherbourne's *Index Animalium* and similar works which serve to bring together information on systematic zoology and botany.

Another type of publication of increasing importance is the *review*, especially the review journal or review annual designed to summarize the progress made by the most recent research in the subject fields concerned. Annual Reviews, Inc. at Stanford University, California, began the *Annual Review of Biochemistry* some twenty years ago, and has since established similar annuals for physiology, microbiology, physical chemistry, plant physiology, and psychology. Without such publications it would be virtually impossible for any but the most active specialist in a given field to comprehend the advances in many subjects.

This matter of organization and synthesis of new scientific knowledge, however, is not the primary concern of this Conference. We should understand its importance to the scientist and be aware of projects and accomplishments; but our primary concern is with the increasingly difficult problems of bibliographic organization.

BIBLIOGRAPHIC ORGANIZATION

The problem of organizing keys to the published literature of science is no new problem. It has engaged the attention of scientists and bibliographers for many decades. Some of the outstanding early projects undertaken abroad, for international attack on the problem, were the publication of *The Royal Society Catalogue of Scientific Papers*, 1800–1900, founding of the *International Catalogue of Scientific Literature* in 1901 (a casualty of the First World War), and before these, the establishment of the International Institute of Bibliography, from the efforts of which there developed the Brussels expansion of the Dewey Decimal Classification, now the Universal Decimal Classification.

There have been many special publications established to index the literature in particular subject areas; but the problem of overall control of the pyramiding mass of information in scientific publications has yet to be solved. Among the most important efforts made since the war, have been the UNESCO conference on indexing and abstracting held in Paris, and the Royal Society Scientific Information Conference which followed in London, in the summer of 1948. The UNESCO meeting has already been reviewed during this Conference. The Royal Society Conference is represented by a thick volume of the proceedings. A summary of the Conference by Ralph Shaw, who represented the United States Government, appeared in *Science*, August 13, 1948. It is tempting to cover some of the same ground here, but perhaps a quotation from Mr. Shaw's evaluation of the Conference will epitomize its purposes:

"Summarizing the purposes and operation of the Conference, it might be stated that the central theme of the Conference appeared to be removal of blocks, whatever their nature, which interfere with free communication among scientists, wherever they may be located and whatever their fields of specialization.

"If it is agreed that the advancement of science rests primarily upon the genius of each scientist in his laboratory, whether the laboratory be in a great center of research or in an isolated corner of the world, and that each scientist, no matter where he be, must profit from the work of his colleagues, all over the world and of all times, then it must follow that anything which contributes to the freedom and ease of communication among scientists is, per se, a contribution to science."

Serious as the problem of bibliographic organization remains, no discussion of the problem can have the right perspective without initial recognition that researchers in the natural and applied sciences are immeasurably better off than their fellows in the social sciences. It is well for us to review some of the accomplishments as a background for assessing the work yet to be done. We will do this, briefly, through a partial calendar of the subjects.

1. *Mathematics*, in some respects, has coverage of the literature in more complete form in terms of both time span and subject matter than most other subjects, although there are sharp breaks between sources, as in many other subjects. The Royal Society of London *Catalogue of Scientific Papers*, 1800–1900, has a subject index for mathematics. There was published one of the great German bibliographies, *Jahrbuch über die Fortschritte der Mathematik* for 1868–1934, succeeded by *Zentralblatt für Mathematik*, 1931–1941. And since 1940, the field has been covered by an American publication, *Mathematical Reviews*.

2. *Physics* has a similar bibliographic portrait, with an index to the Royal Society *Catalogue*, two German abstract services covering the period since 1845 (*Die Fortschritte der Physik*, 1845–1918; *Physikalische Berichte*, 1920——), and *Physics Abstracts*, 1898 to date, a British publication issued as Part A of *Science Abstracts*. American physicists, however, have been far from satisfied with the current coverage, and through the American Institute of Physics have made an intensive study of the use made of scientific literature by physicists and the usefulness of existing abstracting services. The practical outcome has not been forthcoming as yet, but it seems reasonable to believe that the urgent interest in the rapidly expanding knowledge of physics will force more satisfactory services into publication.

3. *Chemistry* is almost the fair-haired-boy among sciences for several reasons. While there is no index of the Royal Society *Catalogue* outside the fields of mathematics, mechanics, and physics, chemistry has the German *Chemisches Zentralblatt* of long-time fame going

back into the 19th Century (established in 1830 as *Pharmazeutisches Centralblatt*), and *Chemical Abstracts*, of equal, and in this hemisphere greater, fame which covers chemistry from 1907. It publishes some 50,000 abstracts per year in all aspects of chemistry from approximately 5,000 journals, and has annual and decennial indexes which interpret the abstracts in great detail.

4. *The Biological Sciences* are represented currently, since 1926, by *Biological Abstracts*, which in its general features appears to parallel *Chemical Abstracts*. But it covers a much smaller fraction of the total literature and does not have the advantage of decennial indexes. In-so-far as it covers the biological sciences, *Biological Abstracts* is our primary source of information on current publications in botany, zoology, bacteriology, physiology, and their various subdivisions. As with chemistry and physics there are German, and to some extent British, French, etc., counterparts for the various biological sciences. For example, two German *Berichte*, one for general biology and the other for physiology, give coverage of the literature of physiology comparable to that given chemical literature by *Chemical Abstracts*. The accompanying chart shows the relationship of these two *Berichte* to each other and to their lineal predecessors running back to 1856. This chart serves to illustrate, in general, the kind of continuity which is needed for bibliographic organization in all fields.

5. *Applied Physical and Biological Sciences* also have their representatives in the complex fabric of bibliographic journals. The *Bibliography of Agriculture*, for example, is the most nearly complete index for this field that has been published, and it is paralleled for selected English language publications by H. W. Wilson's *Agricultural Index*. Engineering has the *Engineering Index* and *Industrial Arts Index*, both good, but neither as complete as the changing scene in technology needs. Medicine has the current index published by the Army Medical Library, the *Quarterly Cumulative Index Medicus*, *Excerpta Medica*, and others; but here, as in engineering, there is much to be desired in both coverage and currency of publication.

In overview, bibliographic organization in the sciences appears to be a great family of indexing and abstracting journals covering the current literature of all fields. This is, unfortunately, an illusion. There are a number of problem areas responsible for preventing the interest and effort of many agencies from effecting complete coverage of all literature, current and retrospective.

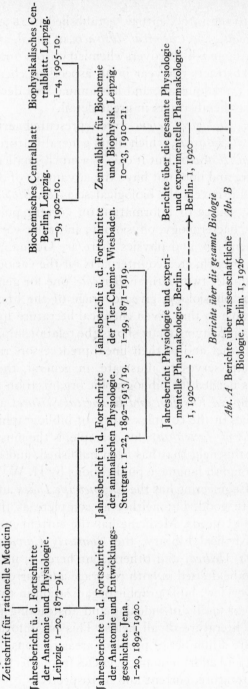

BIBLIOGRAPHIC ORGANIZATION OF PHYSIOLOGY*

GERMANY—BEGINNING 1856

Bericht über die Fortschritte
der Anatomie und Physiologie.
Leipzig. 1–16, 1856–71.
(1856–68 as supplements to
Zeitschrift für rationelle Medicin)

Jahresbericht ü. d. Fortschritte
der Anatomie und Physiologie.
Leipzig. 1–20, 1872–91.

Jahresberichte ü. d. Fortschritte
der Anatomie und Entwicklungs-
geschichte. Jena.
1–20, 1892–1920.

Jahresbericht ü. d. Fortschritte
der animalischen Physiologie.
Stuttgart. 1–22, 1892–1913/19.

Jahresbericht ü. d. Fortschritte
der Tier-Chemie. Wiesbaden.
1–49, 1871–1919.

Jahresbericht Physiologie und experimentelle Pharmakologie. Berlin.
1, 1920 ——— ?

Biochemisches Centralblatt
Berlin; Leipzig.
1–9, 1902–10.

Biophysikalisches Cen-
tralblatt. Leipzig.
1–4, 1905–10.

Zentralblatt für Biochemie
und Biophysik. Leipzig.
10–23, 1910–21.

Berichte über die gesamte Physiologie
und experimentelle Pharmakologie.
Berlin. 1, 1920

Berichte über die gesamte Biologie

Abt. A Berichte über wissenschaftliche
Biologie. Berlin. 1, 1926 ———

Abt. B

* From the John Crerar Library, July, 1950.

PROBLEM AREAS

1. *Conflict of needs.*—The first of these is a conflict of needs. We have noted the statement, "science is progressive and, therefore, ephemeral." Actually this oversimplifies the definition of science with reference to bibliographic problems. It is progressive; and its present rate of progress is very fast. There are many sources attempting prompt reporting for special groups. Such small subject areas as iodine, aluminum, powder metallurgy, atomic energy, and helminth worms, for example, have special abstracting journals—some sponsored by corporations, some by societies, some by government agencies—all trying to help the specialist keep abreast of his own narrow field of research.

The progressive character of science, however, varies from subject to subject and from time to time in the rate of progression. Often, because of the speed of progress, failure of communications, or other contingency, science overruns its front lines; and progress ceases at given points. These points are myriad. There exists, then, the need for organization behind the front, so that investigators who have lost contact with their bases can go back and reestablish liaison with the work already done. It is to the great indexing and abstracting journals referred to above that the scientist or technician goes for aid under such circumstances.

There is a conflict of need in these two situations which leads to great confusion and waste in bibliographic organization. To illustrate this, we can note the fact that in chemistry there are many problems so "hot" that even *Chemical Abstracts*, one of the best, is too slow in its reporting. This may justify—at least, is used to justify—the expenditure of large sums of money in many agencies to fill the relatively brief gap between the publication of original papers in journals and their secondary publication in *Chemical Abstracts*. Examples can be cited for many other fields where there is active research in progress.

2. *Lack of coordination.*—The second general problem area is lack of coordination. There appears to be no operating program of any consequence designed to channel the great investment in bibliographic services of immediate usefulness and the basic indexing and abstracting journals. If the latter were complete in their coverage, this waste might be condoned. Where it is not, and in some fields it is far from complete, this lack of coordination is a serious defect in

our activity. The use of the word, "activity," is purposive. What we need is a program, rather than scattered action.

3. *Duplication.*—A third general problem is wasteful duplication. The problem of duplication in bibliographic publications has troubled librarians and scientists for a long time. It wastes resources that might be used to make coverage more nearly complete. It wastes the time of researchers who must look in two, three, or a dozen places for publications that might be found in one or two. And both kinds of waste contribute to the unmeasured and unmeasurable waste of new research that doesn't get done.

Two examples will serve to accent the problem. The first is that created within the past three years by the establishment of *Excerpta Medica,* a much needed abstract journal in medicine, published in Amsterdam in fifteen sections. The first three sections cover general biological and physiological literature in a high degree of duplication of *Biological Abstracts.* The library which would like to recognize this unjustifiable imposition on libraries and scientists and refrain from subscribing for the offending sections is faced by the "delightful" fact that the subscription price for all fifteen sections is less than the total for the twelve less-duplicating sections at their individual subscription prices. The term "less-duplicating" rather than non-duplicating is used here because the section of *Excerpta Medica* on surgery is in obvious competition with abstract publications already published in Britain and the United States. UNESCO has worked on this particular case without any practical results.

A second example is supplied by data in one of the analyses of abstracts made in the Study of Physics Abstracting sponsored by The American Institute of Physics. Of 1731 abstracts which were published in *Physics Abstracts,* 47 per cent were also published in *Chemical Abstracts;* and 55 per cent of these appeared first in *Chemical Abstracts.*

Before we throw this problem into the hopper with the other problems requiring concerted attention at the national and international level, we should mark it with a large red tag for special attention. The tools on which scientific libraries depend as the keys to their collections, receive only crumbs from the huge lump of "dough" which our country is feeding into the research mill. We should insist that the crumbs be as nourishing as possible. If this metaphor is confused, it is probably all the more apt, to point up the seriousness of the situation.

NEED FOR UNION RECORDS OF LIBRARY HOLDINGS

One of the problems of use which must continue to receive a large part of our attention in the study of bibliographic organization is the further development of aids for location of publications which come to the attention of the potential reader. The problem in the natural sciences is essentially the same as that for the other disciplines. The sources to which the user turns are the National Union Catalog at The Library of Congress, the regional union catalogs, and various kinds of union lists. In one respect, the natural scientists are more fortunate than their fellow workers in the social sciences and humanities. There are numerous sources of information to assist in the location of scientific periodicals; and the fact that a high percentage of use of scientific literature falls within the periodical field makes the locating of needed publications somewhat simpler in the natural sciences than in other subject areas. But the locating of *books* is no less of a problem than in other subject fields.

Because of the extensive amount of thinking devoted to this problem there is no point in dwelling on it at length here, except perhaps to spotlight the problem with one example. Dr. C. Wilbur Rucker and Mr. Thomas E. Keys of the Mayo Clinic in Rochester recently published a catalog of *Atlases of Ophthalmoscopy*. This was prepared to illustrate an exhibit at the 1950 San Francisco meeting of the American Medical Association, designed to celebrate the 100th anniversary of the discovery of the ophthalmoscope by Helmholtz. For each of the 117 atlases there are recorded the holdings of twelve medical libraries in the east, midwest, and far west. An examination of this record demonstrates the need for a union catalog. Not one of the 117 atlases is held by all twelve of the libraries; one atlas is in eleven libraries; three atlases are in ten libraries; and larger numbers of the titles are contained in fewer of the libraries. Nineteen of the titles are in only one library; three of the titles could be located in private libraries only; and six of the atlases could not be located for the exhibit. The largest number of titles, eighty-nine out of one-hundred-seventeen, is held by the Army Medical Library.

ROLE OF GOVERNMENT IN RESEARCH

No discussion of bibliographic organization is complete without examination of the role of government in research. In the issue of *Chemical and Engineering News* for August 23, 1948, there appeared a double spread of pictures headed "Washington: Science Center of the Nation." In February, 1948, the *Oil, Paint and Drug Reporter* carried news of the appointment of Dr. Alexander Wetmore, Secretary of the Smithsonian Institution, as chairman of the Interdepartmental Committee on Research and Development, which had been established in December, 1947 by the President. The agencies represented on this Committee are the Atomic Energy Commission, National Bureau of Standards, Department of Commerce, Federal Security Agency, National Advisory Committee on Aeronautics, Department of Agriculture, Veterans Administration, the Departments of the Army, Air Force and Navy, and the Smithsonian Institution.

These two news items, selected at random from among many, make very obvious the necessity for examining the role played by the Federal Government in the production of scientific literature, either directly by a publishing program or indirectly through the support of research which leads to publication by other agencies. The magnitude of the Government's participation is set forth in the report on *Science and Public Policy* submitted to the President in 1947 by John R. Steelman, chairman of The President's Scientific Research Board, established in 1946.

Of the 137,000 scientists, engineers, and technicians engaged in research in the United States, 30,000 or 21.9 per cent are employed by the Federal Government. And Steelman indicated that the number would be higher except for the fact that "most government agencies . . . have vacancies on their staffs."

The percentage of money expended for research and development by the Government in comparison to industry and the universities is much higher. Steelman's report estimated the total expenditures for 1947 to be $1,160,000,000, with $110,000,000 going to basic research and $1,050,000,000 being devoted to applied research and development. Percentage-wise the Government spent, in 1947, 58.9 per cent of the national expenditure, or $625,000,000. Steelman projected "normal" growth of research and development in the United States to an estimate of $700,000,000 in 1950. Compared with the actual expenditure in 1947, it is apparent that the rate of increase had been greatly accentuated during the war, having jumped more than 300 per cent from 1940 to 1947.

The importance of government activity in scientific research and development is made startlingly clear by noting percentage increases of university, industrial, and governmental research expenditures from 1940 to 1947. These were: university, 45 per cent; industry, 84 per cent; and the Federal Government, *more than 800 per cent*.

These vast expenditures by the Government have thrown the production *and control* of scientific literature out of balance in several serious ways:

1. Normal university expenditures dropped about two-thirds from 1940 to the average for 1941–45, tending to dry up the flow of fundamental research papers going into standard journals;

2. Security classification prevented publication of results of vast amounts of research sponsored by the Government during war; and there is still inadequate machinery for communicating results of scientific information which has been released from such classification;

3. The Government devotes an insignificant portion of its research funds to publication, throwing an all but impossible load on privately supported journals; and

4. The Government has spent sums running into six figures for secondary publication in the form of indexes, abstracts, and other bibliographic services, which have made little or no contribution to strengthening already established publications in these categories.

SUMMARY AND CONCLUSIONS

This paper has attempted to give insight into the nature of science and scientific research adequate to assist in understanding the importance of scientific literature, the ways in which it is used, and some of the inadequacies in bibliographic organization.

The cumulative, yet "ephemeral," nature of science, the interrelationships between the sciences, the vast increases in scientific research, and hence of scientific literature, all combine to make the business of keeping up with front line advances a very difficult and often impossible objective. The scientist needs quick reporting of new publications and solid bibliographic guides to research literature running decades into the past. And he needs to have these in a pattern of bibliographic organization which will make it possible for him to devote a maximum proportion of his time to original research.

The researcher in the natural and applied sciences is more fortunate than his fellows in the social sciences in the amount and quality of indexing and abstracting journals available for his use. But his needs are far from met in coverage of the literature, and in the bibliographic "organization" (and here the word is placed in quotes) the delays in publication and extensive duplication greatly reduce the economy of his research.

And finally, the problem areas have been increased in number and in the seriousness of their effects by the great unbalance in the expenditures of the federal government in research and development on the one hand and the government's contribution to bibliographic organization on the other.

"Science, the Endless Frontier." The endless frontier—no phrase could more aptly describe the quality of continued growth which characterizes science. One of the committee reports on which Dr. Bush based his well known document bearing that title, opens with the statement: "The frontiers of science must be thrown open so that all who have the ability to explore may advance from the farthest position which anyone has attained." This statement related to the freeing of government research reports from security classification. It has wider usefulness as a statement of purpose for all those who struggle with the problems of disseminating scientific information.

Man's curiosity concerning the unknown is so impelling, his need for the values which come from new discoveries so great, that no effort should be spared to develop programs for publication, and procedures and devices for making existing information quickly available. It is obvious that the problems inherent in this briefly stated objective are of such magnitude and complexity that they cannot be overcome except by national and international effort. Individuals, associations, institutes, and government must cooperate to assure that new discoveries are not lost and that all research is conducted at the farthest position on the frontier which anyone has attained.

THE MANAGEMENT APPROACH

THE PROBLEMS OF PHYSICAL ACCESSIBILITY

HERMAN H. FUSSLER

AN INTERESTING pamphlet, probably of the 18th century, the contents of which need not concern us, has as its title *A New Project for the Destruction of Printing and Bookselling; for the Benefit of the Learned World*[1]—perhaps a natural sequel to those famous words, "Of making many books there is no end; and much study is a weariness of the flesh." By far the most interesting part of the book title is the phrase that indicates that the destruction of printing was intended for the benefit of the learned world.

INTRODUCTION

Had printing and bookselling been destroyed, or had the many efforts that man has made to destroy books succeeded, the problems of physical accessibility to books would probably be simpler today—if in fact there were problems at all. Physical accessibility, in a general sense, envisages the establishment of some sort of working relationship at some point in time between a reader and a text. The reader may be any reader and the text may be in any form and may be located anywhere in the world, but until some relationship between the reader and the text has been established, accessibility may not be said to prevail.

The complexity of the subject grows out of the steps or conditions that are precedent to this simple relationship. Many of the conditions that must concern us are the subjects of papers in this conference; others are folklore; while still others are yet emerging and poorly perceived. The bearing of many of the relevant factors, one upon the other, is, on the whole, very intricate. Therefore it is not our intention in this paper to treat of physical accessibility exhaustively or even very systematically; instead we shall endeavor simply to describe some of the more important aspects and problems that are related to the topic. By way of apologia and for the sake of brevity and simplicity we have in several instances made statements

---

1. "[Anonymous] . . . London: printed from the Dublin copy and sold by J. Roberts at the Oxford Arms in Warwick-lane [n.d]."

which for complete accuracy would require much greater qualification and elaboration than we have given them. It is hoped that the consequences of this approach will yield more clarity than confusion.

Many of the current problems of accessibility grow predominantly out of the plethora of books and related graphic materials. You will recall that plethora means "an unhealthy repletion or excess." We must recognize that the immense mass of existing literature is, or may become, unhealthy unless methods are found of digesting, finding, and generally handling it in ways that make us feel that we are the masters of print—rather than its slaves or subjects. In using the words "print" and "books," it is intended throughout that they shall cover the entire spectrum of the ways and forms through which knowledge, usually graphic, has been recorded by man and collected into libraries.

A distinguishing feature of modern culture or non-primitive civilization is its dependence upon the written word as the principal device through which (1) the knowledge of our time is recorded for the future, (2) the state of contemporary knowledge and ideas is communicated, and, finally, (3) the knowledge of the past becomes available to contemporary man. If this is true, or even approximately true, the critical role of the library in relation to the advance and to the preservation of modern civilization becomes obvious, for the library is the major social organization that systematically acquires, organizes, and preserves the books that make the activities described under (1) and (3), above, possible and its role is a major one in connection with the communication of contemporary knowledge as well.

Technological changes, which would modify or supplant the form of the book, are unlikely to make the library obsolete with respect to these activities nor are they likely to alter the essential difficulties of its role with respect to them.

We may, somewhat loosely, say that it is the function of a book to transmit beauty, facts, knowledge, or ideas in some form from man to man. The book or its substitute becomes socially useful actually only when it does so. A book may be ugly or beautiful, it may be a work of art, showing an elaborate and skilled craftsmanship in its physical design and fabrication, it may be owned or purchased because it is valuable or gives prestige rather than because of its contents, yet these purposes are ancillary to the process of communication that I have described.

The modern growth in the bulk of graphic materials, the probable continued acceleration in growth, the growth in the number of persons requiring access to graphic materials with increasingly complex patterns of use and need, and new techniques of publication or reproduction, all are contributing to shifts of fundamental importance in the very foundations of library economy—especially for research, special, and advanced reference libraries. These shifts have affected or will affect the patterns of acquisition, the nature and form of materials to be collected, the methods of bibliographic organization or control of materials, and will greatly sharpen our understanding of what I shall refer to as immediate, as compared with deferred, access to materials. Putting the matter in an over-simplified form, it is my conviction that our professional emphases will shift from a preoccupation with parochially organized and collected resources to a preoccupation with a service based upon local, regional, national, and even international organization and collection of materials.

By way of preface, we must recognize that immediate and deferred access merge one into the other, but that, nonetheless, we may recognize general distinctions between that material which we have at hand in our homes or offices, that which is readily at hand in a local library, and that material which must be acquired when we need it from a distant library, bookseller, or other source. Related to this concept is one which requires that we distinguish between actual use of books and potential use. This leads us to a proposition: *Books, and thus libraries, are useful only insofar as they meet actual or potential needs for use.* This proposition may seem perfectly obvious, but it would appear to have some theoretical, if not practical, relationship to our topic, for, if we observe its conditions carefully, it means that libraries must have use or potential use as a constant criterion for their existence and for their operation; secondly, it implies what *is* obvious but here more formally stated, namely, that physical accessibility, of some sort, is an essential part of use and that we must, in considering access to materials, concern ourselves with at least some aspects of the factors and circumstances that lead to, or are pre-conditions to, the use of books.

Many of these factors could be included under such typical rubrics as: (1) the working methods of readers, (2) the objectives of different readers, (3) the variations in methods for the same reader as his objectives change, (4) the characteristics of books (in the mass) themselves and the generalized patterns in their use, (5) the ways in which readers are led to particular books, (6) the uses they actually make of them, and (7) the relationships between the books that are used in any particular set of circumstances and those books that are relevant to the circumstances, but which, for various reasons, are not used.

In order further to direct our discussion, perhaps this second, and somewhat contradictory, proposition governing access to materials would be useful: *Many libraries do not have sufficient access now to recorded knowledge, yet many libraries are larger than necessary, and access to many parts of recorded knowledge is not distributed according to need.*

Improvement in the accessibility of materials may be expected from the following, closely interrelated sources:

1. An improved understanding of the actual needs of readers and the working methods used by readers in relation to books and other sources of knowledge;

2. An improved understanding of the internal procedures and the economics of operations of libraries in relation to their contributions to the objectives and needs of readers;

3. An extension on a major scale and in several directions of co-operative action between libraries, scholarly societies or institutions, scholars themselves, and other interested agencies or organizations;

4. Greater utilization and development of scientific and technical knowledge and devices applicable to library operations and procedures, and to the learning and scholarly processes that are antecedent or parallel to library operations; and

5. Some shifting of emphases in the expenditures of libraries, preferably accompanied by increased support of many of them.

GENERAL LEVELS OF ACCESS

The very great range in levels of access to books that may be needed by individuals is a conspicuous phenomenon of libraries. In a major simplification of this matter we may observe with some assurance that out of the fifteen to twenty million titles[2] in the world only a relatively small fraction are in potential demand at any one time, and that a far smaller fraction are in actual use. A cumulative extension of the time period would add to the totals for both the books in potential demand and those in actual use, but in any reasonably finite period of time the total number of books covered by

2. Cf. Robert B. Downs (ed.), *Union Catalogs in the United States* (Chicago: American Library Association, 1942), pp. 77–82.

these two kinds of need would remain small relative to the total number in existence. To a very high degree, the major use of books is concentrated among relatively few titles, even in the humanities, and complementarily, there are many, many books for which even the potential demand is almost zero. At this point we simply need to observe that our library economy does not reflect an adequate understanding of this observation.

Because of this relationship between the mass of literature and use, including potential use, we formulate a third proposition: *The frequency of use should be a major—but not an exclusive—factor in controlling accessibility, if conditions of availability do not interfere.* By conditions of availability we mean such prosaic things as rarity, bulk, cost, etc. High frequency of use may exist for a period of either long or short duration—the total period is the relevant factor. The proposition may be applied either to an institution, i.e. a library, or to an individual, but may not be applied to both simultaneously if there is a conflict between them. That is to say, the individual who says to the library, "I use this book more than anyone else and therefore I should be allowed to take it out for a year until I finish using it," must yield to the librarian who finds that the book is extensively used by many other individuals also and must therefore be taken off the shelves for general circulation in order to make it more accessible! Both have the objective of promoting accessibility, but the end result is quite different.

Use must not be used as an exclusive criterion for accessibility, however. It should be supplemented by at least two other factors: (1) qualitative evaluations of use and materials—libraries do not need to provide access to everything that is printed; and (2) an evaluation of potential need or use, as distinguished from actual use.

Accessibility clearly needs to be maximized where use, or potential use, is most frequent or most likely. It can be least at the end of extreme specialization because the number of people using such materials is so small. This may lead us to a fourth proposition: *The general level of accessibility of materials in libraries may vary inversely with the degree of specialization of the materials.* It is important to note that this applies to *general* accessibility, and therefore may not, in the same terms, be applicable to an individual, who is himself a specialist. We also hasten to say that this proposition, if carried too far in the physical division of materials, may have highly undesirable and unforeseen consequences. The proposition is sufficiently dangerous to require many other qualifications also, but the general principle it describes appears reasonably valid.

With these general observations about accessibility in mind, let us examine a few of the methods and techniques of libraries and scholars that have a critical bearing upon access. In the first place, most libraries have thus far tried to serve their constituencies as though the serving library were the only one in the world. Despite some real measures of cooperation, the guiding principle of most libraries has been to be as complete and as autonomous for their constituencies as possible. Our distinctions between real use and potential use have not been realistic. Our definitions of scope and readers' needs have been lax and crude, if they have existed at all. As a consequence, buying is often a random, buck-shot technique, partially intended to provide for the ill-defined needs of the future as well as those of the present. Our techniques and methods of organizing our holdings have shown similar traits of rugged individualism.

In the United States we have conspicuously cultivated and promoted another aspect of access which I will call the "spot," "immediate access," or "delivery-on-demand" theory. We have been prone to regard our services as seriously deficient if we could not produce and deliver one volume out of a million or two upon request and within a very few minutes. This is a laudable achievement, and because of it we have tended to look with a certain hauteur upon our European colleagues who frequently insisted upon at least twenty-four hours' notice from a reader of his desire for any book not in the reading room. There are at least three questions we ought to ask ourselves: What does it add to our costs to deliver *all* books instantly as against some other system? What are the benefits or losses to scholarship of instant access? What would be the consequences of access to a major fraction of research literature under a system that required, say, twenty-four hours' notice? In short, instead of treating all books alike, what are the favorable and unfavorable results, both in cost and service, of a library pattern that would distinguish between books to which immediate, high speed and "spot" access is provided and books *to which a very well organized system of deferred access is provided?*

We have treated a book, once added to a collection, as sacrosanct, and, as a consequence, collections or parts of collections have become static. Obsolescence and utter desuetude have subjected the use of books to the risks of a Gresham's law effect which we have been prone to ignore or to defend as virtuous.

I hasten to say that these things have not been done deliberately nor through neglect or ignorance. The words in a recent article concerning another profession are conspicuously relevant to librarians as well. I have substituted librarian or its equivalent in the appropriate places.

"No one can work with librarians without being keenly aware of their high-minded devotion not only to their immediate duty but to the cause of American education. They are agents, not masters, of those interested in libraries, and their anxiety to do what is best is constant. Like all good agents they are bound by economic facts, by most material and practical considerations, by the wishes of those they serve, and by a specific duty to weigh the merits and demerits of all suggested change. They are also professionals and specialists, keenly aware of amateurish vagaries. By rushing from one quick idea to another they could obviously do a great disservice. If real changes are to occur they must come not by the highhanded will of the agents alone, but by the wish and consent of the parties concerned. A great deal of thought has already gone into the problem, and, judging from past experience, changes will take place and remedies will doubtless be found for all these dangers."[3]

The academic profession is highly conservative in its methods and, even if it were not, the habits, customs, and traditions of generations of scholars are neither lightly nor easily changed. The nature of books themselves and the book market in particular has had much to do with our customs and procedures. One must still seize one's opportunities to buy books when they are offered or often do without. A book once discarded could not be recalled. The evolution of strength in a field, occasionally as a result of a gift, bequest, or endowment, has created its own peculiar pressure to maintain and improve that strength if at all possible. These are things with which all librarians are familiar; therefore, we shall not labor the points. These are among the many customs and traditions, however, that have strongly influenced the approaches to the problems of accessibility. They must be considered in any step directed toward a solution.

3. F. D. Ashburn, "How Do You Test a Student?" *Atlantic Monthly*, CLXXXVI (July, 1950), 57.

THE SIZE OF LIBRARIES AND THE QUANTITIES OF LITERATURE

There are a few items that are too conspicuous to be dismissed with the casual listing above; one of these relates to the amount of literature to which immediate access may be required.

It is reasonably apparent that a consideration of general levels of access and the objectives and control of any one library will reveal certain broad categories of use and reading levels that require access to entirely different quantities of literature. The number of books in a school library (excluding duplicate copies) may be a few hundred or a few thousand and they will be found completely adequate for the potential and the actual needs of the library's constituency. A high school library might need a somewhat more extensive library. A college and a general public library would usually need even more. The graduate student and the advanced specialist need access to progressively more, until finally one may reach a situation where the probable scope of a field may require access to all the literature that exists on a particular topic without reference to its location, language, form, bulk, or cost. The interesting thing about the later parts of this progression is that, within very broad limits, the actual amount of material used by any one individual within any fixed period of time may not vary too much, or, more accurately stated perhaps, the use is unlikely to exceed certain quantitative limits. The *potential* or *probable* use pattern may require a very large number of titles—sometimes an enormous number—but the actual number used in a month or in a year or even ten years will under most circumstances be only a fraction of the required accessible title span— and frequently a very small fraction indeed. Since access presents increasingly difficult problems in direct proportion to the amount of literature that must be secured and controlled, we will, from this point on, give most of our attention to the very large library—and especially to the research library.

It is for this reason that the vast majority of books in a research library are not used in any one year, and it is the reason why a surprising number of them will never be used. This pattern of disuse, if we may call it that, occurs however even in relatively small public libraries.

In the general university library or the specialized research library, the existence of seldom—or never—used books does not necessarily mean that the book selection has been bad. It means simply that the pattern of probable use cannot be met by the few hundred best known or most readily available titles in a field, but may require tens of thousands of titles. As any investigator or librarian knows, this pattern of potential need, but little actual use, has its antecedents in the characteristics of advanced study and investigation.

In fact, the area of potential need for many investigators goes well beyond the resources that even the larger libraries can provide now or have any hope of providing in the future. Thus we see the dilemma of the library with a clientele having such needs: many, if not most, of the books that the library has on its shelves are but very seldom, if ever, used, yet access to more books is both desired and needed. Furthermore, at the outer limits of specialization our criteria of what to add to our collections tend to be determined more by the funds available, and the accident of booksellers' offerings, than by any realistic appraisal of current or potential need.

The dilemma is accentuated by several other factors. Library space is not free. Congestion ought not to become a chronic disease of libraries or it may one day choke them to death. If we must rely upon our present techniques and any likely scale of future resources, our chances of winning the race to keep up with our—admittedly unsatisfactory—definitions of potential need are not very attractive in view of the continuously expanding scholarly interest in the books and records of the present as well as of the past, of which we have only partial holdings. Under a continuation of these conditions access would continue to become worse rather than better.

The emphasis upon the size of libraries as measured by the volumes they contain is a tradition that has appealed to scholars, to librarians, to accrediting agencies, and to the general public over a long period of time. Under this tradition, quantity and quality have been synonymous and it is still the custom to think of the largest library as the "best" library for all practical purposes. It may have its antecedents in the past when most of the books that were in existence were potentially desirable acquisitions for a library. Books were then scarce and carried a value and prestige that no longer prevails in economic terms, but still lingers in our prestige values. Under these early conditions it was not unreasonable to assume that the largest library was—other things being approximately equal—the best library. It is still hard to refute the claim that if one is promoting easy access to books, the best way to do it is to get more books. But refute it we must.

The fact that rapid and indefinite growth of libraries has dire consequences for us has received attention, but not always of the kind it deserves. The rate of growth not only exceeds the building capacities of most institutions, but is now probably well in excess of the rate of functional obsolescence of library structures quite apart from their book capacities. The economic burden of rapid obsolescence of library buildings is certainly to be avoided if at all possible.

This does not mean that libraries have spent or are spending too much money nor that all of them are too large, nor that they can or should stop growing. Quite the contrary, it is probable that most libraries today are seriously undersupported in relation to their services both for current operations and for physical plant. It does mean that large capital expenditures for physical plant may be more difficult to secure in the future. And it does mean that librarians must examine their services and their operations more critically to make sure that we are producing the maximum service for each dollar that is spent. It does mean that growth based upon pride, emotion, and tradition, rather than upon functional requirements, should stop.

THE ECONOMICS OF RESEARCH LIBRARIES

To place a dollar value upon the cultural experience of reading a book or a poem that enlightens or stirs one profoundly is clearly impossible. Yet to assume that, as a consequence, no economic principles apply to libraries is equally unrealistic. Presumably, the services of libraries to society are worth what the libraries cost, or society would stop paying for them. Yet this oversimplifies the matter, for society may not quickly grasp the costs nor the values of such intangible services, nor the alternatives that may be available.

The task before the librarian should be one of appraising the effectiveness of his services, the costs of alternative kinds of services, and the economic impact of various levels or kinds of service upon his constituency. For the sake of simplicity, let us arbitrarily agree that in their internal operations libraries are reasonably efficient from an economic point of view based upon the existing concepts of the organization of materials and the nature of physical accessibility to be provided. It is, however, toward these two points that we should direct our most critical scrutiny.

While Library of Congress and H. W. Wilson unit cards have become widely used in cataloging processes, the fundamental view of the technique and its related procedures is that of unique performance. Every library tends to catalog every book as though it were doing so in a vacuum. The economic waste must be substantial *if* there is any alternative way of securing adequate bibliographic control of holdings. Secondly, we need to redefine our objectives in cataloging, to determine whether the process is, or should be, intended: (1) to produce a variety of bibliographic information about particular books; (2) to supply a finding list for the holdings of a particular library; or (3) to provide all possible approaches to knowledge contained in a particular library. To encourage more critical scrutiny of this problem, I am willing to assert that if our orientation must be shifted from the purely local level of resources to encompass resources beyond the holdings of an individual library, then some of the premises underlying the present cataloging procedures are unsound, uneconomic, and functionally inefficient.

Nor can we ignore the economic aspects of our handling of resources. I have indicated: (1) that our traditions require us to secure locally as many books as we can lay our hands on; (2) that we organize, house, and service these books as if they were all of equal importance; (3) that, of the books in any large library, only a few are in actual use and that even the number for which there is a potential demand is likely to be substantially less in many subject areas than are the actual holdings of the library.

This situation, even if it is only approximately true, represents substantial economic waste and inefficiency *if there are alternative methods of securing prompt and economically and scholarly efficient access to materials that are not held locally.* The increase in efficiency would come from savings in the non-productive purchase, organization, and housing of materials. As we shall indicate below, alternative methods are not now in effect, except on a very limited scale, and as a consequence the existing pattern of providing for physical accessibility has evolved naturally enough. It is our thesis, however, that the alternatives can be developed and that their development is critically important in the face of a growing failure of traditional techniques.

CHARACTERISTICS OF THE LITERATURE AND PATTERNS OF USE

There are certain characteristics of literature, too, that are closely related to questions of accessibility. Of particular significance are the findings of those studies that describe in general terms the literature that is most likely to be required in some general reading situation. Thus far, these studies have been largely concentrated in the sciences and technology. In the sciences it is abundantly clear that most of the literature required in a field will have certain very definite characteristics: for example, far more use will be .nade of journals than books; the literature of certain countries is far more important than that of others; there is an exponential relationship between total references and total periodical titles (a few titles supply a high proportion of the references); and there are real limitations by period.

It is not expected that such sharp patterns can be established for non-scientific disciplines, but we believe that further investigation will show definable patterns that will enable a librarian to predict more precisely than he now can the probabilities governing the use of literature. Such studies should be allowed to govern access only in part, however, for otherwise there would tend to be a narrowing and self-reinforcing effect. Such studies can be most useful in distinguishing general levels of accessibility.

The existing studies in this field and general empirical observations will almost certainly reveal a growing complexity in the subject interrelationships in patterns of use. These interrelationships are themselves sufficient to present an increasingly difficult accessibility problem to libraries quite apart from problems growing out of the growing mass of literature.

COOPERATION

It should be apparent, at once, that no single panacea is going to be found which will greatly extend our physical access to materials. One of the most important of the various steps that may be directed toward an improvement of the situation is increased cooperative action. The fundamental problem we must solve is maintenance of, and improvement in, the access to an existing body of literature and an ever-expanding increment to it. There is little reason to doubt that the maintenance of general, broad, and relatively inclusive access to the literature of any major subject or series of subjects will become increasingly difficult of attainment for any one institution. Yet in opposition to this trend there is, and will continue to be, an increasing pressure for access to broad literature coverage. At least one implication of these divergent trends is a fragmentation of the literature. This presents serious intellectual hazards. If no one institution can command the needed or the desired literature through traditional methods because of limitations in its resources of space, personnel, and money, then we must try to accomplish it through joint effort and other means. It is important that these means be constructive and progressive rather than admissions of defeat or expediency. They must offer us so much more than we are likely to be able to achieve, acting individually, as to show an obvious and major intellectual gain.

What elements in the situation are indicative of greater success through joint library action than seems possible through individual library action? The most important and fundamental element is our observation that the books in larger libraries are, as a mass, relatively inactive and unused. As we have indicated, this is not a desirable economic situation, because of the unproductive capital investment in getting the unused book to the shelf, and the net addition to current operating costs in keeping it there.

The pool of books which are actually not used and for which use is predictably low represents a real drain on institutional resources which might be spent to greater advantage by the library. A possible analogy is in investing a great sum of money in land and a dam for a hydro-electric system when the generator capacity of the plant needs only a small fraction of the water backed up in the unnecessarily large reservoir. The reservoir may be beautiful and a source of great pride and prestige, good for fishing or sailing, but it contributes nothing to the functional system for which it was created. To carry the analogy a little further, the present pattern of libraries might be said to represent a wide-spread scattering of hydro-electric reservoirs where some are, at times, too large, while others may be too small, and the whole system has an antiquated or non-existent electric distribution system. In order to bring power to the points of need, with greatest flexibility, we erect a distribution system for the power, rather than attempt to move or store the water.

We know that unnecessary duplication exists in both our existing holdings (with mal-distribution of access) and in our current acquisitions, and that through this duplication in effort we actually add to the external costs of acquiring materials, and the internal costs of maintaining them.

We should at once point out that some—and perhaps extensive—duplication of material is necessary. The relation to duplication might be stated as a fifth proposition: *Our goal should be the avoidance of unnecessary duplication of both current and antiquarian materials which are in such slight demand that a high level of access is unnecessary if alternative access of some sort is assured.*

Since cooperation is hardly new to libraries, one may ask, what would cooperation offer in connection with these problems that is not being done now? At present, substantial though certain aspects of cooperation are, it has not greatly affected our operations. The Farmington Plan has perhaps made the greatest step in this direction, but important as it is, it has not yet seriously affected the acquisitions or the resources of most libraries. There is in fact no reason why it should. We shall not see major consequences or derive significant advantages from cooperation until our interrelationships generally make us interdependent. Under these conditions a library will acquire the works that it needs currently and the ones for which it is *sure* there will be a substantial future need. For less needed current and antiquarian publications it will rely upon a pattern of institutional cooperative coverage of the world's literature, based upon period, language, country, form, or subject categories in which it will share the obligations of coverage. These obligations would be similar to those assumed in the Farmington Plan, except that they would be chosen to fit the needs and resources of the associated institutions more carefully. In this way no one's freedom to acquire anything is in any way restricted, one assumes an obligation to collect in a certain definite area, and *one assumes an obligation to make the materials in this area readily available to other institutions.* Through these reciprocal obligations the freedom *not to acquire* would be greatly extended.

This seems so simple that one wonders why more has not been done. A principal reason is easily stated. Plans for the broad cooperative acquisition of materials cannot succeed on any general basis unless, at the same time, steps are taken *to insure the actual availability or accessibility of materials cooperatively acquired,* and this, in general, we have not done. Availability implies not only adequate bibliographic coverage of the materials but an acceptable means of securing actual physical access to the materials. This is so important in fact that a sixth proposition might be stated in this way: *The extent to which the cooperative acquisition and sharing of materials may be carried is directly dependent upon the actual accessibility of such materials.* Actual accessibility in turn is dependent upon the mobility of the book or reproductions of it, the costs and speed of such mobility, and adequate bibliographic information concerning the existence, relevance, and location of the cooperatively acquired book. This information must be available to the users of libraries; it is not enough to have it in the hands of librarians.

I will give but one illustration of this point. One might expect to find a substantial saving and consequent extension of resources in a cooperative relation such as that now prevailing between the libraries of Duke University and the University of North Carolina because there has been an exchange of all main entry cards between the two libraries, there is a daily delivery service, and there are agreements on area specialization. In contrast, if Duke has even marginal interests in one or more of the Farmington Plan subjects for which the New York Public Library has assumed an obligation, Duke will probably feel a much stronger obligation to collect these same books than if the subjects were being covered by the University of North Carolina. It would feel this way because catalog cards for such items, instead of being available to its constituency and in its own catalog, would be in the Union Catalog of the Library of Congress; the New York Public Library will not loan the items; copyright might prevent the microfilming of any items that were located and wanted; and finally the New York Public Library is too far away to visit easily.

The common ways in which we have secured bibliographic knowledge of each other's holdings have been through correspondence, the Union Catalog of the Library of Congress, or regional and other special union catalogs, and the *Union List of Serials* and other union lists. We have secured physical access to each other's holdings largely through personal visits, interlibrary loans, and photographic reproduction. We should see at once that while all of these steps are important, they are too cumbersome, slow, and expensive to offer accessibility in any way comparable to that which results from ownership of the book. Further cooperative action therefore must be contingent upon greatly improved accessibility and a more critical definition of local needs and objectives.

STORAGE LIBRARIES

A second method of attack upon access, the storage library, has, on more than one occasion, been accused of making access more difficult of attainment. The storage library at the present time exists in at least three different varieties: (1) a storage depot for the deposit of books from a single library, or library system; (2) a cooperatively owned and operated building in which the cooperating institutions may rent space for the separate deposit of their own materials; and (3) a cooperatively owned and operated library in which the deposited materials are available to and shared by all member institutions. The deposit library exists because libraries find, when they become congested, that certain materials are so seldom used and so unlikely to be used that they do not justify the same degree of accessibility that other kinds of material in the library require. The segregation of these little-used materials to space that is usually less expensive, that permits more compact shelving, that eliminates shifting, that need not be kept lighted and heated to the same extent necessary for a working library, frequently may offer economies that more than compensate for the apparent loss in accessibility and the increased costs of serving the individual item when service is required. The gain in the most cooperative plan above, over individually owned or rented storage, would presumably grow primarily out of savings in sharing overhead and operating costs, through the elimination of duplication, and through the major addition it may make to the resources of any one library.

The difference in this kind of cooperation is dramatic for it offers a particular library a net reduction in the number of volumes it must retain for immediate access at the same time that it yields a net addition to the total resources of that library for deferred access. The over-all gains may thus be of striking importance. The new Midwest Inter-Library Center has been planned by a group of middle western university libraries to achieve exactly these goals as well as other kinds of cooperative access to materials.

It is evident that in a plan of this type one must consider carefully the losses and gains of sacrificing instantaneous access to a part of one's resources, and substituting for it delayed access to much greater resources. The Midwest Inter-Library Center intends to give service by mail with ordinary shipments arriving in 24 to 48 hours to all of its members. Communication to the Center or to any member library may be by teletype. The freeing of space in local libraries for more urgently needed materials, the gain in access to a larger body of materials, and other real and tangible benefits are believed to be sufficient to outweigh the loss of instantaneous access to infrequently used materials. With the distribution of copies of the original catalog cards of deposited materials to member institutions, with the provision of two-way teletype communication, and with the member institutions all within a 24–48 hour parcel post delivery area, the conditions of our sixth proposition, governing ease of access, have been met to a very high degree. For many kinds of material the gains would far outweigh the advantages of an unnecessarily wide-spread distribution of microcards which has recently been suggested as an alternative to the storage library.

We expect to see more—though not too many—regional libraries based upon this pattern since they offer advantages that are not attained through cooperative acquisition, and which no one institution can attain for itself. The areas which they cover should be as large as the transportation system of the region and the pattern in the concentration of materials will permit.

INTER-LIBRARY LOANS

That there is already cooperative access to much of the nation's resources is amply demonstrated by the number of inter-library loan transactions that are now current. Inter-library loans are becoming a big business and are an extremely important auxiliary form of access for many research purposes. This should not obscure certain defects in the present system. The method of locating materials is often haphazard and is certainly expensive. Plans for using the National Union Catalog at the Library of Congress for the clearing of all inter-library loans have yet to come to fruition. The general methods and techniques of borrowing tend to be expensive and slow. Finally, the burden of expense is not equitably distributed and does not fall equitably upon the principal beneficiaries of the service. The large libraries almost without exception loan more than they borrow. The University of Chicago, for example, last year loaned almost five books for every one borrowed, and to compound the difficulty, the ones to whom we loan are not identical with the institutions from which we borrow. We believe the fundamental principle of generous inter-library loaning of books is sound and should be extended. We believe, however, that the time may be very close indeed when all borrowing libraries should expect to pay a reasonable fee for the staff time required in the loaning library. Such charges would not invalidate the principle of access, but they would require that the beneficiary would pay a fair part of the actual labor cost of the service which is requested. Such fees would still cost the borrowing library less than other ways of getting access to the material and may be appropriately borne by the borrowing library as extensions of service or book resources. Obvious difficulties are presented in the application of this principle on the part of state and federally supported libraries, and this is hardly the place to venture possible approaches to the problem. We believe that the present system is important in providing access to certain kinds of materials and that its further extension may require a more equitable distribution of costs.

BIBLIOGRAPHIC ORGANIZATION

The relation of bibliographic organization to physical access is of very great importance. Since this is the subject of this Conference, extended remarks on the topic within this paper are out of order. We shall therefore merely mention some of the more obvious aspects of the relationship.

The traditional arrangement of books on the shelves in American libraries was an admission that the catalog might not serve all users satisfactorily. We will treat this aspect of bibliographic organization under the heading of "Local Accessibility" below.

A far more important aspect of bibliographic organization is the extent to which it may expand or reduce the need for access. We are all familiar with the way in which inclusion of a periodical title in one of the more widely available general indexing services may increase demand for that title, quite apart from its merits. It should be recognized that one of the great potential gains of good bibliographic organization is an opposite effect. Under these conditions, the bibliographic coverage of the field is sufficiently broad to indicate the existence of relevant literature, and the nature of the bibliographic data is such that the reader may make, with confidence, both positive and negative decisions as to his need for the original materials. If this becomes a general characteristic of a part of the bibliographic organization of the major fields of knowledge, it can be extremely beneficial in relation to problems of immediate access, and especially in connection with deferred and cooperative access. The absence of such bibliographic information means that we will always have to acquire, borrow, or reproduce materials which will subsequently be found irrelevant to the study in process. This is economic waste indeed.

Actually, one may hypothesize that many of the traditions and customs in the organization and growth of libraries have their origins in the inadequacy, or sheer absence, of bibliographic coverage. In the absence of adequate bibliographic coverage, the only way in which a library could bring together information or knowledge concerning a subject was to collect as many books as possible. You will see the improvement in practice if we examine the procedures of a few modern industrial organizations, which may maintain very small working libraries, but which systematically acquire microfilm or photostats of *all* articles that appear relevant to their interests by a careful and systematic checking of abstracts and bibliographies. The situation is one of considerable efficiency in comparison to the maintenance of an exhaustive library, though if extended too far, the impact upon the support of original publication might become a problem.

We should also look forward to an increasing number of devices in which the original literature might carry with it its own bibliographic organization.

PHOTOGRAPHIC REPRODUCTION

Photographic reproduction, and particularly microphotographic reproduction, is one of the most important modern techniques for increasing the accessibility of many kinds of scholarly materials. Cameras have filmed manuscripts at Mount Sinai and Mount Athos, as well as in most of the great archival depositories of the world, and the copies thus made have become easily available to readers halfway around the world. Each day thousands of journal articles are being microfilmed and sent to libraries, industrial organizations, and readers all over this country, and to foreign countries as well. The texts of newspapers and other files of materials on wood-pulp paper that would otherwise have been lost and thus made completely inaccessible have been retained and made even more readily available. Most of the work on the Jefferson papers is being done through photographic facsimiles. There are hundreds of other applications being made of photographic reproduction in the solution of scholarly problems. Because libraries still have books and look much as they did before the wide-spread use of photography for library and scholarly purposes, there has been some tendency to belittle the importance to scholarship of these techniques. While we should not belittle, we should not be blind to the limitations of the techniques either. Some basic observations may aid us in placing these techniques more precisely in their proper relationship to accessibility.

Other things being equal, a reader under most conditions would still prefer to read from an original rather than from a machine.[4] Most readers would prefer to read materials in reproduction, even using a projection machine, rather than travel to the originals (unless the distance is very short) or do without them entirely. Photographic

4. A growing number of readers seem to prefer old newspapers on microfilm to the originals, however.

reproduction offers, in addition to a wide variety of important services, two major essentials to libraries and readers. The first service comes through the way in which it can supplement the printed book in increasing the material which a library may acquire, in more or less conventional ways, to add to its resources for relatively immediate accessibility. The second service is one which deserves more attention than it has received—the extension of deferred accessibility-on-demand to materials which are not held by the local library. Microcards and microprint, both of which require editions—even though the editions be smaller than those conventional in printing—can now be used in extension of normal forms of acquisition. Microfilm can economically be acquired either as an edition copy or as a single acquisition to meet an existing need —in contrast to acquisition in anticipation of a future need. The gains in the latter are very great, for it means that large masses of highly specialized and peripheral literature—systematically and cooperatively collected—would be available on a deferred basis, when needed, at costs less than multiple acquisition, cataloging, and storage. Further, we should note that microfilms made from master negatives will not go out of print, and may therefore be acquired when and if needed. This to a slightly lesser degree is fine for microcards also.

To make such a system more effective, what are the essential requirements? In the first place we must be able to learn easily, quickly, and inexpensively of the existence and the precise location of relevant materials. There must be good photographic services to which the materials may be taken. The book must be gotten to the camera quickly, the reproduction must be made well and quickly too, and the reproduction must reach the reader promptly and at a cost that is reasonable in terms of the need or use and the direct and indirect cost of alternative methods of securing access.

The copyright laws should be amended in the interests of scholarship to permit those kinds of reproduction of textual materials which do not impinge upon the basic and substantial rights of authors and publishers. And finally, the product must lend itself to easy, widespread, and inexpensive use.

We should also look forward to major extensions of photographic and partial-photographic techniques in improving the local access of individuals to materials within a particular library, and in extending the means of communication for current information, in part by-passing the library.

This topic is again one of some complexity, but in many respects photographic access is of critical importance in relation to the success of any broad plan for the cooperative acquisition of original materials. Suffice it to say that I do not think microfilm, microcards, or microprint, as they exist today, are the final and perfect solutions to this particular application of reproduction. I believe we will see further major important technical developments in this area, and that such technical advancements will inevitably increase accessibility by promoting ease of use, by reducing costs, and by faster availability.

LOCAL ACCESSIBILITY

Perhaps we should, before concluding, recognize the existence of important aspects of accessibility on a purely local level. Even on the local scale, the distribution of library facilities appears to have great importance in their use. Thus we see an increasing amount of attention given by public librarians to the location of regional and branch libraries because they have long since recognized that the main, central libraries in the downtown areas of large cities will not suffice for the needs of their constituencies, and that physical accessibility, much more intimate in character, is an essential part of use. There are many situations in which the absence of reasonable physical accessibility will result in a complete absence of use.

The problem is an important one in connection with colleges and universities. The extremely compact college or university campus can develop a more closely centralized library system than can the university which spreads through many acres of land or even finds itself in various parts of a city. It is my understanding that a member of the faculty of the University of Chicago has said that a faculty member can walk two blocks to get to the University Library, but that he can go no farther. The psychological and physiological implications of this two-block limitation involve knowledge that has been withheld from me, but there is something to it nonetheless. There is something to it in the sheer expenditure of time involved. We must recognize that students and faculty members, as well as housewives and other users of libraries, have things to do other than read books in a library. This means that they can afford a certain expenditure of time to get to and from a library from their other tasks wherever these may be conducted, but that if the time is disproportionately high the social cost may be too great. Clearly the factors are complex; the time of all individuals is not equally valuable; the motivations are not equally strong; and the patterns of use differ markedly for various subjects, as well as for various individuals, and for various purposes at different times.

Thus one can easily see that it would be possible for a busy faculty member to spend fifteen minutes crossing a university campus to get to a main library, if when he got there he could be sure that his time might be efficiently spent and if his purposes justified a stay of half a day or so for serious work. On the other hand, if his need at the moment is the verification of a single reference, the derivation of a word, or some similarly detailed factual problem, requiring short-duration use of bibliographic resources, his vexation will be extreme if he must expend a disproportionate amount of time in getting access to the material as compared with the time spent in using it. It would be difficult to ascertain the limits of an acceptable ratio of time spent in securing access to time spent in use, but that we need such a ratio is fairly evident. There must be limits in the ratio that one cannot repeatedly cross successfully; better reference and communication facilities may be the answer to a part of the short-duration use.

On the other hand, we should recognize that accessibility under some circumstances may be so great as to cause unrecognized harm. This is particularly true in large libraries where there is a natural tendency to divide the library by some sort of subject and form division, presumably because of the convenient physical access and for administrative reasons. This division can easily be functionally undesirable, depending upon the way in which the library is used, the number of people who use it, and the relationships that may exist to other subject disciplines. Having immediate and convenient access to one subject may entail undesirably distant and inaccessible relationships to other subject fields.

It is also important to note that libraries, although they are composed of individual books—which seem capable of ready subdivision into various kinds of associated groupings—are in reality perhaps more organic wholes than we have thought; that a good library serving serious purposes of study and investigation must have a certain array of books and associated facilities to operate effectively. A library implicitly requires a working relationship between books, staff, and bibliographic apparatus together with an appropriate physical plant. The dispersion of these kinds of facilities into very small units will inevitably produce some attenuation in them and we may once again be faced with the interesting problem of determining whether or not over-all efficiency is improved or hurt by such dispersion.

Finally, in this connection, we should note that accessibility is relative even within a library structure and the kind of accessibility of the old, closed, and isolated stacks of the library in which no books were evident, except to the initiated few who had permits which would take them into the stacks, and the new Princeton Library or the new Lamont Library at Harvard are of entirely different orders. Immediate physical accessibility has always been regarded by public librarians as being of substantial importance in the use of the library. Motivations of librarians and readers have not always been the same, but in recent years especially, the increasing trend to direct access has been unmistakable—today one might as well deprive a graduate student of his right arm as of access to the stacks. It is not my desire in any way to take issue with this trend, but I would like to point out that: (1) studies have shown clearly that reliance upon the subject classification of books as a device for revealing information is likely to leave one in considerable ignorance of relevant materials; (2) the maintenance of such an arrangement of books is a very expensive operation in both time and space in a large library; and (3) some very respectable investigation, reading, and studying have been done in libraries in which the reader was never allowed to go near the books in the stacks and where, as a consequence, they could have been arranged in any pattern to suit the librarian's whim. If his whim led him to arrange them by size, however, he might be able to shelve perhaps twice as many books in the same space.

Despite these major reservations concerning the lack of economic and functional efficiency in the subject arrangement of books, I feel that for many kinds of use, direct shelf access to books in some sort of subject arrangement is, for the present at least, desirable and may actually be relatively more efficient than an approach to the books through intermediate bibliographic devices. The current problems seem to me to grow out of our failure to appraise critically the effectiveness—or lack thereof—of the existing methods of arrangement and of the kinds of books and uses for which such arrangement may be useful or necessary as compared with those for which it is not. Such direct access may be a vestigial residue of tradition—with the Rapid

Selector in sight—but I am not convinced that we can, or that we should try to, channel all approaches to books through the Selector or even related bibliographic devices. We should certainly educate our constituencies in the realities of direct use and its limitations.

CONCLUSIONS

Both explicitly and implicitly, I have tried to indicate several major trends that seem to me likely to carry into the future, yet there are many aspects of the topic that remain untouched. The whole question of how readers approach books and their methods in finding and using books deserves far more research attention than it has received. The effects of ultra-high-frequency communication, demonstrated a few months ago under the name of Ultra-fax, open up possibilities of extremely high speed transmission of very large masses of material that may have a critical bearing upon future patterns of accessibility. Less exciting but more immediately prospective is the gradual linking of libraries, first by teletype, then by some type of facsimile circuits, perhaps of more conventional design than Ultra-fax.

We have unfortunately ignored the whole topic of accessibility to knowledge without the library. It is a fertile and extremely important field. We should certainly look forward to seeing the library by-passed—to the advantage of the reader, I hasten to say—in the handling of certain kinds of current information especially. The list of omissions could easily be extended.

We must recognize that emotion, pride, tradition, and library and scholarly methods will have to be set aside or modified if we are to succeed in greatly increasing cooperative access. While some aspects of any program for greater coverage of bibliographic resources will require greater financial resources, we must acknowledge that our present facilities could go much further than they now do if we were able to integrate our resources for our common needs. Let no one minimize the difficulties which we face, but at the same time, no one should minimize the importance of the objectives which we must seek. Our goal is not the "destruction of printing and bookselling," but is, indeed, "for the benefit of the learned world."

SUBJECT CATALOGING IN THE SUBJECT-DEPARTMENTALIZED LIBRARY

RAYNARD C. SWANK

THIS paper is written to explore the case for decentralization of subject cataloging and classification, together with subject bibliography, in university libraries organized along subject-departmental lines. For the sake of argument, decentralization is favored. Nothing is immediately urged or recommended, however, except that each of us flex his imagination and apply himself to a major cataloging problem.

My interest in this problem has a fourfold origin.

First, three years ago I wrote a paper called "The Catalog Department in the Library Organization."[1] After acknowledging the close relationship between order work and cataloging, I said that the relationship between cataloging and bibliography is still more close and that their functional unity might be expressed administratively by creation of a combined catalog and bibliography department. I then described how such a department might function in a centralized library with a general reference service of the traditional kind. But I begged a question rather badly by devoting only one paragraph at the end of the paper to the status of a central bibliography department in the subject-departmentalized library. The present paper is intended to finish that paragraph.

Second, I find no clear evidence that the implications of subject-departmentalization for cataloging have ever been squarely faced. Our present system of subject cataloging is a logical complement to centralized service, as exemplified by the general reference department. As long as the spotlight shines on general reference and circulation, with the departmental libraries remaining in the background, the general subject catalog, supported by its departmental offspring, is appropriately cast in the lead role. But when the light shifts to the departments and the emphasis is placed on their special subject interests, the general subject catalog slips into shadow. The light

1. *Library Quarterly*, XVIII (January, 1948), 24–32.

has already shifted insofar as the grouping of library services under broad subject divisions constitutes an acceptable compromise between centralization and decentralization. General reference is already vestigial in a few university libraries, and departmental libraries are being consolidated or coordinated into larger units. The emphasis is on specialization in these larger units, yet cataloging is still aimed primarily at general service. It may be time to see whether subject cataloging can be adapted to meet the needs of decentralized service through subject-divisional organization.

Third, the old cry is still heard that subject cataloging is poorly integrated with published bibliographies, that much subject cataloging unnecessarily duplicates the bibliographies, and that the bibliographies are not being fully exploited. To the extent that this is true, I have an abiding interest in effecting whatever reconciliation is necessary to release for other purposes some of the big money now spent on cataloging. Progress is being made, but no change in the essential structure of the catalog has yet occurred. There seems to be no really practical way of reconciling the nature and methods of general library cataloging with those of specialized subject bibliography. Sometimes I think that only a basic reorganization of library services could effect that reconciliation. It might be that specialization through subject divisions will provide the necessary upheaval and that the opportunity for integrating cataloging with bibliography will occur at the divisional level instead of the general level. If a general subject catalog cannot be synchronized with subject bibliographies, which are decentralized as a matter of course in the subject-divisional scheme, perhaps special subject catalogs could be.

The fourth reason for this paper is the appearance in book form of the *Library of Congress Subject Catalog*. In past years there has been much speculation about the possibility of delegating some of the functions of the general subject catalog to the *Cumulative Book Index*, the *Cambridge Bibliography of English Literature*, and other fairly general bibliographies. These schemes have never come off, even experimentally. Now we have this new tool which clearly duplicates a large part of the subject catalog. Can it be put to work in place of that part of the subject catalog which it duplicates? If local subject catalogs were decentralized, perhaps the *LC Subject Catalog* could satisfy any vestigial need for a general subject list. In any case it is important that the potentialities of the new *LC Subject Catalog* be conscientiously investigated.

As a basis for discussion let me describe a proposition—an imaginary scheme for decentralization of subject cataloging and classification in a university library organized into subject divisions.

This hypothetical library has four subject divisions for upperclass, graduate, and faculty use: a humanities division, a social science division, a biological science division, and a physical science and engineering division. Each division has a central reading room (not necessarily in the main library building) with a well developed reference service and an open-shelf collection of frequently used books and journals. The smaller departmental libraries in each of these subject areas operate as branches of the related division and are administered by the division chief and his staff of subject specialists.

There is no general reference department, periodical room, or reserved book room, these services being allocated to the subject divisions. For lower class students, however, there is a general education division consisting of an open-shelf library of the books, journals, reference works, etc. used in connection with freshman and sophomore courses.

In addition to the four subject divisions and the general education division there is an acquisition division of the conventional sort, with purchase, gift and exchange, serial, and binding departments. There is a bibliography division which includes the catalog department and a central bibliographic service. The bibliography and acquisition divisions could, if desired, be consolidated into one division.[2]

A circulation division controls the physical disposition of books throughout the system and maintains and lends books from the central stack, which serves as storage for seldom used books. A division of special collections handles rare books and manuscripts.

Within this subject-divisional library bibliographies and catalogs are disposed as follows:

The heart of the bibliographic system is the central bibliographic service, administered by the chief bibliographer. This service employs a union author-title catalog of the resources of all parts of the system. No general shelflist is used. The subject card catalog is separate from the author-title catalog and contains only books published to 1950. No general subject catalog is maintained for books published after 1950. Beginning with 1950 the *LC Subject Catalog* is used for

2. Cf. John J. Lund, "The Cataloging Process in the University Library: A Proposal for Reorganization," *College and Research Libraries*, III (1942), 212–18.

general purposes, together with the *CBI* and other general subject lists. The service also employs the *LC Author Catalog*, other library catalogs (such as the British Museum catalog), the trade and national bibliographies, the general periodical indexes, etc. With this equipment and a card index to bibliographies located in the subject divisions, the service functions as a clearing house for bibliographic information and for the referral of inquiries to the appropriate subject divisions.

In each subject division an author-title catalog and a shelflist are maintained. These cover all books, including those stored in the main stack, which fall within the relevant subject areas. Author lists only are kept in the smaller branches, and these are limited to the books actually located in the branches. The divisions and branches are equipped with as good a collection of subject bibliographies, indexes, annual reviews, and abstract journals as is needed or available.

To the extent that the published tools leave significant gaps to be filled, special subject catalogs and indexes are compiled locally by the divisions. These special catalogs are made only when necessary, only as long as necessary, and are designed to satisfy the specific needs of specific readers. The extent and nature of local subject cataloging varies from division to division according to the adequacy of the published bibliographies. In some areas (for example, geology) no subject catalog is compiled. In others (for example, business) full subject catalogs are compiled. Between these extremes is a wide variety of practice. All such catalogs and indexes are special in purpose and design and are supplementary in the sense that they are discontinued as soon as the special need passes or is satisfied by a new bibliography.

In this bibliographic system it is a function of the central bibliography division, which includes the catalog department, to prepare the unit cards for the author-title catalogs, both main and divisional, for the divisional shelflists, and for the central card list of bibliographies. For books published after 1950 the bibliography division sends all copies of these cards without classification numbers or subject headings with the books to the service divisions. For books published before 1950 subject headings are assigned and subject cards included, but classification numbers are still omitted.

The subject specialists in the divisions then classify the books within exclusive blocks of numbers assigned to the divisions and decide where the books go—to the divisional reading room, a branch, or the main stack. The cards for the main author-title catalog and the main subject catalog for books published through 1950 are returned with call numbers and location symbols to the bibliography division for filing. The divisions file their own cards and prepare the entries, if any, for the special subject catalogs and indexes needed in the divisions.

The coordinating authority is the chief bibliographer, who approves the plans for all subject cataloging and classification done in the divisions and reviews the work from time to time. The subject cataloging of the divisions, however, need not be uniform, since the cards are not interfiled in a general catalog. Within the blocks of numbers assigned to the divisions, the classification schedules are applied without possibility of conflict and the call numbers identify the divisions to which the books belong.

That is briefly the hypothetical organization. Now let us see what elements in the present situation tend toward that kind of organization and then consider some of the angles. The decentralization of the subject approach to books may not be as alien to present practice as at first it might appear.

First, to the extent that subject divisions and branches now exist, subject bibliography and reference service are already decentralized. It has been taken for granted that the bibliographic apparatus in special subjects belongs in the subject departments, whether duplicated elsewhere or not. The general reference service may be entirely gone, as at the University of Nebraska; it may be vestigial, as at the University of Colorado; or as at Stanford, it may be fragmentary. At Stanford half of all library use, including nearly all service in the physical and biological sciences, occurs in the departmental libraries; and the so-called general service is actually specialized in the humanities and certain social sciences.

Second, the hypothetical organization is already approximated to the extent that subject catalog cards are now made for the general catalog without being supplied to the subject departments, or for the subject departments without being filed in the general catalog. At Stanford, out of 28 departmental and special libraries, subject cards for 9 are now made only for the departmental catalogs, and subject cards for 15 are made only for the general catalog. For only 4 are duplicate sets of cards now filed in both the general and departmental catalogs, where service is concentrated. These situations qualify or cast doubt upon the theory of the general subject catalog.

Third, the hypothetical organization is further approximated to the extent that analytics and other entries for serials (especially periodicals), government publications, and other materials are omitted from the general subject catalog in deference to published indexes and bibliographies. The approach to periodical literature is almost entirely through special indexes. The significance of this fact to the research worker ought not to be underestimated. Herman Fussler, in his study of the literature used by chemists and physicists, showed that over 90 per cent of the references cited by research workers in these fields are from serial publications.[3]

Fourth, to the extent that subject departments now perform special cataloging or indexing activities, our hypothetical organization is again approximated. It is fairly common practice for a central catalog department, in processing books for departmental libraries, to prepare subject cards for the general catalog but to supply only author cards with tracings to the departments. The departments then make for themselves whatever subject catalogs or indexes are needed to supplement the published bibliographies. Seventy-seven departments at the University of California operate on this basis. A few maintain full subject catalogs; most probably do not. Some may engage upon special indexing or abstracting projects in place of, or in addition to, straight subject cataloging. At the Los Angeles Public Library, in which all departments are supplied with subject catalogs by the central catalog department, the subject specialists in the departments were recently found to be compiling a total of 111 special indexes and catalogs, large and small. At Stanford, a good example is the biological science division, which regularly operates without a subject catalog but carries on a variety of special indexing and abstracting activities.

Fifth, while centralized cataloging is clearly the vogue in university libraries, there has always been the exception of a few departmental libraries, usually autonomous or located at a distance from the main library, which have done all their own cataloging. These exceptions may or may not be important to this discussion, but they may be kept in mind as a further tendency toward our hypothetical organization.

These present conditions, the extent of which I am not able to measure, should at least remind us that the elements of our hypo-

---

3. "Characteristics of the Research Literature Used by Chemists and Physicists in the United States. II," *Library Quarterly*, XIX (April, 1949), 126–27.

thetical organization do now exist in one form or another. How would the reader be affected if these elements were combined and elaborated into the kind of decentralized pattern which has been outlined?

The crux of any argument about decentralization of subject cataloging is probably the ability of the reader to get along satisfactorily without the general subject catalog. Special catalogs and indexes made in the departments would obviously be useful, as the bibliographies are now. But is the *general* subject catalog dispensable? No reliable answer can be given, although a little information and a lot of argument are available.

It appears at present that the advanced student, graduate or faculty, is less dependent upon the general subject catalog than the undergraduate student, but that he still uses the subject catalog to an extent that must be reckoned with. At the University of California, according to data recently compiled by LeRoy Merritt,[4] graduate students, who comprised 18.3 per cent of the university population during the period of study, borrowed from the main loan desk 16.2 per cent of all books derived from the subject catalog, 21 per cent of those derived from the author catalog, but 46.3 per cent of those borrowed without reference to either author or subject catalog. Faculty members, who comprised 4.7 per cent of the population, borrowed 2.1 per cent of the books derived from the subject catalog, 3.4 per cent of those derived from the author catalog, but 10.1 per cent of those obtained without reference to either catalog.

Unfortunately, we cannot say whether this use of the subject catalog is large or small, important or unimportant, in relation to the use of other subject tools. No data are available on the extent to which these same readers depend upon subject bibliographies, indexes, abstracts, etc. in quest of books obtained not only from the main loan desk but also from the departmental libraries—data that would enable us to see the facts of subject catalog use in broader perspective. The existence of the bibliographies, their acceptance as part of the scholarly equipment of special fields, and the interest of the scholarly world in perfecting them are presumptive evidence that they are extensively and necessarily used. It could still be that the general subject catalog plays a minor part in the scholars' subject approach to the literature of many fields. It was possible for the authors of the recent study on "Bibliographical Services in the So-

4. His "Subject Catalog Inquiry," as yet unpublished.

cial Sciences" to report on present services and make recommendations without discussion of any role that the subject catalog might play.[5] My own study of "The Organization of Library Materials for Research in English Literature" indicated that the bibliographies in that field are more useful than the subject catalog.[6] Before it can be concluded that the general subject catalog is indispensable to the advanced student, it will have to be shown that the present use of the subject catalog is important and desirable and that the same job cannot be done better by other and cheaper methods. In our hypothetical organization, it is assumed that for the most part the job can be done better by other methods and that the advanced student can and should be taught to use the special apparatus of his field, supplemented only when necessary by locally compiled catalogs or indexes.

With respect to the beginning student, the logic of our hypothetical organization is more clear. At the University of California undergraduate students, who comprised 70.8 per cent of the population, borrowed 72.8 per cent of the books derived from the subject catalog, 63.7 per cent of those derived from the author catalog, but only 17.6 per cent of those derived from no catalog. The bulk of subject catalog use was therefore undergraduate. This fact may have either of two meanings: the extent of a good thing or the extent of a bad thing. Is heavy undergraduate use of the general subject catalog of a large research library a good thing?

The underclassman is typically engaged with the acquisition of a general education. It has been variously estimated that he needs for that purpose a library of several thousand, 50,000, or even 100,000 books, depending upon the nature of the curriculum. But patently he does not need a large research library and is not equipped to use one. A million-volume research library without stack access is an obstacle to his finding the comparatively few books he really needs. He gets in the way of the advanced students who do need a research library. The small, select, open-shelf library of the liberal arts college is better suited to his purpose. It follows that if his use of the research collection is inappropriate, so also is his use of the subject catalog of that collection.

Our hypothetical organization provides a separate general education division—a special library which would contain the books which

5. *Library Quarterly*, XX (April, 1950), 79–100.
6. *Library Quarterly*, XV (January, 1945), 49–74.

freshmen and sophomores are expected to consult. Since there is no standard bibliography for such a literature, the divisional staff would be obliged to make some kind of subject catalog. Whatever kind is made, it should be sufficient for the collection and for the users of the collection and should be more direct and helpful than the general subject catalog. The staff of the division, moreover, being responsible for the orientation of new students, could teach the use of this smaller collection with some hope of success. When the student begins to specialize during his junior and senior years, he would be graduated to the subject divisions, where from the beginning he would be taught the bibliography of his chosen fields.

There is, then, the possibility that the general subject catalog is dispensable, that the advanced student could be served better through published bibliographies, supplemented by catalogs made in the divisions, and that the beginning student could be served better by the catalog of a select, general education library. But let us suppose that there is still left a significant residual need of a general subject catalog. To what extent could the new *Library of Congress Subject Catalog* fill that need? Any number of copies could, of course, be supplied, and we could hope for some fat cumulations in future years.

We know that university libraries now use LC printed cards for about 50 to 70 per cent of the books cataloged and therefore added to the subject catalog. In 1948–49 Stanford cataloged 60.5 per cent of its books with LC cards, the University of California about 67 per cent. That leaves 30 or 40 per cent not covered by LC. LeRoy Merritt, in connection with his "Subject Catalog Inquiry" at the University of California, recently analyzed a small sample of 1,784 books actually loaned through use of the subject catalog to determine the incidence of LC cards. 67.9 per cent had been originally cataloged with LC cards. But since LC cards had been subsequently printed for another 12.6 per cent, cards were available *at the time the books were used* for 80.5 per cent. If these proportions were to continue, that would leave 19.5 per cent not covered by the *LC Subject Catalog*. With an 80 per cent display in this one list, with such other general lists as *CBI* available, and with well developed subject approaches in the subject divisions, there is reasonable doubt that the general subject catalog would be worth while.

Let us examine more closely now the relationship which our hypothetical organization would establish between subject cataloging and bibliography. As already noted, our heart has been willing but our hands unable to arrange any really effective coordination between local subject cataloging and published bibliography. Two reasons may be suggested.

First, cataloging is a distributive or book-to-subject process, while bibliography is a collective or subject-to-book process. The cataloger takes books in hand and distributes them among subjects in a prearranged schedule. The bibliographer takes a subject in hand and collects books around it. There is no way for the cataloger to avoid duplication of the bibliographies, and yet provide full coverage, without searching the bibliographies for the titles being cataloged. Second, because of the existence of the general subject catalog, the pressure for uniformity and consistency of practice is not between cataloging and bibliography in any field, but between cataloging in different fields. Cataloging for chemistry is coordinated with cataloging for economics, history, and romance languages, not with chemical bibliography.

To some extent the decentralization of subject cataloging would get around both of these difficulties. The subject specialist in a division would take stock of the adequacy of the bibliographies in his field and define the areas not covered or the functions not performed. With a knowledge of the field, its bibliography and its readers, he could take the necessary subjects in hand and list only the relevant books which the division acquired. He could reason that this book treats of an area which is already covered, but that one does not. By defining his work in terms of subjects a larger degree of coordination should be possible.

Regarding the other difficulty, lack of a general subject catalog would release at once the bond of uniformity around cataloging in different fields. Whereas the pressure is now toward coordination of all subjects by one bibliographic method, the pressure would then be toward coordination of all methods for each subject. The cataloger would join the bibliographer in serving the community of scholars in each field, wherever they may be. The institutional inter-departmental dimension would be superseded by the departmental inter-institutional dimension.

If subject cataloging were coordinated with bibliography and oriented to the more specialized services of the subject divisions, several changes might be expected in the nature of the cataloging

still to be done. These changes are inherent in the idea of specialization.

First, in our hypothetical organization subject cataloging would
become less extensive but more intensive. The scope of the work
would be narrowed as large subject areas are relinquished to bibliography; but in those specific areas in which local work is done, the
subject specialist would be inclined to do a more thorough job—a
job more nearly approximating the best work found in the best bibliographies, for lack of which he would be trying to compensate. He
might indulge more freely in analytics for both journals and books,
seek out the more ephemeral and peripheral materials, and dig into
the primary sources. With any given potential it is possible to do
much with few subjects or little with many subjects. We can have a
shallow lake across a wide plain or a deep pool in a narrow valley.
To the extent that breadth is no longer needed we can have depth.

Second, a change might be expected in the nature of the subject
headings or classifications used. The approach of the central catalog
department to the organization of knowledge is panoramic, that of
the subject specialist is focal. The cataloger stands on a hill, views the
world all around him, then makes a picture which is unrolled scene
by scene before the spectator. The specialist goes down into the fields,
selects a particular scene, then makes pictures of that scene from
every angle—close-ups to which all the rest is background. He has a
slant on the world, and all he sees is oriented to his particular interest. In the background he does see other specialties, but the whole
is arranged and interpreted from his point of view. So with books,
his arrangement or interpretation is different from those of specialists
in other fields; and none is like the cataloger's, except possibly the
philosopher's. To the extent that we can do without the panoramic,
as far as subject headings are concerned, we can develop the focal
approach. We can try to see the literature through the specialist's
eyes, use his language, and arrange things for his convenience.

Third, a more selective and discriminating treatment of books
might be expected. A general catalog department tends to handle
books uncritically, and with good reason. Lacking the focal approach,
it has no specific orientation and therefore no criteria for evaluating
them. The panoramic method is by nature undiscriminating, since
discrimination involves reference to special purposes or needs. Those
needs would be more keenly felt and more readily defined in the sub-

ject divisions, where every new book, journal, and pamphlet could be examined with an eye for research in progress, the requirements of the curriculum, and the interests of a known clientele.

And fourth, one further change—toward change itself. The more intensive, focal, and discriminating a job becomes, the more quickly it becomes obsolete. Again, there is a price to pay for the value received. The price is temporality; the value is adaptability. The ideal of the stable, omniferous catalog would be gone; that of the ephemeral and individual would take its place.

Since decentralization might change the nature of subject cataloging, a corresponding change might be desirable in the qualifications of those who do the work. Let us end this discussion with a quick look at the manner in which the library staff might be affected.

We have come to think of two general qualifications of a good cataloger: a knowledge of catalog techniques and subject or language competence. For the present objective, which is the construction of a general catalog, we are probably right in assigning the greater value to techniques. A good cataloger can get along in our present system without unusual subject background, but a subject specialist can get nowhere without a knowledge of cataloging. If there were, however, no general subject catalog and if that part of cataloging were delegated to the subject divisions, the balance might tip in the other direction. A knowledge of cataloging techniques would still be important, but subject background would be indispensable. For the new objective, which would be intensive, focal, selective cataloging closely coordinated with bibliography, the emphasis would be reversed.

Catalogers would not be out of a job, however. They are already subject specialists to some degree and could pursue those interests further with profit and pleasure. As a group they are still one of the most able in the library profession, and they have long since been ready for change. If they are on the defensive now, it is only because they are afraid of being shelved. Our hypothetical organization would bring them out into the open and make their presence felt throughout the library system.

One of the attractive aspects of the decentralized plan is the possible redistribution of staff. We now have a heavy concentration of staff in the so-called technical departments, while in the service departments, especially the departmental libraries, the staff is thinly spread. Important service units are often left with no professional supervision at all. A very large part of our real professional know-how never reaches the reader in a direct personal way. In our hypothetical organization, some of the catalogers could be transferred to the subject divisions, where their cataloging abilities would be welcomed and where they could vary their work with service responsibilities. The central catalog staff would then be reduced to the size required for descriptive cataloging only.

Another shift, however, would probably occur from the general reference department, which would be discontinued, to the central bibliographic service, which would be combined with the catalog department into a new bibliography division. Some reference workers might become general bibliographers, others might be allocated to the subject divisions. The new bibliography division, then, might be almost as large as the original catalog department, although its functions would be quite different. This difference would be important to the professional outlook of the staff.

The functions of the new bibliography division would be narrower in one way and broader in others than those of the present catalog department. The delegation of subject cataloging and classification to the subject divisions might be regarded as a loss by some who stay on with the bibliography division, but the central catalogers or bibliographers would still have authority over the subject cataloging activities of the subject divisions. Also their sphere of interest would be extended to embrace the entire field of bibliography, and they would have specific responsibility for the operation of a service department. This service would bring them into direct contact with the reader. All in all, their opportunity would be substantially greater than now to make a distinguished contribution to the library program; and those who transferred to the subject divisions would have an equally good opportunity to extend their bibliographic horizons and to work directly with the reader.

MANAGEMENT, MACHINES, AND THE BIBLIO-GRAPHIC PROBLEMS OF THE TWENTIETH CENTURY

RALPH R. SHAW

THE level of development of bibliographic services has always been dependent in some degree upon the level of development of bibliographic tools and machines and the intelligence applied to their management.

In the simplest and most accurate sense, even catalog cards or slips of paper are tools. The development of bibliographic management took its first step forward when the listing on slips in multiple places made it possible to make a shortcut over placing a copy of the publication in turn in the several places or placing multiple copies in the several places simultaneously. In some cases, such as files of patents, it is still the custom to attempt to organize the knowledge contained in literature by placing copies of the publication under the various subjects contained in each, although generally this is supplemented by more detailed indexing on cards or in bibliographic forms such as the *Official Gazette of the U.S. Patent Office.*

Bibliography—the listing of literature—is never free from the handling of physical objects, regardless of the form of the artifacts used to represent the book. All of the attempts to bring out a book or article under two or more subjects or ideas involve the handling of physical objects, and even the new electronic machines handle objects which require space and are recorded in physical form; the chief difference between placing two copies of a patent in two different places and placing two sets of magnetic impulses on a tape, or two sets of holes in a punched card, or two lines of entries or two numbers in a bibliography, or two cards in a card catalog, is a difference in the physical bulk to be handled, and a difference in speed and ease and cost of handling these physical objects by the various manual and/or mechanical means available *for achieving the objectives for which the entries have been made and are being handled.*

In other words, one of the basic elements in the bibliographic problem of all times—and more particularly of the twentieth century, because of the great masses of materials to be handled—is the problem of scientific management of exceedingly large masses of physical objects.

Scientific management can not be confined to the mechanical problem of handling materials, without regard to the purposes for which the material is handled. However, the nature of the bibliographic problems of the twentieth century has been treated in another paper[1] which should be read in connection with this report; so this discussion will be limited to the scientific management approach to the use of machines for bibliographic purposes, bringing in the purposes and requirements only insofar as they are requisite to understanding of the limitations and useful attributes of the mechanisms.

It should be noted that scientific management will not yield quick and easy solutions of bibliographic problems. As stated by Braum, Person and Cooke, "Scientific management exists primarily as a concept and a mental attitude towards achievement. It exercises a basic systematic technique for discovering and establishing objectives, plans, standards, methods, schedules, and controls of an enterprise, all within the laws of each situation and in an environment of high morale. It thereby exemplifies the best use of human and material energy."[2]

It might be well to stop for a moment to consider the extent to which the above criteria have been met in our planning of bibliographic programs.

Coming now to the subject of machines for use in handling bibliographic problems, it must be noted that whatever machines may do in the future, they do not now offer any promise whatsoever for elimination of the intellectual effort involved in bibliographic work; and fuzzy thinking about the creation of new knowledge by assembling unrelated data mechanically is probably responsible for a large part of the delay in applying machine techniques to the parts of the job they may be able to handle. Tools and machines of some types appear to be indispensable and have always been used for storage,

---

1. R. R. Shaw, "Machines and the Bibliographical Problems of the Twentieth Century," *Windsor Lectures* (to be published by University of Illinois, 1950).

2. M. C. H. Niles, *Middle Management* (rev. ed.; New York: Harper & Bros., 1949), p. 238; see also H. B. Maynard, "The Role of Scientific Management in World Recovery," *Mechanical Engineering*, LXXI (March, 1949), 229–31.

selection, and reproduction of bibliographic materials. Those aspects of the problem appear to constitute the field of application of machines. Machines do not now, nor will they in the foreseeable future, handle the intellectual aspects of bibliography.

But even as a purely mechanical problem, it is by no means certain that the machines available or in sight at the present time will enable us to forget about the problems of bulk of the written record; and even the most enthusiastic statements of the most able designers of electronic equipment leave much to the imagination and are limited by the fact that their imaginations, magnificent as they are in the field of machine design, are limited by lack of knowledge of the frequency of use and other factors involved in meeting bibliographic requirements.

For example one of the most outstanding designers of electronic equipment, Dr. J. W. Mauchly,[3] indicated that Univac, the most advanced of the electronic computing devices from the point of view of handling bibliographic material, could search the collection of the Library of Congress in twenty hours. It probably could, provided that all the preliminary work had been done, and it might record the answer to the inquiry on a magnetic tape. The magnetic tape would then have to feed a battery of electric typewriters at a maximum rate of 120 words per minute, and the time in the typewriters would depend upon the amount and type of material selected. But even disregarding the preparatory work and the time required for getting rolls into the machine and for translating the answer from machine language into usable form, and assuming that an answer can be provided to any inquiry, from the whole collection of the Library of Congress, in only 20 hours, the obvious question is: "So what?" An average of 2,500 members of the general public use the Library of Congress each day, and Verner Clapp, Associate Librarian of Congress, estimates that staff use of the catalogs on research and information problems is about double public use. Assuming that each person who uses the catalog looks up only one subject and that the number of staff uses is only equal to, instead of twice, the number of public uses, we find that the minimum number of questions which the Library of Congress has to handle in one day will be at least 5,000. Now 5,000 questions at 20 hours each will require 100,000 hours of machine time

3. "No-Slip Library Machine," *Science News Letter*, LVI (November 5, 1949), 295.

per day to do what the Library of Congress is now providing. If we are to provide 100,000 hours of machine time per day, assuming no lost time on any of the machines during the normal 12-hour library day—no time for getting the instructions prepared for the machine and no time for machine repairs—but just the actual running time required, it would require some 8,333 such machines to provide the minimum service now being provided at the Library of Congress by our obsolete manual methods. Let us assume that if a sizeable run of these electronic machines were produced at one time, it would lower their cost considerably, so that they would cost only about $100,000 each, a modest price for so intricate a machine. In that case, the Library of Congress would need to make a capital investment of only $833,300,000, to buy the machines to handle this minimum reference and research load. It hardly appears worth while to analyze the operating costs.

There are several morals in this story. One is that, if we try to apply our present methods to machines which were not designed to handle our problems, we will get frustration; a second is that, while it is quite possible to revise our thinking to take advantage of the potentialities of machines, our thinking will have to be revised first before we can install and use the machines economically. A third is that the volumes of material with which we are faced when we talk about total sorts of knowledge contained in literature are so much greater than those of mathematical and business problems, for which the machines were designed, that entirely new orders of machine speeds and especially of machine outputs will have to be designed before we can shake off our problems and let machines handle them automatically, at the "speed of light." And a fourth moral pointed by this story is that machines may be bottlenecks. While 100 or more people can use the public catalog of a large research library at one time, if the catalog is put into a machine so that the entire catalog has to be run, the machine must make a complete run for each question and it may reduce the potential for service instead of increasing it, regardless of the speed of the machine. A machine used as outlined above would be a gadget. Unless we are willing to assume responsibility for making studies required by the scientific management approach so that we can use machines to help us achieve necessary objectives, we would be much better off if we just forgot about the use of machines.

MACHINES FOR STORAGE

As noted above, the areas of bibliographic management in which machine techniques would appear to be most likely to yield useful results are: (1) condensed storage of text and of index entries; (2) speedy and economical selection of pertinent entries; and (3) speedy and economical reproduction of entries, abstracts, or the original textual materials.

In terms of storage capacity, the basis of the discussion is 100,000 word storage, which is the unit of storage in the Univac, the most advanced for bibliographic purposes of the digital computers.

STORAGE CAPACITY OF MACHINES[4]

A. *Text.*—A 250-page book $5\frac{1}{2} \times 8\frac{1}{2} \times 1$ inch can easily store 100,000 words (400 words per page). Thus in conventional book format with average 8 point type we require about 46.75 cubic inches for storing 100,000 words—exclusive of shelving, etc.

Punched cards, storing 80 characters per card, would require somewhat more than 6,250 cards for storage of 100,000 words (500,000 characters). Six thousand two hundred fifty Hollerith cards would require $7.375 \times 3.25 \times 62$ inches, or 1,488 cubic inches, to store the content of this book.

Elliot stencils 4.5×2 inches, with 6 lines of text, will store almost 60 words (300 characters). Thus 100,000 words will require about 1,666 stencils. Elliot stencils are about one-eighteenth of an inch thick, so 1,666 stencils will require $\dfrac{1,666 \times 4.5 \times 2}{18}$ cubic inches, or 833 cubic inches.

Addressograph slugs with selector tabs are approximately 2.6×4 inches and about 0.1 inch thick. Each slug, therefore, occupies approximately 1.04 cubic inches. The six-line area will store about 48 words, so 100,000 words would require about 2,080 slugs. Two thousand eighty slugs at 1.04 cubic inches each will require 2,163 cubic inches.

Using reduced facsimile, at 50%, as was done in the case of the Library of Congress Catalog of Printed Cards, would reduce the storage space required in printed form by about three-fourths, and would store 100,000 words in about 12 cubic inches.

4. Since shelving and trays vary widely, all dimensions used are exclusive of cabinet space and shelving, but rolls are considered square for purposes of storage. For the purposes of all these computations, five letters equal one word.

A 3 × 5 inch catalog card can store about 160 words (800 characters), so 100,000 words would require about 625 cards, or about 141 cubic inches.

Notched cards (Keysort) are commonly about 5 × 8 inches and run about 16 inches in thickness per thousand. Thus 1,000 cards occupy 640 cubic inches, and one card occupies 0.64 cubic inch. The area available for text is about 4×7 inches, which will store about 450 words (2,250 characters). Thus, 100,000 words will require $\frac{100,000}{450}$, or 222 notched cards, occupying approximately 142 cubic inches.

The Univac will store 100,000 words magnetically on a 7-inch roll, about 0.4 inch in width. This requires 19.6 cubic inches, or a little over one-third of the space required by the original book.

35 mm. film, at usual reduction ratios, with 2 pages per frame, would require 125 frames or .156 roll. A 100-foot roll is about 3.5 inches in diameter and about 1.5 inches in width, or 18.375 cubic inches. Therefore, in full roll form, conventional microfilm storage of these 250 pages would require .156 × 18.375 cubic inches, or 2.87 cubic inches.

Microcards store 46,000 pages per catalog tray (assuming 1,000 cards per tray, and a catalog tray of about 3 × 5 × 15, or 225 cubic inches). Therefore, 250 pages in this form require $\frac{250}{46,000}$ of 225 cubic inches, or 1.22 cubic inches.

If 16 mm. film is used, at the same reduction ratio as is used on microcards, but considered as stored in 100-foot rolls, 250 pages require 83 inches, or approximately 7 per cent of a roll. The roll is 3.5 inches in diameter and 0.75 inches wide, or 9.18 cubic inches, and the storage space for these 250 pages is approximately 0.64 cubic inch.

The Rapid Selector, solely because of the greater storage economy of its 2,000-foot roll, will store the same 250 pages in less than 0.4 cubic inch.

If 300-power reduction ratios reported experimentally were developed for routine use, then microcards would store these same 250 octavo pages in 0.0017 cubic inch; and at 300 diameters 16 mm. microfilm in one-hundred-foot rolls and the Rapid Selector would require considerably less space for storage of 100,000 words than would microcards.

B. *Index entries.*—It is theoretically possible to do rough indexing by placing a copy of each book under each subject. This is done in patent search files. Assuming books of the same size as for the discussion of storage of content, and assuming five subject entries per item, which is high for library catalogs but is about the average of the better bibliographic tools, indexing by this method would require five times the size of the book, or approximately 234 cubic inches per title.

The normal card catalog, requiring five catalog cards for this purpose, would involve storage space of 1.12 cubic inches per title.

The Library of Congress Catalog of Printed Cards, printed in reduced facsimile, at 50 per cent of full size, occupies approximately 33,450 cubic inches to store somewhat less than 2,000,000 cards. Five subject cards on this same basis would occupy $\dfrac{5}{2,000,000}$ of 33,450 cubic inches, or about 0.8 cubic inch per title.

Five addressograph slugs would require 5.2 cubic inches; and five Elliot stencils would require 2.5 cubic inches. In very narrow fields two or more subjects may be placed on one slug, or stencil, or punched card, or notched card, but in broad fields it would be difficult to code even a single subject on one stencil or card.

Indexing on notched cards, at 0.64 cubic inches each, will require five cards, or 3.2 cubic inches.

Punched cards containing the same amount of basic data as a research library catalog card would require about seven cards for the information, or 35 cards. Punched cards are longer and wider, but thinner, than average catalog card stock, and 35 punched cards would occupy about 1.75 cubic inches per title.

Conventional microfilm would not be suitable for this purpose because it would be uneconomical to find the subject entries scattered along a strip of microfilm.

Microcards use abbreviated conventional size entries for indexing, and sets would have to be filed in five places. Thus, microcards would occupy 5 × 1.22, or 6.1 cubic inches.

Printed indexes vary widely in method of storage of entries. Two relatively economical formats are that of *Chemical Abstracts* and the *Bibliography of Agriculture.*

Chemical Abstracts annual index, which repeats titles, averages around 203,000 index entries in 187.5 cubic inches. Five entries, therefore, require approximately 0.004 cubic inches.

The Bibliography of Agriculture does not repeat titles and averages 270,000 index entries in 37.9 cubic inches. Five index entries in this form require $\dfrac{5}{270,000}$ of 37.9 cubic inches, or 0.0007 cubic inches per title.

The Rapid Selector wastes one-sixth of its storage space for index entries when there are only five per entry, but even at that it stores five-sixths of 432,000 index entries, or 360,000 entries, in 165 cubic inches. Five entries per item, therefore, occupy only 0.0023 cubic inches.

Storage of index entries on Univac, assuming three words per entry, would require $\dfrac{15}{100,000}$ of 19.6 cubic inches, or 0.003 cubic inches per title.

According to Table 1, which summarizes the above data, if storage of text were our sole problem, the logical solution would be to develop 300 diameter reduction ratios to commercial practicability. If storage of index entries in a form in which they might be found were the sole problem, then further development of printed bibliographic indexes would appear to be the fruitful approach.

However, the purpose of storage of books and of storage of index entries is use. Thus usability of the form in which both are stored is the determinant factor. Ease and speed of finding and ease and efficiency of use are fields in which practically no objective data exist.

The third column of the table does indicate that, of the available devices for storage of both index entries and text, so that the end product delivered to the user is the text he desires, the first in order of efficiency is an electronic device using microfilm for storage, followed by microfilm in card form, reduced facsimile, and an electronic device using magnetic tape storage. If the usual furniture required for storage, card catalogs, shelving, microfilm file cases, and similar equipment were included in the computations, the order would probably be changed somewhat. The Rapid Selector would stay far out in front, but Univac, storing almost 100 rolls on a standard three-foot shelf, would soon catch up with reduced facsimile, and Univac might even overtake microcards stored in conventional catalog cases, in which a large amount of space is wood and air.

SPEED OF SELECTING

Almost no objective data are available on the relative speeds of servicing a given number of readers per hour or a given peak load of readers. At the present time, as noted above, we tend to confuse speed of operation with speed of service. An electronic machine which can digest five hundred thousand, or even five million, digits

TABLE 1

SUMMARY OF STORAGE EFFICIENCY UNDER THE CONDITIONS STATED,* FOR
TEXT AND INDEXING

	A STORAGE OF TEXT		B STORAGE OF INDEX ENTRIES		C BOTH TEXT AND INDEX ENTRIES	
	Cu. In. per 100,000 Words	Order of Efficiency	Cu. In. for Five Entries	Order of Efficiency	Cu. In. (Approximate)	Order of Efficiency
Printed book................	46.8	8	234	12	280	7
Addressograph slugs........	2,163.0	13	5.2	10	2,168	10
Hollerith cards.............	1,488.0	12	1.75	7	1,490	9
Elliot stencils.............	833.0	11	2.5	8	835	8
Notched cards.............	142.0	10	3.2	9	145	6
Usual card catalog.........	141.0	9	1.1	6	142	5
Univac....................	19.6	7	0.003	3	19.6	4
Reduced facsimile (50%)...	12.0	6	0.8	5	12.8	3
35 mm. microfilm.........	2.87	5	....		....	
Microcards...............	1.22	4	6.1	11	7.3	2
16 mm. microfilm.........	0.64	3	....		....	
Rapid Selector...........	0.40	2	0.002	2	0.4	1
Bibliographic indexes:						
Chemical Abstracts.....	....	....	0.004	4	....	
Bibliography of Agriculture	....	....	0.0007	1	....	
300 diameter microfilm†...	0.0017	1	....		....	

* See preceding pages. There are dozens of possible variables, and variations from the above should be made, but this table applies only to the conditions cited, which are common at present. It is offered as an approach to the problem rather than as a definitive solution, and its indications should not be overgeneralized. Rather, they should be considered the starting point of much needed research.

† Not commercially available.

per second, does not necessarily answer more questions faster or cheaper than a card catalog which stands still and permits hundreds of humans to walk slowly about it. So long as this speed complex continues to make us think in terms of sorting every page in the Library of Congress to find the birthday of George Washington, machines will be gadgets.

The fallacy of speed is traceable to the fact that the number of units to be handled is incomparably greater in great research libraries than in business, computing, or other types of manipulation of data.

Argument by analogy from a machine capable of storing 130 twenty-three digit numbers and manipulating each in a fraction of a second to the idea that we can handle the intellectual content of the world's literature by random total sorts is fallacious.

Take for example Dr. Berkeley's estimate[5] of the content of the Library of Congress expressed in machine language. Assuming 7,000,000 volumes in the Library of Congress, Dr. Berkeley estimates that the Library stores about 300 trillion units of information. Now, in view of the fact that we are not able to agree on a uniform method of counting whole volumes, Berkeley's estimate, which involves estimating the number of alphabetic characters in the collection and converting them into machine units at six to ten machine units per letter, must be considered a rather rough approximation, and may be a few hundred trillion units off in either direction—particularly since illustrations can not yet be duplicated in machine language. Nevertheless 300 trillion is a nice round number, and, assuming that it bears some relationship, no matter how remote, to the actual load, it might be interesting to compute the time required for a total sort. Univac can manipulate several million digits per second. Assuming that it can handle 3,000,000 machine language units per second, every second all day long, Univac would require $\dfrac{300,000,000,000,000,000}{3,000,000}$ or 100,000,000 seconds to sort through these three hundred trillion units. Since 100,000,000 seconds is just under 30,000 hours, it is obvious that even 3,000,000 transactions per second is far too slow for random searching of the whole of knowledge.

It should, therefore, be evident that speed alone is not enough to serve any useful bibliographic purpose. We do not read through every book in a great research library every time we want to find a fact that may easily be found in the *World Almanac*, nor do we read through the entire card catalog when we want to find one publication by a known author. There appears to be no basis for assuming that machines will ever be fast enough to eliminate the use of judgment in the selection of the best approach to any reference problem; and even if a total sort of the Library of Congress by machines were faster than consulting the *World Almanac*, it is doubtful that it would be the more economical method. The point here is that machines as tools will not automatically replace all other available tools regard-

5. E. C. Berkeley, *Giant Brains* (New York: John Wiley & Sons, 1949), p. 15.

less of their speeds, and that machines will have a difficult time competing with other tools for achieving the same purpose; some of which, such as some printed reference works, bibliographies, and card catalogs, are remarkably efficient in terms of the objectives for which they were created. In other words, while it is theoretically possible to do almost anything by machines properly designed and applied, there are many operations which do not justify the use of machines.

If machines are to be used for bibliographic purposes, then more attention will have to be paid to the other elements of *getting an answer from a selected block* of information. That requires much more attention to the question of getting the logically selected block of information into the machine and getting the answers out of the machine, and less emphasis on the running speed of part of the machine. This leads to consideration of the fallacy of confusing part of an operation with the whole operation.

THE FALLACY OF CONFUSING PART OF AN OPERATION WITH THE WHOLE OPERATION

This is a common fallacy. In discussing most machine operations or mechanical devices, we commonly emphasize the one or two spectacular advantages, skipping over the other details. This disease is chronic and prevalent, and this speaker must admit that he has at times been guilty of this all too common failing. Yet in terms of scientific management, it does not matter that Katisha's "left shoulder blade . . . is a miracle of loveliness, . . . and her . . . right elbow has a fascination that few can resist," so long as the summation of her attributes leads Ko-Ko to his famous lament.

Starting with microfilm, for example, we have been guilty of confusing part of the operation with the total operation. The cost of supplying a page of text to a user in microfilm is lower than the cost of supplying a single copy in some other forms. But the cost of reading machines not required for other forms, the time spent in going to and from reading machines, the time spent in the special handling and indexing required, and in similar operations, *all of which are part of the cost of the end product*, must be computed as part of the total cost of supplying and using microfilm, if comparisons are to be valid.

Similarly, in speaking of using Hollerith cards for bibliographic purposes, we commonly speak in terms of the speed of the sorter, using the rated speed of the sorter rather than the actual speed

which can be expected over a considerable period. This totally neglects the fact that the cards have to be brought to the machine. In
large files this involves a great deal of walking time. The cards must
be placed in the machine. They must be taken out of the sorting
pockets and, in many cases, re-run through the machine, the cards
selected must be printed in another machine—involving carrying to
the other machine, inserting them, and printing them at a theoretically possible speed of 80 cards per minute only; they must then be
re-assembled and then placed back in their trays and carried back to
their places in the storage files. It is, therefore, exceedingly doubtful
that the total operation, counting all of the time involved in obtaining the end product from large files of punched cards, even if the
time for preparing the cards in the first place is disregarded, will
average out to as much as fifty cards handled per man-minute,
rather than the four or six hundred per minute figure which we commonly cite.

Or as another example, take the Univac. While Univac may sort at
millions of digits per second, its output is in the form of a magnetic
tape which is of no use to anyone until it is translated by an electric
typewriter at a theoretical maximum speed of 120 words per minute.
Furthermore, Univac's memory, the best electronic memory developed to date, can store up to 12,000 bits. At ten bits per letter and
five letters per word, this means that the mercury memory can store
only 240 words at one time, and it takes at least two minutes to type
that information off. It is possible to postulate searches involving a
great deal of transcribing of data in which the selector mechanism of
Univac, operating at say 3 million choices per second, would overload
the memory in .004 seconds. Even if the memory can feed into a new
magnetic tape as fast as the selection mechanism feeds into the
memory, the tape would still have to be transcribed at 120 words
maximum per minute. Thus, the tape produced in a one-second run
of the machine working on a bulk search or a translation—representing up to say 3 million bits—would require typing time of eight
hours and twenty minutes, at the theoretical maximum speed of
typing, after the tape came out of the Univac before the material
"produced in one second" would actually be ready for use.

The same factors on the output end apply to practically all tools
and machines, and it would be fruitless to go into all of them. However, it should be noted that the author's statements on searching on
the Rapid Selector, likewise, do not give the time required for obtain-

ing the final usable end product. After the machine-run at 78,000 to 120,000 choices per minute, it is still necessary to develop the film which results. That can be done in five seconds if there is any good reason for such speed, so that the added factor is less in the case of the Rapid Selector than it is for most other tools. Nevertheless, there is an added factor in the output end which should be added to the running time to get accurate comparisons. For most purposes it would not appear worth while to produce the end result as fast as five seconds after the end of the machine run, so that this may, in some cases, be an appreciable factor.

Of course, what has been said about the output time applies to the input time required for preparing the material in machine language. Unfortunately, there is even less information available in this regard than in regard to the output end.

Before we can use any machines as tools for the efficient execution of bibliographic projects, we shall have to have a great deal more information about the total operation involved in getting the desired information to the reader in a form in which he can use it—including in our computations any of the reader's time wasted by the form in which it is presented.

THE PRINCIPLE OF EQUAL QUALITY

A corollary to the problem of comparing various systems on the basis of the total operations involved is the necessity of basing our comparisons on products of equal quality—using the term quality in the sense of the intellectual as well as the mechanical or physical product. This is fundamental to comparability. This principle has been widely disregarded in bibliographic circles. While the discussion below uses Hollerith cards as the basis, it would apply equally to addressograph slugs, Elliot stencils, and other devices. It is not feasible in one preliminary report to cover all situations, so the cases cited below are offered just as examples.

We frequently read about the relative efficiency of punched cards for performing library or bibliographic operations. Take the simple operation of charging books. In the case of the Montclair installation of punched cards, the end product of the machine operation, when a book is overdue, is the accession number of the book. To find out what book is overdue, it is necessary to establish or maintain an accession number list, a device which has been given up by many libraries, and to consult that list, manually copying off the information. Most other charging systems produce the author, title, and other necessary information as the end product of the charging system and do not require either the maintenance of the accession list or the extra step of consulting it. Now perhaps the information is unnecessary. Perhaps charging systems using accession numbers are adequate. If so, accession number charging should be the base of comparison in comparing the systems. It is not sound scientific management to compare methods yielding different qualities of end product as if the quality of the end product were identical; nor is it either sound management or intellectual honesty to omit steps which are required by one system but not required by the others in comparing the two systems for the purpose of determining which is the most economical.

We now come to Hollerith cards for bibliographic purposes. Not only have we discussed speed of one part as if it were total speed, but we have discussed products of different quality as if they were the same.

Abbreviations may be used on catalog cards filed manually. They may not be used on punched cards filed mechanically because the machine has no way of differentiating between N. D. for North Dakota and N. J. for New Jersey, for example, and would file the former first. It is necessary, therefore, either to insert an extra, and costly, step of coding abbreviations or names in order to make sure that they will file right, or to eliminate abbreviations, thus wasting space by use of the punched card. Since the punched card has a theoretical capacity of only some 80 or 90 characters or spaces, while the catalog card has a theoretical capacity of 540 characters, this is proportionately much more wasteful in the case of punched cards than it is in the case of elite type on catalog cards.

To store as much information on punched cards as is stored on an average Library of Congress printed card would, according to preliminary estimates made at that Library, require an average of six or seven punched cards. So for equal quality, the Library of Congress Catalog would be much larger if it were to contain in punched card form the information it now contains in conventional catalog form.

Assuming only five punched cards per catalog card of equal content, the following comparison shows what would happen in terms of storage required.

Filed in standard 15-tray catalog units, and using standard light-weight catalog stock, we use 409 cubic inches per thousand for three by five cards. While punched cards are generally thinner than catalog cards, they are much larger in cross section. A standard 20-tray punched card filing unit uses 540 cubic inches of space per thousand cards filed. This is about 32 per cent more space than required for filing 1,000 catalog cards. Since at least five punched cards are required for the same amount of information and each card occupies 32 per cent more space, it is obvious that a punched card catalog containing the same amount of information as a normal library catalog would occupy about six and one-half times as much space as the conventional card catalog.

Thus, economy in space can be achieved only by providing so small a fraction of the information included on the conventional catalog card that space is left in the 80 spaces for coding of at least two subjects per card.

Clearly these are not comparable. If the amount of information given on the conventional catalog card is unnecessary, it should, of course, be reduced. But so long as the amount of information given on the punched card is different from the amount of information given on the catalog card, there is simply no basis of comparison.

Only one more of the many types of non-comparable factors which have been compared will be cited. This example deals with the quality of the end product of machine operation. One machine provides an end product which is merely a key to the information which is desired, a patent number, call number, or the like. After the machine-run it is necessary to use conventional steps in addition to the machine-run to reach the objective, which is placing the pertinent text before the reader in usable form. Another machine delivers the text as its end product. The two can not, therefore, be compared in terms of machine-running time alone, even though the latter is incomparably faster than the former. Such a comparison has no validity because the end products are not the same. Yet such comparisons as these are constantly being made in discussing bibliographic problems.

Without delving further into this subject at the present time, it should appear obvious that even the most rudimentary regard for the principles of scientific management would require that comparisons be made only when it is possible to include the factor of quality of the product in terms of the objectives which the methods or machines are supposed to achieve.

THE QUESTION OF THE BEST METHOD

Closely related to the question of comparability in terms of quality is the question of determining the best system or method or machines for achieving a certain required end product of a determined level of quality.

While a proposed system may have advantages over the system in use, that does not necessarily make it the optimum method. We fre quently encounter cases in which a new machine method is recommended to replace inefficient manual methods, and in most of these cases it appears likely that the new method will effect a saving. Nevertheless, both systems may be inefficient, with the proposed one somewhat less inefficient than the old one. While it is possible to show that a machine will, in many cases, make a saving over a very inefficient manual method in use, it is possible in many of these cases to show that an efficient manual system will be more efficient than the proposed machine system, and in some cases it is quite possible by intelligent combination of efficient manual methods and efficient machine methods to devise a system which is more efficient than the efficient manual method. The scientific management approach requires not merely that some improvement be made; it requires that the system developed be the optimum which can be developed for the particular end purposes involved and under the conditions of operation involved.

The example given below shows that, in some cases at least, proper combinations of machine and manual methods make possible certain results which can not be attained by either alone.

The manufacturers of punched card equipment generally agree that machine filing of punched cards alphabetically, when filing must be done on all 80 or more columns, is uneconomical. To file alphabetically on 80 columns requires running the cards through the sorter twice for each column, or 160 times. Assuming a speed of about 250 cards per minute, which is a good day-to-day output for a sorter, running ten thousand cards through the sorter 160 times would require about 106 hours. Of course, if abbreviations were used, hand sorting would be required in addition. This example does not include punching time, but is limited to filing, assuming for comparability that in this case punched cards are necessary and that they must be filed alphabetically.

Now filing these same ten thousand cards completely manually takes only 56 hours of labor, so it would appear that the manual procedure is more efficient.

However, the largest part of hand filing time is the time for handling the large bulk of cards in making the preliminary sorts on the first few letters. Experiments were conducted on performing the preliminary sorting by machine, with the final filing done by hand. The result of this experiment was that filing the cards mechanically on the first five columns required eight hours of machine time. The final sorting by hand (including correcting the filing of abbreviations) required only 15 hours. Thus total machine and manual time was reduced to 23 hours per ten thousand cards, as compared with 106 hours by machine alone or 56 hours for hand-filing alone.

It should be borne in mind, therefore, that the objective of scientific management is not that of finding a machine or system which is slightly less inefficient than the system in use, but rather it is to develop the most efficient system for performing that which needs to be done, at the level of quality at which it needs to be done, and under the conditions under which it must be done.

The machines which have been discussed in the literature as providing bibliographic services or promising to solve bibliographic problems are, in most cases, in competition with existent tools and machines. One of the important factors which must be considered in determining which machine or method is most suitable for any purpose is the cost of the end product. While some of the factors involved have already been noted, one of the important special factors in considering machines is amortization of machine cost.

MACHINE COSTS

The direct outlay for a machine, whether it be a typewriter or a digital computer, must be charged against the cost of doing the work by means of the machine. In many bibliographic operations, this means that purchase or rental of the machine is prohibitively costly. A machine for alphabetic printing from Hollerith cards may cost $3,600 to $10,000 a year just for rental of the machine. Unless such a machine is kept busy, the cost per hour of use is very high. On the other hand the cost per hour may be negligible if a commensurate saving per hour of running time as against other known means actually does result. In one bibliographic job for instance, the actual printing time involved was only about 70 hours per year. At $3,600 per year rental for the machine, it would have cost over $50 per hour for machine rental alone. The solution in that case was contractual service, which yielded the printing time required at a much lower rate. *The decision in each case must be made on the basis of the facts in that case.*

Electronic devices are developing so fast, however, that they are generally out of date before they are run through their first tests. They should probably, therefore, not be amortized over a longer period than five years. Assuming operation of six hours per day, which would probably be high, for five days per week, all year, this would mean that the cost of any electronic device for library purposes would have to be amortized over about 8,000 hours of use as a maximum. Thus a machine which costs $100,000 will represent a minimum machine cost of about $12 per hour and will probably represent costs of ten times that amount for the next ten years at least, until enough material has been translated into machine language to keep the machine busy for more than a few minutes each day. When we add to this cost of probably $100 per hour for machine depreciation alone the cost of preparing the vast amounts of material required to keep the machine busy, and the cost of operating and maintaining the machine, it seems clear that we shall have to study all the factors carefully to determine what the information we can get from machines is worth, whether new orders of bibliographic budgets are justified, and what alternative measures are possible for solution of our problems.

Of course, if we are successful in producing an electronic bibliographic machine for around $10,000 so that the theoretical minimum machine cost would be reduced down to about $1.25 per hour of use, and so that numerous places could afford to buy machines, thus making it possible to divide the cost of original preparation of the material in machine language among 100 or more institutions, then all these factors will be changed, and the machine might well compete with other tools.

This factor of machine costs is obviously related to the amount of time the machine is kept busy. Since it is axiomatic that machines are most inexpensive when they can be kept busy every hour of every day, this means that expensive machines are not normally suitable where the load fluctuates greatly. Not only does the machine cost go up if the machine is not kept busy, but, on the other hand, if the machine is kept busy, then it is not capable of responding to peak loads. This means that expensive machine installations, if they are to be economical, are suitable only where there is a fairly uniform load, and are not particularly efficient when their capacity must be designed to take care of a peak load which is several times as great as the normal day to day load. This lack of flexibility in response to peak loads requires serious consideration in study of cost of machines for normal bibliographic operations.

As noted in Table 1, the Rapid Selector provides more economical storage of text and index entries than any other tool now available. It requires additional study of the input rate, since it is now arranged to handle 4-minute units, and might well be more flexible and more efficient if it handled five- or ten-second units of input. But it does require less expensive preparation of the material in machine language than the others, after the original intellectual work, which is common to all, has been done. Also it does supply a usable end product much more directly than do the other electronic devices. The problem of producing the Rapid Selector in the cost range of ten to fifteen thousand dollars does not seem out of the question, and its form of storage lends itself readily to inexpensive duplication of the master records for use at other installations. It might be well, therefore, to describe the Rapid Selector in some detail.

THE RAPID SELECTOR

The fundamental principles upon which the Rapid Selector operates are very simple. Like digital computers and individual brain cells[6] it gives only "yes" or "no" responses; nothing happens when the answer is "no" and something happens when the answer is "yes." While digital computers require at least four relays per digit to express digits from zero to nine, and some use ten vacuum tubes in flip-flop arrangement to express a single digit, the Rapid Selector can identify a seven-digit number or more with a single photocell, thus simplifying the circuits and greatly reducing the number of parts required.

This device is really nothing but a slightly sophisticated version of the common electronic door opening device. In the electronic door opener the parts involved are a light source, a photocell, an amplifier,

6. W. S. McCulloch and J. Pfeiffer, "Of Digital Computers Called Brains," *Scientific Monthly*, LXIX (1949), 368–76.

a relay, and a motor. The photocell is merely a device which converts energy received in the form of light into an electric current. Since the electric energy emitted by the photocell is tiny, it must be amplified before it can do useful work. As shown in Figure 1, the electronic door opener operates by shining a light across the door opening onto the photocell. So long as the light shines on the photocell, it emits a current. The current is amplified and run through the relay, which is energized as an electromagnet so long as current runs through it, and keeps the contact for the electric motor in the open position. When someone walks between the light source and the photocell,

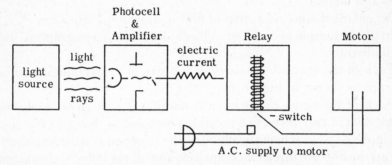

FIG. 1.—Block diagram of electronic door opener

he interrupts the light energy. The photocell stops delivering its electric current, and the instant that happens the relay loses its electro-magnetism, permitting the motor contact to close. As soon as the motor receives current, it operates to open the door.

The major difference between this operation and the Rapid Selector operation is that, in the Rapid Selector, black dots are used as keys to the number sought, and the light reaches the photocell only through holes punched in an opaque card. When the black dots on the film coincide with all of the holes in the card, the light beam to the photocell is interrupted and it permits something to happen. So long as light comes through a single one of the thirty-six holes used for keying, the photocell continues to receive enough energy to prevent anything from happening. The other major difference is that the Selector uses a stroboscopic light flash, lasting only 2 millionths of one second, to make a copy of the data side of the film when the photocell is blacked out. This flash is of such short duration that it effectively stops the motion without requiring that the film be stopped or slowed down. Thus, the Rapid Selector does nothing but match dots and holes, answering "no" or "yes" to each match. So long as there is not a perfect match, the answer is "no" and nothing happens. When there is a perfect match, the answer is "yes" and the light flashes, making a copy of the related data. The Selector does not care what it is matching, nor does the number of holes and dots involved make any appreciable difference. The major problems in building the first Rapid Selector were really mechanical rather than electronic, since the film must track almost perfectly while running at speeds up to 500 feet per minute, and very small amounts of side-play in the running film would result in failure properly to match dots and holes.

An enlarged copy of a strip of film is shown in Figure 2.

In this example six sets of subject codes are photographed with each abstract.

Each of the six code numbers in this case is a seven-digit number written as shown in Figure 3.

Each of the seven digits in each number is written by using two black dots in two of the five possible positions, as shown in Figure 4.

Figure 5 shows schematically how the selection is done, representing all the dots by three black squares, and all the holes in the opaque mask by three circles. If we consider a film running along at high speed, with light reaching the photocells only through the holes in the mask, it is obvious that, when the dots on the film in Figure 5 reach the holes, they will cover all the holes for a tiny fraction of a second. This will block off all light from the photocell, and the electronic contact which results from blacking out the photocell will trigger the flash lamp for two microseconds. Even though the film keeps running along at 500 feet per minute (i.e., 100 inches per second) in two-millionths of one second it would move only $\dfrac{2}{1,000,000}$ of 100 inches, or 0.0002 (two ten-thousandths) of one inch, which is not enough to cause any appreciable blur, so effectively the speed of the flash "stops" the motion while making the picture—even though the master film runs on at 100 inches per second.

While, as noted in Table 1, the Rapid Selector has the advantage of economical storage on microfilm together with high speed selection and reproduction, it may be that the roll of 2,000 feet is too large for flexible handling, since it requires runs of four minutes, and that our conception of the amount of storage should be changed to allow for more detailed selection, as is done in approaching the catalog and

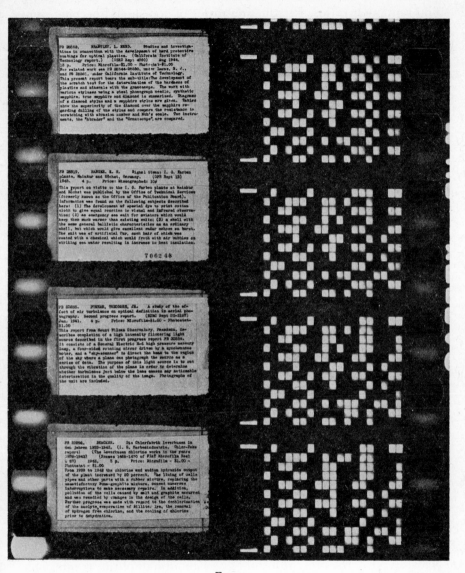

FIG. 2

reference questions at the present time. The data for storage of material on the Rapid Selector is based upon storage at normal 16 mm. film reduction ratios. If reduction ratios of 300 should become commercially feasible, that should increase the storage capacity of the

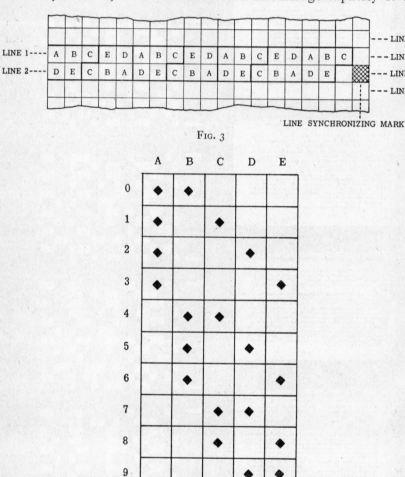

FIG. 3

FIG. 4

Selector. Also, the present format gives about half of the 35 mm. film to text and half to coding. In copying a catalog, the space for filming a three by five card could be reduced and the storage capacity of a 2,000-foot roll, about one-fourth of a cubic foot, could be increased from its present level of 72,000 pages of text or abstracts and 432,000 index entries to about one million catalog cards. If that were done, the Library of Congress catalog would represent about 2.5 cubic feet of storage space, and about 40 minutes of running time in any case in which it is necessary to run the entire catalog. If the rolls were mounted in cartridges of five-second runs, it should then be possible for one machine to answer at least twelve questions per minute, or about 8,000 per day, and one machine might then, if

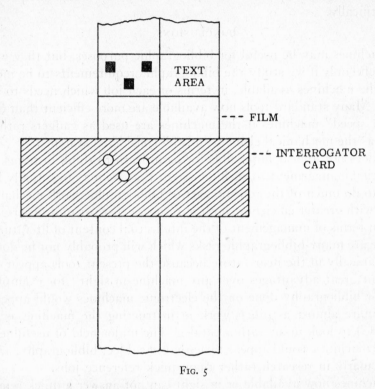

Fig. 5

properly used, handle all the reference uses of the public catalog of a great research library.

In general it would appear that the Rapid Selector opens up the possibility of coupling the advantages of microfilm for storage with a simple and speedy electronic sorter, so as to make possible economic use of microfilm for storage, finding, and reproduction of bibliographic entries or text. It appears to make possible the use of machines for cumulative indexing in place of manual searching through multiple indexes—assuming that the problem of grouping of the materials from the various indexes is properly solved to hold the running time per question down to reasonable limits, and, third, because it greatly reduces the physical problems of indexing and of finding, it should free many hours of the scholar's time for performing higher orders of bibliographic work than have heretofore been possible— if we can find out just what is needed to advance learning.

None of these results will accrue automatically. All will require further research before we can hope to manage the mass of literature scientifically.

CONCLUSIONS

Machines may be useful for bibliographic purposes, but they will be useful only if we study the bibliographic requirements to be met, and the machines available, in terms of each job which needs to be done. Many standard tools now available are more efficient than the "high speed" machines if the machines are used as gadgets rather than as the mechanical elements of well-considered systems.

It does not appear impossible for us to learn to think in terms of scientific management to such an extent that we may eventually be able to do much of the routine part of bibliographic work mechanically with greater efficiency, both in terms of cost per unit of service and in terms of management of the intellectual content of literature. There are many bibliographic tasks which will probably not be done mechanically in the near future because the present tools appear to present great advantages over any machine in sight—for example, author bibliography done on the electronic machines would appear to require almost as much work in instructing the machine as is required to look in an author catalog. The major field of usefulness of the machines would appear to be that of subject bibliography, and particularly in research rather than quick reference jobs.

Machines now available or in sight can not answer a quick reference question either as fast or as economically as will consultation of standard reference works such as dictionaries, encyclopedias, or almanacs, nor would it appear worth while to instruct a machine and run the machine to pick out one recent book or "any recent book" in a broad subject field. It would appear, therefore, that use of high-speed electronic or electrical machinery for bibliographic purposes may be limited to research institutions for the next five or ten years at least, and will probably be limited to research problems in those institutions. It seems quite probable that during the next decade electronic machines, including the Rapid Selector, which was designed with bibliographic purposes in mind, will find application in administrative, office, and business uses to a much greater extent than they will in bibliographic operations.

The shortcomings of machines used as gadgets have been stressed in this paper. Nevertheless, the use of machines for bibliographic purposes is developing, and it is developing rapidly. It appears quite certain that several of the machines and mechanical devices can now perform certain of the routine operations involved in bibliographic work more accurately and more efficiently than these operations can be performed without them.

At least one machine, the Rapid Selector, appears potentially capable of performing higher orders of bibliographic work than we have been able to perform in the past, if and when we learn: (a) what is really needed for the advancement of learning in the way of bibliographic services; and (b) how to utilize the machine efficiently.

There is no magic in machines as such. There will be time-lag in their application, just as there was with the typewriter. The speed and efficiency in handling the mechanical part of bibliographic work, which will determine the point of diminishing returns, depend in large measure on how long it will be before we approach these problems from the point of view of scientific management.

This report cannot solve the problem. Machines alone cannot solve the problem. We need to develop systems of handling the mass of bibliographic material which rest upon discovering and establishing our objectives, our plans, our standards, our methods and controls, within the laws of each situation. This may take twenty years and it may take one hundred, but it will come. The determination of how long the time-lag will be rests upon our time-lag in gathering objective information upon which scientific management of the literature can be based.

THE PREPARATION OF THE BIBLIOGRAPHY
OF AGRICULTURE

MARGARET C. SCHINDLER

THIS is a case study of one current bibliography. Other papers presented at this conference have dealt with theoretical aspects of bibliography, with surveys of existing services and services needed but not yet provided, and with new methods and techniques to help us control the ever growing literature with which the scholar and the scientist must keep abreast. This paper discusses a continuing experiment in providing bibliographic control in one subject field.

The *Bibliography of Agriculture* is an index to the world literature in agriculture and the related sciences, prepared in the library of the U. S. Department of Agriculture and issued monthly. As the national library of agriculture, our library is obligated to collect and preserve the literature of agriculture and the related sciences and to make it available to employees of the department and others engaged in agricultural research and in agricultural extension and educational work all over the country.

Employees of the Department of Agriculture are stationed in all parts of the United States, in the territories and the island possessions, and even in foreign countries. For them, the most complete and best organized library is inadequate unless they can be kept informed of the literature available and can have access to it.

The *Bibliography of Agriculture* combined with loans and free photostat service brings the resources of the library in Washington to the supervisor of a national forest in Oregon or the American technical advisor in a Mexican experiment station, to the soil conservation technician in Maine or the entomologist in Texas. Each can receive the *Bibliography of Agriculture*. He has only to scan it and to send to the library a note of anything he wants to read, and a photostat, or sometimes the original, is mailed to him.

The *Bibliography of Agriculture* is sent not only to offices of the department, but also to libraries in the land grant colleges and experiment stations, and to other institutions where research in agriculture is carried on and to foreign institutions on exchange. Workers in these institutions also have access to the library collections through inter-library loan and the photo-copying service, but they must pay for their photo-copies.

Because the *Bibliography of Agriculture* serves so large and diverse a group of people, its scope must be wide and its coverage as complete as possible. Its scope is shown by the main heads in our scheme of classification: PLANT SCIENCE, SOILS AND FERTILIZERS, FORESTRY, ANIMAL INDUSTRY, ENTOMOLOGY, AGRICULTURAL ENGINEERING, AGRICULTURAL PRODUCTS: PROCESSING, DISTRIBUTION AND STATISTICS, AGRICULTURAL ECONOMICS AND RURAL SOCIOLOGY, FOOD AND HUMAN NUTRITION, and, that necessary evil, MISCELLANEOUS, where we put obituaries of scientists, general reports of research institutions, and other items which do not fit anywhere else. Geographically, the scope is world wide. Publications from all the continents of the globe are indexed regularly. While we are not able to index literature in all languages, anything can be indexed that has at least a contents page in one of the languages of western Europe or in Russian.

With our diversified clientele we have not thought it wise to try to be highly selective in our indexing. This pleases nobody completely, for everyone must read through a great many references in which he is not interested to find those in which he is interested. The practical man on the range in New Mexico complains that we list so many articles in languages he cannot read that he cannot take time to find those in English, and the research man complains that we include so many popular and trivial articles that he can find the few grains of wheat in the bushels of chaff only with the greatest difficulty. We do omit certain minor categories of agricultural literature entirely, such as elementary textbooks, student publications, county farm bureau papers, and quarterly and semi-annual administrative reports. Unsigned articles and those signed with a pseudonym, if we know it is a pseudonym, are not indexed unless they are very important, nor are columns, letters to the editor except for those which report the result of scientific work, prize papers below the college level, and similar publications. We exclude narratives of personal experience which contribute nothing new to the subject, "How I Got My Start in Chickens," for example, and we are selective in the indexing of articles in the borderline fields of home gardening, the culture of ornamentals, and home processing of food.

Items in the *Bibliography of Agriculture* are arranged in broad subject groups according to a classification scheme, the main classes of which have been given above, and within each group alphabetically by author. An item is listed only once under its principal subject, but may have as many subject index entries as necessary. Each issue from January to November includes an author index referring to item numbers. The December issue contains author and subject indexes for the volume, references being made to item number.

I shall begin with a brief outline of the process of preparing and issuing the *Bibliography of Agriculture* which will help to make more meaningful detailed discussion of some of the procedures which will follow. Each day at noon a messenger brings from the Current Serial Record and the Preparations Unit the serials checked in and the separates prepared for the shelves since the preceding day. These are sorted by subject and language and given to the bibliographers. For separates the procedure is very simple. The bibliographer takes the cataloger's process slip, which comes with the publication, assigns the classification symbol, adapts the subjects to those used in the *Bibliography of Agriculture*, and passes the slip on to a typist. For serials, which have no process slip, he marks the articles to be taken and indicates the correct entry for the author's name if there is any doubt, decides on the classification and subjects. We do not go beyond the publication for the author's name. We have rolls of paper five inches wide and perforated every three inches made up for us, giving us 10,000 3 by 5 slips in one continuous roll. The roll is inserted in the typewriter. On the first slip the bibliographer writes any instructions for the typist; on the second he puts the classification symbol in the lower left corner. The next slip or slips are left blank for the author index slips, and on the succeeding slips are typed the subjects, one to a slip. After each article in a given issue of a journal has been so treated, the bibliographer tears off the paper on the next perforations and inserts the whole strip in the journal. The typist, using an IBM proportional spacing bookface typewriter and a carbon paper ribbon, types an entry slip according to forms which she has learned, and the necessary author index slips, positioning the author's names carefully, and tears the strip between items. A proofreader, after reading the slips for typographical accuracy, folds the group for each item into a fanfold. Each morning the slips are filed by classification symbol and interfiled with the rest of the slips for the month.

At the end of the month each subject is reviewed by the proper subject specialist. Item slips and index slips are numbered with a numbering stamp, and torn apart. The index slips are filed alphabetically, author and subject indexes being kept separate, and the item slips and author slips are pasted up on large sheets of paper with double gummed scotch tape. When a contents page has been typed, the manuscript is ready to go to the printer for reproduction by offset. When the manuscript is returned, the author slips are stripped off and saved for the annual index. Subject slips are interfiled so that the annual index may be typed from them.

The *Bibliography of Agriculture* is a large and growing indexing operation. In the calendar year 1949, 87,200 items were indexed, an increase of 60 per cent over the 54,500 indexed in 1944. These 87,000 items were gleaned from 101,748 separate issues of periodicals which were handled by the bibliographers. To do the indexing, we have a professional staff of seven and three-fifths persons, the supervisor, three subject specialists, two full time language specialists and one who gives three days a week to us and two to Technical Processes, and one general assistant. Our subject specialists have had special training in plant science, animal science, and social science respectively and are responsible for the lists in those fields. They all read French, German, Spanish, and Italian. Our language specialists index material in the Scandinavian languages, Dutch, Finnish, Portuguese, and Russian, working with the subject specialists on difficult questions of indexing. Since our Portuguese specialist does not have enough Portuguese to keep her busy, she establishes abbreviations, reviews subjects, and fills in wherever backlogs develop. Our general assistant indexes farm papers and keeps up the checklists of publications of the department and of the state experiment stations and extension services. Bibliographers handle an average of eleven periodical issues per hour of indexing time, and index better than nine and one-half articles. The average per hour of working time, including time spent on reviewing lists and other duties, is eight periodical issues and six and one-half entries per hour. Both the above figures include some proofreading time, since our one proofreader cannot keep up with all the slips and about 1500 slips per month must be read by bibliographers.

Typing slips for the *Bibliography* occupies practically the full time of four typists who type 15 items an hour on an average. In addition to typing the main slip according to the established forms, they type the author index slips and look up the abbreviation for the serial title. When the abbreviation is not found in the card file on the typist's desk, she passes the issue on to have an abbreviation established. Until very recently we have used the abbreviations in Miss Whitlock's *Abbreviations Used in the Department of Agriculture for Titles of Publications*[1] and set up abbreviations for new titles as they appeared. A stencil was cut for each new abbreviation and cards were run off for each typist, and for several other files. In our new *List of Serials Currently Received in the Library of the United States Department of Agriculture, November 1, 1949,* we have included a list of words which are abbreviated in serial titles in our bibliographies. Necessary changes have been made in our established abbreviations, and henceforth these words and only these words will be abbreviated. This system should make it easier for users of our bibliographies to interpret the abbreviations.

Proofreading of the slips is done chiefly by one editorial clerk who can read 45 items per hour. Up to the present our Russian specialist has done her own proofreading. Now, however, our proofreader has learned to transliterate Russian and is reading the Russian titles also. Several years ago, one of our typists learned to transliterate the Cyrillic alphabet, and she has worked from the Russian originals marked by our Russian bibliographer ever since.

Indexing, typing, and proofreading are all continuous activities occupying the full time of twelve people. The preparation of the issues for the printer occupies seventy per cent of the time of three additional clerk-typists and one editorial clerk, who supervises the makeup of the *Bibliography*. Monthly issues go to press one month after they are closed. Reviewing the lists occupies approximately 125 hours a month and is scheduled so that it covers seven working days. On the eighth day, the first boxes of slips are turned over to the preparations workers, and the makeup begins. After quick review of the filing to be sure that no slips have been misplaced during the review of classification, the slips are torn apart without disturbing the order. They are then numbered with a numbering stamp set for repeat and changed after each group of slips. The stamp is mounted in a jig so arranged that when the slip is placed in one position the

1. Miscellaneous Publication, No. 337; Washington: U.S. Dept. of Agriculture, 1939.

item number is correctly placed just before the author's name, and when it is placed in the other position it is correctly placed for stamping the number on the author slip. Since subject slips are not pasted up, the positioning of numbers on those slips is unimportant. As the clerk numbers the slips, she places them in three boxes, citation slips in one, author slips in another, and subject slips in a third. Tearing and numbering slips for an issue of 8,000 items requires about 60 man hours and is done over a period of seven to eight working days.

The boxes of citation slips are passed on to a clerk who does the pasting. He has a large pine board with heavy black lines marking the position of the two columns. He thumbtacks his paper to the board, and fastens a strip of double gummed scotch tape to the paper at the left edge of the column. Slips are fastened to this tape overlapping so that the blank space at the bottom of the slip and the classification symbol are covered by the next slip. It takes 19 minutes to paste a page containing 45 items. The various headings of the classification have been previously typed on slips and inserted in the file of numbered slips and are pasted in their proper places.

Each day the author and subject slips are separated by their first letters, using filing boxes with 25 pigeonholes. A study of the distribution of initial letters in the index was made to give a breakdown of letters so that the packs will be approximately equal in each pigeonhole. No further filing is done until all the slips have been sorted. Then they are arranged in alphabetical order and numbers for the same subject are combined on one slip. The over-all rate for arranging author slips including both sorting and arranging is 230 slips per hour; for arranging and combining subjects, it is 200 per hour. As soon as the author slips are filed, the author index is prepared by pasting them up in much the same way as the item slips, except that there are five columns to a page instead of two and the overlapping is much greater. It takes a little more than an hour to paste one page of the author index. In the monthly indexes, an author's name is repeated for each article by him in the issue. In other words, we do not combine numbers after an author's name in the monthly issues. If Mr. T. C. Smith has three articles in one issue, the index will read Smith T C 34672 Smith T C 34673 Smith T C 34879, not Smith T C 34672, 34673, 34879. By combining numbers we would save one to two pages at a cost of $6.80 for printing and $3.30 for pasting. Combining the numbers, besides slowing up the index at a critical point, would use up $15 to $20 worth of typing time. In the annual index with its much greater proportion of repeated names, there is a slight saving in combining numbers and it makes the index much easier to use.

While the index is being pasted, headings are typed at the top of the pages and the table of contents is prepared. The manuscript is then ready for the printer.

Scheduling the monthly issues presents no very great problems except those common to all operations having deadlines to meet. Scheduling the annual indexes is more complex. The indexes are the last issue of the year. Because we recognize the importance of getting them out promptly, we give ourselves only one month in which to prepare them. Obviously the final preparation cannot begin until all the slips from the November indexes are in, and they go to press on December 5. This does not mean that nothing is done on the annual indexes before November. On the contrary, we are constantly looking for means of spreading as much work as we can over the rest of the year. In 1949 we tried preparing our index on punched cards and printing from them. This did enable us to spread our work more evenly, but the resulting index was not legible enough to be satisfactory.

Work on the annual indexes really begins in January when we strip the author index slips from the manuscript returned to us by the printer and put them away. We do not interfile author slips until March because we find that it does not take twice as long to combine February and March with January as it takes to combine February alone. On the other hand, if we try to combine too many files at once, more mistakes are made. As the slips are interfiled, those bearing the same name are clipped together. As soon as the June manuscript is returned we add April, May, and June to the file and begin to combine numbers.

Numbers are combined by inserting the first slip for an author in the typewriter and adding the other numbers in predetermined positions. As you can see, the author's name is given but once, followed by all the numbers for articles written by him. Obviously the time spent in inserting slips in the typewriter and removing them is an important part of this operation, and is the same whether one number or twenty are typed on the slip. The most economical way of doing this combining would be to wait until the end of the year so that no slip would have to be inserted more than once. This, however, would prevent us from using the pasteup of the author index as a means of spreading the annual index over the year. We now wait until the end of the first six months to begin combining because our experience shows that in about 40 per cent of the cases we will not have to add more numbers to a slip on which numbers were added at the end of June. Numbers from the July, August, and September issues will be added in October, and in November we shall type the author index instead of pasting it, so that the slips need not be sent to the printer but can be retained for the annual index. As soon as November numbers have been added to names beginning with A, B and C, we are ready to start pasting the annual author index, usually only a day or two after the November issue goes to press.

Preparation of subject indexes for the first part of the year is limited to interfiling the subject slips into the master file each month. The filing of subject slips and combining of numbers is more complicated than the filing of author slips, and interfiling several files at once has not proved very practical. Subjects are reviewed each month after they are filed and any inconsistencies are corrected before they are interfiled. In September, we begin to check cross references and review the combined file. When the November subjects have been added, we are ready to begin typing.

The annual author index is prepared in exactly the same way as the monthly indexes, except that, because there is not time for one person to paste all the pages in eighteen to twenty working days, we have had two persons paste slips on the rolls of tape while a third cuts the strips to the proper length and pastes them to the pages. The subject index is typed on rolls of paper five inches wide without perforations. Slips are distributed to five typists who type long strips which are proofread, cut to the proper length, and pasted in the right order. This method was devised because our first typewriters would not take the full sized sheet. Now we have a wide-carriage typewriter for typing headings and for other work, but we shall stick to our paste-up for the subject index because it enables us to have any number of typists work on the index at once without breaking it. Another advantage is that if a group of slips is misfiled, as will happen, we can cut out that section and insert it in its proper place if the error is found in proofreading before the strips are pasted. The same thing can be done if a group of slips or even a single slip is omitted in typing.

Even though leave is granted in November only for the most urgent reasons, all this cannot be done entirely by the regular staff of the *Bibliography of Agriculture*, which must, at the same time, keep up with at least enough current indexing to release the important journals for circulation. Help must be found in other parts of the library. For professional assistance, our first reserve is our Special Bibliographies Section, the other section in the Division of Bibliography. We do not schedule work on any but the most essential special bibliographies during November, and our special bibliographers are on call when their help is needed. Typing in that section comes to a stop, and the two typists devote their full time to the index. In addition we plan this year to use two typists from the Division of Technical Processes and one from the Division of Administration. In return we shall detail two of our typists to the Division of Technical Processes for the month that they are working on the periodical bid, their busy time, which fortunately does not come in November, and one to the Division of Administration when they need her. Bookface typewriters are in use in both these divisions so that the detailed typists will be able to operate them. We shall have to train them in the forms used in the index after they get to us.

We have considered the possibility of spreading our typing on the subject index over the year by preparing it on slips and pasting it as we do the author index. Our experience with the punched cards does not lead us to believe that it would be a satisfactory method. At least, we have not worked out any very good way of doing it yet. In preparing punched cards for the subjects, our two greatest problems were the difficulty in getting main heads and subheads of all degrees in their proper places and keeping them there, and the waste involved in preparing thousands of cards in the proper form and then throwing them away. We would have the same problems in a pasted subject index.

As we do not want to have the complete pedigree of each subject appear in the finished index, we would have to type at the top of the slip to be pasted only the last subhead, just as we punched on each card only the last subhead. The main head and any superior subheads would have to be placed at the bottom of the slip. For example, if the subject were BULBS—CULTURE—NETHERLANDS, we would type NETHERLANDS at the top of the slip and BULBS—CULTURE at the bottom. The filing difficulties of this arrangement and the possibility of errors in combining are increased by the fact that we use standard subheads under our main heads. We must be sure that both BULBS and [BULBS]—CULTURE will appear in the finished index. Not infrequently we have no references at all indexed under large main heads. We must, therefore, go through the index looking for these armies without generals before it can be pasted.

The combining of numbers is much greater in the subject than in the author index. In 1949, after counting numbers in a sample, we estimated that of the cards punched for subjects from January to April, 70 per cent were thrown away and only 30 per cent appeared in the file for the completed index. By September, the number of cards retained had dropped to 9 per cent of those made. In September, 90 per cent of the slips which were prepared with exact positioning of subject and number and filed more slowly than slips could be filed which had the subject in its expected form would be thrown away. With punched cards we had at least the advantage of doing part of our filing by machine, which would not be true of typed slips. Without having tried a pasteup for the subjects, we are convinced that the extra time taken by filing difficulties, careful positioning and combining on the typewriter would outweigh any gain from having our index at least partly typed before the rush in November, unless we can figure out some way of preparing and pasting our index that would solve these problems.

The whole cost in round numbers of preparing the *Bibliography of Agriculture* for the fiscal year just ended was $75,000. Salaries accounted for $63,700, printing and mailing for $9.000, supplies $800, miscellaneous, including depreciation on typewriters, and telephones $1,500. Because there are no items for heat, rent, and light in the library budget, these costs are not included in the figure quoted. Each item in the *Bibliography of Agriculture* costs about $0.86.

This concludes our case study of the *Bibliography of Agriculture* as it is prepared at present. We are constantly watching for new methods, or modifications of old ones, which will help us to do a better job, or to do it more easily or more economically. As new methods are developed, we shall experiment with them and adopt those which we can adapt to fit our needs. By the time this paper is in print, we shall probably have made major or minor changes in the methods here described.

IMPLICATIONS AND CONCLUSIONS

IMPLICATIONS FOR SERVICE ASPECTS
OF LIBRARIANSHIP

JOHN MACKENZIE CORY

IT IS apparent that there are many possible channels for development in the field of bibliographic organization. Time does not
permit considering the implications of all the new developments
and new discoveries in this field. However, it does seem appropriate
for us to explore the relationship between at least the most probable
developments and our practical problems of daily service and administration.

My topic is "Implications for Service Aspects of Librarianship."
The first question we should ask is, obviously, "Implications of
what?" I am assuming that we are discussing the principal implications of the previous papers as they relate to bibliographic organization, technological changes in recorded communications, and the
implications of the very processes by which we review and analyze
problems and opportunities in bibliographic organization.

For instance, we have seen that the present structure of our bibliographic apparatus is capable of extensive improvement. Printed
bibliographies in book form, revised classification schemes applicable
either to books or to card catalogs, mechanical and electronic selection equipment and new opportunities in international cooperation,
all offer hope for changes and improvements in our bibliographic
organization. We are also faced with the need for organizing bibliographic knowledge relating to far more than the customary fields of
the written and graphic records of our communication. We see the
possible desirability of placing the bulk of such records on film or
coded cards so that even the "bits" or units of bibliographic information will change considerably from those with which we are familiar.

Finally, in the process of reviewing the steps which should be taken
to improve our bibliographic organization, we have learned that
there are unforeseen opportunities for international and inter-disciplinary cooperation. These opportunities have service implications
extending well beyond bibliographic organization.

The second obvious question we must ask in setting the framework for this discussion is, "Implications for whom?" Immediately, we are concerned with the implications for ourselves, the audience of the preceding papers; more generally, however, we must consider ourselves as representatives of other librarians and bibliographers and must consider the implications for the various types of institutions which we represent. For purposes of convenience, I shall categorize these institutions as follows: public research libraries (national, state, local), university research libraries, special research libraries, public lending libraries, college libraries, secondary school libraries, elementary school libraries. We shall return to these categories later as we attempt to relate the processes and problems which have already been presented to the library organizations by whom the chief impact of these changes and problems will be felt.

Third, we have the problem of deciding the chronology of our discussion. We might consider the implications of new trends in bibliographic organization in the near future, the middle future, and the distant future. While I shall remark later and briefly upon the possible developments in the near future and distant future, I shall concentrate primarily on the indefinite middle future.

Fourth, we must define our topic geographically, indicating whether we are concerned with the implications in the community, in the nation, or throughout the world. I believe it has been shown already that bibliographic organization is essentially international, and that the problems of the local community are integrally involved with the problems of the nation and the world. Consequently, my discussion will be concerned largely with implications by type of library, rather than by geographic area. It should be assumed, however, that the following remarks will be equally applicable throughout this country and in other countries of the world, allowing for historical differences and the structure of librarianship and scholarly research in those countries.

Finally, and most important, we must determine *what* service aspects are of concern to us as we discuss the implications of the preceding papers. Here I shall try to relate a number of different categories, the first dealing with individual library service vs. library service to groups; the second with reference service vs. loan service; the third with formal service vs. informal service; and the fourth dealing with current values as opposed to permanent values.

In the light of the above introduction, we might choose examples of possible implications or we might exhaust the various possibilities (and probably the audience as well!). It should be recognized that a variety of patterns is possible. Many developments have been predicted, some of them in direct contradiction to others. From each of these possible developments there are many conceivable courses of action and corresponding implications for service aspects of librarianship. In order to conserve time, it would appear desirable to analyze the most likely over-all pattern of development, indicating some possible variations as we progress. We should also avoid the temptation to discuss what *should* be instead of what *can* be. (Aside: "What *should* be" is frequently called, in terms of educational jargon, the "optimum"; to coin a useful sociological phrase, we might concentrate, however, on "what *can* be"—and label it the "possum.")[1]

First, we must note a development in bibliographic organization which must be recognized for its influence on the total picture of library organization and service. We are becoming increasingly aware of the existence of new sources of the "bits" of information with which our bibliographic organization and libraries are concerned. We are familiar with the existence of publishing agencies of many types, producing various kinds of materials for libraries. We are becoming aware, however, of the addition of "recording agencies" which do not exist primarily to publish either for the general public or for libraries, but which, nonetheless, produce records of historical and research value, with which libraries are necessarily concerned. The records produced by both publishing and recording agencies *all* have a potential research value and are the proper subject for bibliographic analysis and organization. Recognizing that a selection process is involved in any useful bibliographic organization, it is nevertheless true that libraries or similar repositories must be concerned with the acquisition of the total product of publishing and recording agencies, and that many of the bibliographic tools which we have been discussing will be based upon the library's access to such materials.

It should also be recognized that service aspects of librarianship are inter-related with a great many other factors. It is clear that library service depends on bibliographic possibilities, technological

1. Native habitat: J. H. Shera's tree (see pp. 84–86).

possibilities, structure and equipment, commercial competition, literacy and educational levels, and the climate of bibliographic cooperation. Library service patterns, in turn, will determine bibliographic organization, physical arrangement of informational items, the use of equipment, administrative organization, governmental organization (geographical, political, financial), relationships with other agencies, library processing methods, and the selection of library materials.

Let us return, then, to the types of libraries for which we seek to determine the service implications. I have been asked to relate the previous papers to *all* kinds of libraries in order to show that this is a significant topic of practically universal concern. You will doubtless share my opinion that the implications are fairly explicit for research libraries but considerably less so for the popular services of public libraries and for the teaching functions of public, college, and school libraries. Nevertheless, there are some important implications for the latter as I shall attempt to show shortly.

I have mentioned three types of research libraries: special research libraries, university research libraries, and public research libraries at the national, state, and local levels. Obviously these are not mutually exclusive since both public and university research libraries will include special library collections and services. Nevertheless, the classification will provide a useful framework for our explorations. (Parenthetically, perhaps that is all we should really expect from any classification for any purpose). Furthermore, since we have been paying so much attention to the classification of materials, we should not overlook the correlated classification of libraries themselves and even the classification of library users. (At times this week I have felt that we were treading perilously close to recommending separate classifications of material for each user, let alone each class of user.)

The special research library may be considered as the "pure" type. It will become increasingly important because of its concentration of materials and its emphasis on personalized service and organization. One very important implication, therefore, of our findings relative to bibliographic organization is that library service will become more and more specialized and personalized.

The university and public research libraries will continue their present trend toward specialization and we may expect them to become congeries of separate collections and staffs, centralized only by top administrative direction and through personnel and fiscal controls. Their classifications and arrangement may vary within the same library system and much greater control will be exercised by the library-bibliographer-specialist in charge. This trend from universality and uniformity to specialization and diversity will be true of both the public and university libraries insofar as their research functions are concerned.

Public libraries have another function to perform however—or several more functions. These include the educational use of leisure time, collateral instructional use, and straight recreational use. There are few research implications here and not as much obvious relationship to the problem of bibliographic organization. I submit, however, that we have touched upon several factors with implications for public library non-research services.

First, we can foresee a growing division between the public library's research and non-research functions and organization. There is no reason why these two functions should not continue to be administratively centralized as they are in the New York Public Library and many state libraries, but with different patterns of bibliographic organization and service prevailing within.

Second, the concept of personalized bibliographic organization and focus is equally applicable to the general user of the public library's less scholarly materials and services. We will need skilled generalists rather than specialists on the staff; the arrangement and guides to materials will be broader and simpler, reflecting not only the more general use but the nature of the materials themselves; and we will be more likely to continue to have access to the open stacks for direct browsing by the library users. All of these developments are a direct outgrowth of our predictions for research libraries since they will flourish under a clearer division of function among libraries and librarians.

Finally, the service relationships of the general public library with the research libraries will be changed. Improved bibliographic organization and communication will mean fewer local public libraries struggling with difficult reference and research services. Requests for such help will be more readily referred to regional, state, national, and other research libraries.

Public libraries share with college and school libraries very definite instructional responsibilities. We have explored principles of bibliographic organization which point clearly to the desirable arrangement of materials for these purposes and to the probable orientation of services. The respective curricula and work habits of the students will continue to be controlling. Electronic sorting will be unimportant in these areas but they nevertheless are an important phase of bibliographic organization.

We previously referred to several different aspects of service for which our discussions of bibliographic organization might have implications. The first aspect was individual service vs. service to groups. Research service is essentially individual and our difficulty is to classify the individual users into a significant order to avoid costly chaos in our bibliographic organization. Some library materials (e.g. slides, films, etc.) are essentially group services; and some library users, particularly in the public library field, are representative of identifiable groups (e.g. labor unions, women's clubs, youth groups, etc.). In the former case the organization and service will necessarily emphasize the materials which are more malleable than the users and their infinite needs; but I believe that in group services the pattern of library organization and service will revolve even more about the users than it does in research situations. There is a definite economic consideration which makes this almost certain. We may sometimes have to compromise with our optimum bibliographic organization as we deal with individual researchers but we can justify and defend more expensive special arrangements for sizeable groups.

The same arguments apply to the formal vs. informal services of libraries. Formal services, supporting class work and closely directed research, will require and justify exceptional bibliographic organization more readily than informal recreational and research needs will, no matter how much we should like to cater to such needs.

Reference and loan services are familiar categories, but they are likely to change more rapidly than we might have supposed before learning of new potentialities in bibliographic organization. For instance, reproduction of materials automatically after their identification (as in the case of the Rapid Selector) merges reference and loan service very effectively. Furthermore loan and reproduction are only two of many ways in which materials may be made available. Mr. Lionel McColvin in England has discussed the possible development of library reference services (public and academic) as centers solely for identification of what exists on any given subject, the materials themselves to be supplied from many possible sources including local loan, interlibrary loan, special purchase, photographic reproduction, teletype transmission, or referral to some other source for personal inspection. Mr. Donald Coney of the University of California has similarly explored the hypothesis that a great research library is primarily, if not exclusively, a great collection of reference and bibliographic aids supported by an extensive communications network.

These developments in bibliographic organization are closely related to our final categories of service, namely current values vs. permanent values. The non-research libraries will be concerned with current values entirely, serious values, let us hope, but based on current needs. They will rely on the organized network of research collections to maintain files of materials for permanent use.

The implications of these developments include the probable strengthening and modification of four types of repositories with which we are familiar. The first is the group of archival and historical societies principally publicly supported but also including some privately supported agencies. These will receive, as they have in the past, primarily the unpublished materials of the recording agencies, and will not generally be concerned with the output of the publishing agencies, except for background and reference purposes.

In addition, we will have, as we are now beginning to have, a series of interlibrary centers which will probably in time receive some materials directly from recording agencies and some materials directly from publishing agencies. These will be in addition to their present chief purpose which is to relieve the over-crowding of existing collections by the transfer of certain categories of less frequently used or easily shared materials.

Next we will continue to have a series of specialized collections, the purpose of which will be to acquire and arrange all useful materials in certain specialized fields. These collections may be divided in a number of ways. The most frequent categories being by subject, by country of origin, and by type of material. Incidentally, the sharper the specialization by category the less elaborate will be our necessary bibliographic organization.

We now find such collections in industrial, public, and academic libraries of all kinds primarily based upon specialization in subject areas, but occasionally by type of material and by country of origin. I believe that we will see a considerable increase in the kind of co-operative acquisition procedure exemplified by the Farmington

Plan. This Plan is at present, however, based upon a division of materials by subject since this method of allocation of materials was probably the easiest to sell to faculties and administrative officers in academic institutions. It would seem, however, to be important from a bibliographic point of view to have these subject collections supplemented or replaced by collections based primarily on country of publication so that the division of responsibility for "exhaustive" collecting can be more simply understood by the average librarian and library user. Such a procedure would also save considerable amounts of money in processing since the national bibliographies of the countries whose materials are collected could serve as the sole catalog for the collections, both for the research library assuming the *primary* collecting responsibility, and for all other libraries seeking to use such publications. As long as we are discussing the inclusion of all materials published in a given country, it would seem to be simplest to adhere to a division of responsibility by country. It is really only when selective acquisition of materials is desired that division of responsibility by subject is more useful.

Finally, we will see the development, from our present research and rare book collections, of what might best be described as "book museums" which will be concerned with the preservation and the use of books as books and similar records of communications as physical examples. These collections will not be primarily concerned with text, but they will be charged with responsibility for preserving the physical records, particularly published books. Their field will be "bibliomorphology" or the study of the form of books.

These, it seems to me, will be the probable repositories of the "bits" of information with which our libraries and bibliographic organization are concerned. An intermediate point of service is also implied. In the case of frequently used or easily accessible "bits" (e.g. materials abstracted in *Chemical Abstracts*) we will need more than archives, interlibrary centers, specialized collections, and book museums. We will need, and can now foresee, files of coded data, possibly on film, possibly on punched cards, possibly in some other form not yet clear to us but easily capable of analysis through rapid mechanical or electronic selection. This intermediate center would also include a laboratory designed to reproduce rapidly material which was known to be of interest to the user. No single name now exists to describe this important intermediate unit. In any case, its function in our future bibliographic organization is bound to be of considerable importance.

The total structure described above does not necessarily assume the existence of multiple agencies providing the various services enumerated. It is entirely conceivable that a single agency would combine all of the repository, laboratory, and reference functions described. However, this is not necessarily the case, and we may find the separate existence of agencies for each of these functions more frequently than we will find them concentrated in a single agency.

Up to this point we have stressed the service implications of bibliographic organization from the point of view of the institution and the user. I cannot forbear to comment on the effect which these changes must have on the librarians concerned. The machines and bibliographic systems which have been outlined in previous papers will never be merged into a single national or international system without the application of wise and imaginative professional guidance. Lacking this, we will simply have new layers of bibliographic organization imposed on our present layers, and increased confusion in the minds of the users of all kinds of libraries. Bibliographic control will not be the result of bibliographic organization without the intermediary assistance of qualified personnel.

The ultimate implications, therefore, of bibliographic organization to the service aspects of librarianship will depend upon the speed with which professional skills can be developed to accompany technological changes and opportunities.

Pertinent also to the future of library services in relation to personnel is the probable weakening of the dividing line which now separates book selection, cataloging, and reference, in all types of libraries. The use and preparation of bibliographic aids require much the same type of knowledge, whether that of the skilled specialist or the skilled generalist. It seems inevitable therefore that more librarians must become better bibliographers, well grounded in the subject needs of the library's users. Correspondingly, subject bibliographers will become increasingly active as members of library staffs. There are many evidences of this trend already, from the Library of Congress to Washington State College. Library staffs of research libraries will more and more closely resemble faculties, and faculties will play an increasing role in the operation of research libraries. Just as the college and school libraries must become better integrated with the teaching process, so research libraries must improve their relationships with research programs.

One final implication for library service personnel is the probable increased use of mechanical and electronic devices which will greatly reduce physical labor and routine work and permit the utilization of higher quality personnel. Such equipment need not alarm the librarians: first because it has generally been found that only nominal technical knowledge is required for their general understanding and use; and second, because we will see the development of technically trained assistants who will have primary responsibility for the problems of storing, duplicating, and manipulating masses of materials for research use.

Many of the possible implications of problems of technological change and bibliographic organization have been alluded to only briefly. Many variations are possible. Furthermore there are limiting factors which may delay the introduction of some of the innovations discussed. Patterns of vested interest, shortage of qualified personnel, and lack of funds and space will limit the immediate impact of the various proposals considered. We may expect to see some intensification of present trends, and their gradual spread to related problems, but we must recognize that the advanced thinking in the field of bibliographic organization is not yet widely publicized and it will be some time before it is acceptable to the professional librarians and bibliographers, let alone the research scholars and the general public who must adjust to it and support it.

In a way, this is fortunate, for there are many decisions yet to be made on possible choices of pattern and ways in which to channel our newly-recognized but long-sought bibliographic potential.

In case these estimates of possible implications appear to be unrestrained and extreme, one might turn for contrast to a generally maligned form of recorded communication. It is of some interest to consider the future of bibliographic organization as shown in science fiction! George R. Stewart, a well known contemporary American novelist, sets the framework for such an exploration in a recent article in the *Pacific Spectator*. Writing from the point of view of the year 2000, he makes the following statement: "The printed book began to dominate literature in the fifteenth century; after a sway lasting nearly five hundred years, it began to decline about the middle of the twentieth century, and by the end of that century had been largely superseded." Curiously enough, Mr. Stewart's prediction of the demise of the book as an important medium of communication is almost automatically assumed by all writers of science fiction. Wherever records are referred to they are either photographic or phonographic; they are preserved in far more indestructible forms than paper and ink and they are more compactly stored and more easily sorted for use. While no one contends that science fiction writers have an assured view of the future, it is nevertheless true that the more serious writers of this genre base their predictions upon current technical developments, the implications of which they project into the distant future. Surprisingly often they have turned out to be right, if not even conservative, in their estimates.

Without attempting to forecast all the implications of bibliographic changes for all future periods, I think we can all agree on several points. There are implications for all types of libraries and all facets of library service. There will frequently be violent changes. Usually their cost will be justified through accompanying savings in other related areas. They will require extensive revisions in our methods of training librarians and bibliographers. They will be subject to influences not now predictable, stemming from technological developments and world events which cannot yet be foreseen. And, finally, they are potentially capable of greatly improving and even completely transforming the research and popular services available to library users.

SYNTHESIS AND SUMMARY

SYNTHESIS AND SUMMARY

MARGARET E. EGAN

URING the past half century there has been increasing and
widespread concern over the problems of subject bibliography. In spite of the almost startling growth in the number
of separate subject bibliographies being published, neither the extent nor the methods of coverage have proved adequate to the
needs of users. Yet the rationalization of subject bibliography is
not in itself a complete answer to the problem, for a mere bibliographic listing will not satisfy the inquirer if he is unable to proceed
from the citation to the original. There was, therefore, purpose in
the choice of the term "bibliographic organization" rather than
"subject bibliography" or even "documentation" as the topic for
discussion at this Conference. The structure of the thinking which
produced the plan for the Conference has, we hope, become apparent as the several papers have been presented. My task, as I see it,
is not to give you a series of abstracts of these papers, with the contents of which you are now familiar, but rather to return to the
central problem, to indicate again its major parts, and to sketch in
lightly those parts which could not be fully presented in separate
papers during the Conference.

SCOPE OF THE PROBLEM

Early in the Conference Mr. Clapp gave us a very good definition
of bibliographic organization—"the pattern of effective arrangements which results from the systematic listing of the records of
human communication." Further analysis of this definition will disclose that it contains, at least by implication, all the various parts
of the problem with which we are concerned.

In discussing the "records of human communication," Mr. Clapp
was careful to point out that we now have permanent records in
other than graphic form and that access to records in other forms
may be just as important as access to graphic records. To assure
such access to the records of the newer media of communication

will present special problems. That no special consideration has been given here to these new media represents postponement rather than rejection of their claims to attention. If we can achieve mastery of our graphic records we shall have, if not a complete solution, at least a pattern which may be adapted to new forms.

It is noteworthy that in the definition given there is no qualification in terms of kind or value of the "records of human communication," yet in practical bibliographic planning some such qualifications must be made. Communication is one of the fundamental social processes, with many functions as well as many forms. Some of these functions are fulfilled immediately and locally, with no need for transmission across space and time and hence no need for the intermediary services of bibliography. We might narrow our field somewhat by limiting our consideration to those records which need to be made available, across the span of time or space which separates the producer from the ultimate consumer, for some purpose which society recognizes and approves. Even a subjective estimate of the social value of a given group of graphic records would serve to eliminate the temporary, the local, the purely personal, and the trivial. Any attempt to explore the possibility of establishing objective criteria leads one into fascinating, if hazardous, intellectual mazes. It is enough for our purposes to suggest that no communication has any social value unless it stimulates or modifies behavior which has some impact upon the community. The greater the impact, the greater the importance to society. Such behavior may be individual or it may be corporate, for in our society corporate behavior is a potent factor; the impact may be immediate, long-delayed, or gradual. Thus, the use of books to develop desirable character traits may result in the modification of behavior throughout an individual's entire life, and such an effect is of considerable social importance. At the other end of the scale, the single item of information that the market for a particular product is contracting may lead a corporation to change its product or to seek new markets in time to prevent a costly failure or shut-down, the impact of which would certainly be immediate and heavy upon that part of the community dependent upon its activities. We may not be able to isolate the use of graphic records as a causal factor, and we may not be able to measure accurately the impact of any single event upon the community, yet the constant awareness of such a criterion might serve to sharpen observation and to give at least a rough scale of priority values in the allocation of always limited resources for bibliographic services.

Discrimination in terms of kinds of communications is not entirely separable from discrimination in terms of value, for some scale of values would be applicable to each different kind of communication. Similarly, each subject field might bring forth examples of most, if not all, the various kinds of publications. For example, in the field of chemistry we find not only the research publications of scholars but also publications dealing with chemical technology, derived partly from chemical research, partly from previous technological publications, and partly from independent experimentation in applied chemistry. In both research and technology there must be production of textbooks appropriate to the education of a new generation of chemists and chemical technologists. Finally, there must be explanations of new discoveries, processes and products suitable for the lay public which must accept, absorb and support the changes brought about by the work of the various specialists. Our "pattern of effective arrangements" must obviously provide bibliographic channels *between* these groups as well as *within* each. If the Conference as a whole has seemed to emphasize the needs of scholars at the expense of other groups, it is only because historically, as Mrs. Murra has shown, scholars have been most keenly aware of their dependence upon bibliographic machinery, most articulate in the expression of their needs, and most efficiently organized to develop their own services.

The "systematic listing of the records of human communication" implies the existence of agencies to do the listing. As we have seen, such agencies may be governmental agencies, professional associations, commercial concerns, libraries, or individuals. At the very heart of the problem of rationalizing and co-ordinating bibliographic services lies the question of responsibility for production and support. Insofar as a complex and highly organized society depends upon effective transmission of graphic records for its smooth functioning and its continued progress, there must be recognition of social responsibility for assuring that effective transmission. A society which has accepted public responsibility for supporting the libraries which collect, preserve and make available the records themselves, but which is unwilling to support the machinery which would maximize the usefulness of those records, is minimizing the return on its already heavy investment. One of the more-than-incidental benefits to be derived from an attempt to measure the use of graphic records of communication in terms of social impact would be the continuing emphasis upon the social value of the intermediary services which make those records accessible.

Finally, in our analysis of the implications of our definition, we must consider the phrase, "effective arrangements resulting from. ..." If bibliographic services are to be effective, the arrangements resulting from them must include the machinery to provide *physical* as well as *content* accessibility. Such machinery includes: (1) the libraries which actually have the document desired, with all their techniques and tools for delivering the volume; (2) the union catalogs or guides to collections which indicate the particular library holding the volume; (3) the loan agreements which make it possible to lend the volume to a distant inquirer; and (4) the equipment for reproducing all or part of the content upon request.

Each aspect of the total problem of bibliographic organization has its own importance, the measure of which is not necessarily reflected in the amount of space given to it here. If undue consideration seems to have been given to subject bibliography at the expense of other types of bibliographies, it is only because subject bibliography seems to be the most immediately urgent problem today. If a seemingly inordinate amount of attention has been given to classification, it is because a workable system of classification is necessary to any large-scale attempt to coordinate subject bibliography and because failure to agree upon a single system has been the rock upon which many previous attempts to achieve coordination have foundered.

NEW APPROACHES TO CLASSIFICATION

In the UNESCO/Library of Congress report the elements of bibliographic description, such as author, title, publisher, date, etc., are likened to the units of a currency system. "These units are of universal acceptance: they make possible a national and also an international traffic in the information supplied by publications; they form a common coinage of the realm of learning. ... But because the subject is a unit of changing form and fluctuating value, its advances have been resisted, and even when not resisted have been found difficult of acceptance."[1] This analogy is particularly apt when one recalls that international exchange in money is possible without the adoption of a single, universal system of currency, for if international bibliographic coordination must wait upon acceptance of a universal classification system it may well wait forever.

The three new approaches to classification described by Taube, Shera, and Ranganathan (the first two embryonic, the last rather fully developed) take account of the "changing form and fluctuating value" of the subject unit. Each provides for the subject description of a particular bibliographic unit by means of a combination of symbols which sum up the significant parts or uses of the whole, and each such symbol may be used as a pivot around which may be gathered all other publications which are characterized by that one aspect, regardless of whether or not they share any other characteristic. All three systems are, then, multidimensional rather than linear, and referential rather than hierarchical. They allow for fluctuating values in that new elements may be added or old ones deleted in classifying new publications without destroying still significant relationships to previously classified materials.

The extent and the speed of such fluctuations in value will depend upon the stability or instability of the interest in concepts, or approaches, considered of importance in any field of investigation. This kind of "deep-level analysis" is, in effect, an attempt to establish a pattern of bibliographic subject description which will correspond as closely as possible to currently accepted patterns of intellectual activity in any given field. At best it will be a costly process, justifiable only in application to a limited range of materials relevant to fields in which intellectual patterns have developed to the point where significant elements or approaches may be quite clearly defined.

The current ferment over classification is not an esoteric efflorescence of the academic mind. It reflects the increasing clamor for closer analysis of publications in many subject fields, as exemplified by demands for extensive abstracting services with intensive analytic indexes to the abstracts. The use of intensive, multi-dimensional classification, like the use of electronic sorting equipment, will no doubt be limited to materials of this kind rather than applied to the book-units in a library.

Obviously, the success of any such attempt depends upon the clarity with which concepts can be isolated and defined in any given field, a process which might best be undertaken by specialists in the different fields. That such a list of significant concepts can be derived from the analysis of the literature itself has been recently demonstrated in the preparation of the "Syntopicon," the concept index to the volumes being published by the Great Books Foundation, at the University of Chicago. This project was not intended to be a contribution to the theory of classification but its techniques and results are remarkably suggestive.

THE SUBJECT FIELDS

It has been said that we need a "taxonomy of bibliography." We do indeed, and in such a classification of bibliography the various forms of subject bibliography would be only one section. If we seem to ignore other forms of bibliography here, it is for lack of space, not lack of interest. Yet when we limit ourselves to consideration of subject bibliography as determined by differences in patterns of intellectual activity between various subject fields we must still be wary of a too limited approach. Quite small and homogeneous groups of users, concentrating upon the same body of literature, may need different kinds of bibliographic tools for different purposes. A biochemist, for instance, may need a comprehensive index to the literature of his field in order to implement a particular research project, while he will also need a much more selective and differently arranged bibliographic service for general browsing in order to keep up with progress in the field as a whole.

We must also remember that within each subject group there are many smaller subject area specialties, each with slightly different literature needs, so that an approach through subject areas as broad as we have used here may be extremely misleading as to the homogeneity within such areas. Within each subject group, furthermore, there may be several distinct groups of users, including (1) the scholar or scientist, whose task is to add something to the body of knowledge in his field; (2) the educator, whose task is to transmit to the younger generation, with varying degrees of thoroughness at different levels of education, that which is already known in the field; (3) the student, who needs literature of a summary nature for his own use; (4) the practitioner, who operates the agencies, businesses, or enterprises which may derive from the various fields of scholarship and which in their totality constitute our social machinery; and (5) the general public, which needs sufficient understanding of the total cultural environment to enable its members to act intelligently within that environment. It is noteworthy that the literature produced or used by the last four groups is to a large extent derived from the literature of the scientists or scholars, or at the least is conditioned by their activities. The production of this derived literature is dependent upon bibliographic tools for convenient access to the parent literature, a need which is generally ignored when scholarly groups plan and produce the bibliographic tools which they themselves use. At the same time, different bibliographic services are required for channeling the completed secondary materials among educators, students, practitioners, and the general public. The need for comprehensiveness is much reduced at these levels because there is less loss in substitution of one publication for another. At the level where each publication is supposedly a unique contribution to knowledge there is no factor of interchangeability whatsoever.

The UNESCO/Library of Congress report summarized these various needs succinctly in its analysis of the task of bibliography as a whole:

"Make it possible for intellectual workers to learn of publications recording the developments in their fields of interest not only in their own countries but throughout the world.

"Promote the effectiveness of particular projects in research.

"Contribute to the cultural development and enjoyment which are derivable from the records of learning and culture.

"Assist in promoting useful applications of existing knowledge and in making the applications which have been developed in one country widely known to all countries."[2]

The last area has been, without a doubt, the most neglected by librarians and bibliographers, yet the individuals and corporate bodies operating within this area are largely responsible for the smooth functioning of our society, and they are becoming increasingly dependent upon communication through print. As society becomes more complex and people with more specialized knowledge than that possessed by the proverbial "man in the street" are needed to staff the various agencies which carry on its essential processes, and as those processes themselves become more complex and cover a wider environment than that within the scope of immediate personal observation, each such group tends to develop its own body of literature as well as to draw upon that part of the general store which it needs. This literature may be roughly divided into two

large classes, one embodying information as to *methods* of conduct-
ing specific operations, and the other embodying the *facts* necessary
to reach a decision upon a particular course of action. Such materials
might be called "operational" or "decision-making" to differentiate
them from the scholarly, the educational, or the popular, although
none of these groups is a completely separate or discrete unit.

As an illustration we might go back to Dr. Taeuber's reference to
the census publications as representing both original research and
the data for further research. It might be pointed out that the government began to collect census data, and has constantly increased
the scope of the data collected, because the government itself realized
the need for such information in order to make intelligent, informed
decisions concerning its own operations. The fact that these data have
been used extensively in social science research is an incidental by-
product, as is their use in the decision-making processes of many business and industrial enterprises. Similarly, many private agencies,
notably trade associations, collect and publish for their own uses
statistical data which are also useful for research purposes.

Many of the special libraries developed in such numbers during
the past few decades are concerned exclusively with operational materials, while public libraries have found it increasingly necessary to
have such materials even though they can not offer the intensive
service demanded of a special library. At least two new types of
bibliographic services have been developed for this new kind of use:
(1) the index to sources of statistical data, which represents an approximation to deep-level analysis in that it points out the location
of specific facts; and (2) the loose-leaf service, which by-passes the
conventional bibliographic apparatus by incorporating with speed
and precision new material directly into the body of already available and still relevant materials, at the same time discarding the
obsolete. This is bibliographic organization at a high level of efficiency insofar as speed and convenience are concerned. Librarians
point out that such services also exemplify a high level of cost, but
one wonders if the costs may not be less than the total costs of processing and providing content access to the original documents from
which such services abstract, especially when for operational purposes the material must be known and used very quickly if it is to
have maximum value. We might do well to study the conditions
under which such services are most effective and economical and
experiment with adaptations for other purposes.

We have seen that scholars in all fields need bibliographic services which give comprehensive, intensive, analytical, and summarizing access to the literature of their own fields, as well as more limited access to the literature of related fields. Those responsible for promoting useful applications of existing knowledge, both social and technological, have equally urgent though somewhat different bibliographic needs—needs which are as yet scarcely appreciated, much less explored.

Service to these two groups can never be adequately measured in terms of the number of users either of bibliographic tools or of the original publications indicated by bibliographies. A single use by a single individual might produce results of considerable importance to the community at large, justifying an expenditure of funds which might be far beyond the resources of the individual or of the group to which he belongs. There is as much reason for public support of the roadways of information as for the roadways along which material goods are transported, for one is as necessary to a healthy and progressive society as the other.

The third important task of bibliography is to "contribute to the cultural development and enjoyment which are derivable from the records of learning and culture." This is primarily the field of the humanities and the function of the public library. This field differs essentially from the others in that the wide-spread use of the original publications is necessary to accomplishment of the purpose. The bibliographic services which indicate which are the most desirable publications for the purpose are much less important than provision of the network of agencies which will make copies of the publications available to many people in many communities. What is needed in the way of bibliographic service may be, not provision of new or different bibliographies, but the development of more exact criteria for inclusion of materials in the existing bibliographies.

PROBLEMS OF MANAGEMENT

We have provided ourselves with a nice example of the dependence of research upon institutional arrangements, or social machinery, to implement its results. If research can isolate and describe the usable concepts of scholarship, relate them in a meaningful way to units of publication, and describe the types of tools necessary to deliver them to the ultimate consumer, the entire effort is sterile if the physical equipment and the social organization to complete the job is not available. We included in our definition of bibliographic organization the necessity for some such arrangements. Opinions as to the best achievable arrangements may be drawn from close observation of previous experience rather than from research. Mrs. Murra has described for us several examples of attempts to produce or to coordinate bibliographic services; Fussler described the physical facilities and types of organization necessary to deliver a given publication or a reproduction of it to the searcher; and Swank suggested a variation in internal organization of a library which might give better access, both content and physical, within a local situation, at the same time contributing to and making use of a wider network of bibliographic services. None of these presentations was intended to be definitive or to point to premature conclusions. It is enough for our present purposes to indicate the problems involved and the kind of observation of experience needed in planning any extension or coordination of such facilities.

We have seen that many agencies—governmental, international, commercial, professional, and private—have been concerned with the production of bibliographies. Perhaps the primary problem here is to try to fix responsibility on a rationally tenable basis for the production of certain types of bibliographic services by certain types of agencies, and then to attempt to secure the necessary support for such agencies. Libraries, the major agency concerned with the collection and physical accessibility of publications, may need to re-examine the distribution of the total responsibility among the several types of libraries as well as among individual libraries. As Cory pointed out, a more rational distribution of functions among libraries and the planned development of each type to satisfy the particular need it is best fitted to satisfy would free all from the weight of incidental and inefficiently performed functions and result in fuller service within the spheres appropriate to each. Historically, libraries have developed parochially, in isolation from each other, and in response to needs felt by a given group at a given time. Fussler indicated how difficult it is to expand the physical and organizational facilities developed under such circumstances as needs expand. Shaw sounded a similar warning in regard to the too-hasty embracing of new technological developments without a preliminary study of utility as well as costs. Librarians need to observe with a critical eye both old and new patterns of machinery for implementing bibliographic organization.

To summarize briefly, we need many types of information before we can plan intelligently. Specifically, we need

1. thorough, taxonomic study of bibliographies, both as to form and as to uses;
2. thorough, taxonomic study of users, by subject field, by level, and by purpose;
3. careful observation and considered judgment of the efficiency of the agencies producing bibliographies, of the agencies handling publications, and of the potentialities of new techniques and machines; and
4. rational estimation of the distribution of the ultimate benefits of effective bibliographic organization and judicious location of responsibility for support.

There are observable in the field today two distinct trends, one toward integration and one toward further fragmentation. Granting that fragmentation usually occurs because of inadequate existing service to a particular group, such a trend should be impeded whenever possible until an over-all plan can be formulated or the impracticability of such a plan fully demonstrated. Fragmentary services are usually short-lived, but every failure makes eventual success more remote and more difficult to achieve.

To formulate a blue print for a system of bibliographic organization is no part of the responsibility of this Conference, but such a formulation will no doubt involve the efforts of many of the individuals who have participated in these meetings. It is cheering to remember, as one of our speakers said, that though the job may be long and arduous we may see the end of the era of bibliographic chaos and enter upon a new era of bibliographic order, convenience, and speed.

When an historical epoch dies and another begins, both events are usually celebrated in imaginative literature, translating history into the immediate personal experience of the individual. Since Mr. Cory has noted that the birth of a new bibliographic era is now being described in science fiction, I can not resist the temptation to quote an old but prophetic story of the death of the era of bibliographic chaos:

"The idea occurred to me, in the month of June last year, to go and consult on the origins and progress of Penguin art, the lamented

M. Fulgence Tapir, the learned author of the 'Universal Annals of Painting, Sculpture, and Architecture.'

"Having been shown into his study, I found seated before a roll-top desk, beneath a frightful mass of papers, an amazingly short-sighted little man whose eyelids blinked behind his gold-mounted spectacles. . . .

"The walls of the study, the floor, and even the ceiling were loaded with overflowing bundles, paste-board boxes swollen beyond meas-ure, boxes in which were compressed an innumerable multitude of small cards covered with writing. I beheld in admiration mingled with terror the cataracts of erudition that threatened to burst forth.

" 'Master,' said I in feeling tones, 'I throw myself upon your kind-ness and your knowledge, both of which are inexhaustible. Would you consent to guide me in my arduous researches into the origins of Penguin art?'

" 'Sir,' answered the Master, 'I possess all art, you understand me, all art, on cards classed alphabetically and in order of subjects. I consider it my duty to place at your disposal all that relates to the Penguins. Get on that ladder and take out that box you see above. You will find in it everything you require.'

"I tremblingly obeyed. But scarcely had I opened the fatal box than some blue cards escaped from it, and slipping through my fin-gers, began to rain down. Almost immediately, acting in sympathy, the neighboring boxes opened, and there flowed streams of pink, green, and white cards, and by degrees, from all the boxes, differ-ently coloured cards were poured out murmuring like a waterfall on a mountain-side in April. In a minute they covered the floor with a thick layer of paper. Issuing from their inexhaustible reservoirs with a roar that continually grew in force, each second increased the vehe-mence of their torrential fall. Swamped up to the knees, Fulgence Tapir observed the cataclysm with his attentive nose. He recognised its cause and grew pale with fright.

" 'What a mass of art!' he exclaimed.

"I called to him and leaned forward to help him mount the ladder which bent under the shower. It was too late. Overwhelmed, des-perate, pitiable, his velvet smoking-cap and his gold-mounted spec-tacles having fallen from him, he vainly opposed his short arms to the flood which had now mounted to his arm-pits. Suddenly a terrible spurt of cards arose and enveloped him in a gigantic whirlpool. Dur-

ing the space of a second I could see in the gulf the shining skull and
little fat hands of the scholar; then it closed up and the deluge kept
pouring over what was silence and immobility. In dread lest I in my
turn should be swallowed up ladder and all I made my escape through
the topmost pane of the window."[3]

REFERENCES

1. UNESCO/Library of Congress Bibliographical Survey, *Bibliographical Services: Their Present State and Possibilities of Improvement: Report Prepared as a Working Paper for an International Conference on Bibliography* (Washington, 1950), pp. 42–43.
2. *Ibid.*, pp. 3–4.
3. Anatole France, *Penguin Island*, trans. A. W. Evans (New York: Blue Ribbon Books, Dodd, Mead & Co., 1909), Preface, pp. xiii–xv.

INDEX

INDEX

U.S. Department of Agriculture, 67, 158
List of Serials Currently Received in the Library, 230
U.S. Department of Commerce, 158
U.S. Federal Security Agency, 158
U.S. Interdepartmental Committee on Research and Development, 158
U.S. National Advisory Committee on Aeronautics 158
U.S. National Bureau of Standards, 158
U.S. National Military Establishment, 158
U.S. Nautical Almanac, 38
U.S. Office of Naval Research, 63
U.S. Patent Office, 89
Official Gazette, 200
U.S. President's Scientific Research Board, 158
U.S. Public Health Service, 137
United States Quarterly Book List, 8
U.S. Research and Development Board, 63
U.S. Superintendent of Documents, *Monthly Catalog*, 10, 16, 18, 136
U.S. Veterans Administration, 158
Unity of knowledge, 74-76
Univac, 202, 205, 209, 211-12
Universal Decimal Classification, 36-37, 45, 64-65, 79, 151
University of California, 192, 194-95, 244
University of Chicago, 129, 135, 179, 183
Carnegie Corporation, grant from, 137-38
Commission on the Future Policy of the University of Chicago Libraries, 144
Division of the Social Sciences, 127

Graduate Library School, 84, 127, 193-94
Oriental Institute, 118
University of Colorado, 191
University of Nebraska, 191
University of North Carolina, 177

Van Laer, H., 33
Vedic period, 97
Vedic Seers, 98
Vienna Academy, 118
Voigt, Melvin J., xii

WPA, 124
Ward, Lester F., 77
Washington State College, Library, 247
Wells, H. G., *World Encyclopaedia*, 45
Weltwirtschaftliches Archiv, 132
Wetmore, Alexander, 158
Whitehead, Alfred North, 83
Whitlock, *Abbreviations Used in the Department of Agriculture for Titles of Publications*, 230
Wilson, H. W., Company, 66, 91, 172
World Almanac, 209
World Bibliographic Repertory, 45
World List of Scientific Periodicals, 47

Yale University, Cross-Cultural Index, 119

Zentralblatt für Mathematik, 152
Zoological Record, 40
Zoologischer Jahresbericht, 34